Popping the Crypto Bubble

Market Manias, Phony Populism, and Techno-solutionism

Stephen Diehl, Jan Akalin, Darren Tseng

What is easy and what is right rarely coincide.

ISBN 978-1-915597-00-7
English (US)

First Edition

0 / 1

Contents

Introduction

Cryptocurrency is a giant scam, although a complicated scam that uses technobabble, heterodox economics and populist anger to obfuscate its functioning. A pitch perfect scam for the post-truth era of social media where trust in institutions and experts is at an all-time low.

The overarching idea of cryptocurrency is based on a complex set of mythmaking built on a simple unifying aim: to reinvent money from first principles independent of current power structures. Rarely in the history of technology has there been any invention that has been the nexus of discussion along many dimensions of human experience and divides technologists on the ethical implications of its existence. the way that cryptocurrency does. It has emerged as one of the most intriguing and destructive socio-technical phenomena of the early 21st century, capturing the zeitgeist in economics, technology, politics, law, ethics, culture, and monetary policy.

Cryptocurrencies are undeniably an economic bubble, but it is a bubble on a scale that we are yet to experience. Nevertheless, the Nobel laureate Robert Shiller gives us a framework for understanding this phenomenon in his Narrative Economics[3], which describes the epidemiology of bubbles that perpetuate "stories that motivate and connect activities to deeply felt values and needs". Cryptocurrency is primarily driven by the twenty-first century narrative of distrust in financial institutions coupled with, the need for continuity of the financial services traditionally provided by these institutions.

While a software is political, some software is more political than other. Cryptocurrency can best be understood as a reaction to the 2008 Global Financial crisis and the synthesis of technolibertarian ideology with growing distrust in financial institutions. Within this context, technology has influenced the financial services sector and had a profound influence on popular economic discourse. It is a technology that remains extremely divisive in its approach to disruption and its political ends. The divisions over cryptocurrency are based on a philosophical question: Do you worry more about the abuse of centralized power, or about anarchy?

For those who fear anarchy, cryptocurrency is the fantasy of a financial system free of democratic oversight whose efficacy is based purely on technology and free-market forces. For those who fear centralized power, cryptocurrency is a hedge against the overreach and corruption of big government and a financial services sector whose greed and excesses were made clear during the financial crisis. This philosophical divide falls loosely along existing political ideologies. The cryptocurrency school is often ideologically adjacent to existing right-wing economic schools of thought, although it is, not entirely contained within that political sphere. It is a phenomenon that many individuals have co-opted[2] for many ends as a result of its general misunderstanding.

In this critique, we will survey the state of cryptocurrency, its political imaginaries, and the outcomes it has achieved in the last decade. In the "fake it til' you make it" culture of Silicon Valley and libertarian ideologies, it is widely accepted to ignore externalities of technology until a critical mass is reached, and the benefits of the technology can be realized in hindsight.

Nevertheless, cryptocurrency in the present moment has profound technical, privacy, economic, ethical, and environmental shortcomings that need to be discussed. The constellation of these shortcomings, lack of innovation, and potential for vast public harm form the case against the cryptocurrency[1].

The History of Crypto

"The concentration of wealth is natural and inevitable, and is periodically alleviated by violent or peaceable partial redistribution. In this view all economic history is the slow heartbeat of the social organism, a vast systole and diastole of concentrating wealth and compulsive recirculation."

– Will and Ariel Durant, *The Lessons of History*

The introduction of bitcoin as a technology is a limited innovation, it presents a quirky and limited solution to a classic problem in computer science. However, for most of the general public, the perception of cryptocurrency is often at the more basic level of:

Bitcoin has something to do with computers / is very expensive / is the future of something / sometimes goes up.

The technology behind cryptocurrency is the product of many people and the fusion of different advances from the last twenty years. Nevertheless, its history is described by a single overarching truth:

Cryptocurrencies were intended as a peer-to-peer medium of payment but have since morphed into a product whose purpose is almost exclusively as a speculative investment.

3

2.1 THE CYPHERPUNK ERA

Despite its most ardent acolytes' claim, bitcoin was not an artifact of divine revelation. Like most technologies, it does not exist in a vacuum and was the product of a long sequence of trends going back to the early days of the internet. Bitcoin was not even the first digital currency and was preceded by multiple attempts along the same idea dating back to the early 1980s. The provenance of bitcoin is best understood through the lens of understanding the various internet subcultures that gave rise to the political ideologies and component technologies behind it.

The first hints of this idea go back to David Chaum's cryptography paper *Blind Signatures for Untraceable Payments* which outlines a theoretical basis for a system of making an electronic payment system using digital signature algorithms.[1] The paper presents this idea as a mathematical formulation and does not provide an implementation. Later in 1989, Chaum started a company that attempted to bring these ideas into production in the financial services sector. The company sold three years later, and its technology was eventually folded into an open-source project called GNU Taler.

At the same time, the Cold War was coming to an end, and the United States Department of Commerce and the State Department were increasingly concerned with the geopolitical implications of allowing exports of strong encryption standards. This led Phil Zimmerman, the inventor of a common encryption standard known as PGP, to challenge the United States munition controls on encryption in what would be known as the first Crypto Wars. The legal precedent, in this case, had massive implications for the early development of internet browsers and internet technology which were starting to rely on strong encryption standards to enable secure communication and eventually e-commerce. This trend created an underground movement on the early internet known as cypherpunks, who were technological activists who advocated for the unrestricted use of cryptography and privacy-enhancing technologies as a vehicle for social and political change.

The first digital currency was launched in 2006 in the United States by a company named eGold. The company allowed early internet users to purchase fractional ownership amounts in offshore physical gold holdings and used this centralized register to make instantaneous transfers to other eGold customers. Businesses like MoneyGram and Western Union had been operating e-money services for many years, however, eGold differed in that it was not denominated or backed by a national currency. This service operated under what the law defines as a money transmitter business that facilitated payments between third parties by creating a central register that records credits and debits. The business quickly rose to prominence during the early internet eGold, and was soon prosecuted by the United States federal government under the Patriot Act as it was found to violate existing money transmitter laws. In 2007 the enterprise was shut down, and the federal government seized its assets.[4]

The story continues with a company called *Liberty Reserve S.A.* that operated out of Costa Rica from 2006 to 2013 and offered an offshore anonymous money transmission service. The service allowed users to deposit money into a virtual dollar account via wire transfer or credit. Customers could then transfer these funds to other Liberty Reserve account holders without validation of the identities of the account holders or any legal restrictions. The FBI raided the offices of Liberty Reserve S.A., and the company was shut down in 2013 for violating the United States money laundering laws.

In the 21st century, most money is digital, represented as numerical values in databases holding balance sheets for bank deposits. The auditing and accounting of money is a regulated part of obtaining banking licenses, and this process of digitization of products and digital straight-through processing began in the 1980s. To most consumers today, this is transparent, although it was first, in the early 2000s that, consumers became aware of the digitization of their money in the form of increasing online banking. These now-common services gave customers a real-time view of their balances and transactions and increasingly allowed consumers to issue and receive payments. However, in the early days of e-commerce, there was still apprehension around receiving and making payments over the internet with credit cards. To fill this gap, PayPal emerged as a service to support online money transfers, which allowed consumers and businesses to transact with a single entity that would process and transmit payments between buyers and sellers without the need for direct bank-to-bank transfers.

This was a particularly well-timed business that capitalized on the rise of online shopping services such as eBay and Amazon.

Contemporaneous to the e-money digital transformation was the digital file-sharing scene, which in 1993 grew out of early file-sharing systems on Usenet and found its way into the mainstream with the development of Napster. Napster was a global peer-to-peer file-sharing network that allowed users to share the newly invented MP3 files with other users without paying for the original recordings of the music. This service was eventually shut down for copyright infringement but spawned an entire generation of new open-source protocols such as Gnutella, Freenet, and BearShare. The most successful of these, BitTorrent, proved more challenging to shut down because of the lack of a single entity to target. The BitTorrent protocol was based on a data structure known as a Merkle tree which allowed large files to split up into individual pieces, transmitted over a network, and reconstructed in parts while maintaining the integrity of the entire data file. This core data structure would be instrumental in advancing peer-to-peer networks to share hashes of incomplete data while maintaining integrity through cryptography.

On the 31st of October, 2008, a person or group of people under the pseudonym Satoshi Nakamoto published[3] the Bitcoin Whitepaper, outlining a new system on a cryptography mailing list. The nine-page essay outlines what is described as a peer-to-peer electronic cash that could operate independently of central authorities.

> A purely peer-to-peer version of electronic cash would allow online payments to be sent directly from one party to another without going through a financial institution. We propose a solution to the double-spending problem using a peer-to-peer network.
>
> – Nakomoto, Bitcoin Whitepaper

Computer science had previously grappled with what was known as the *double-spend problem* since the first networked computers and databases were invented. In short, this problem is concerned with ensuring that a digital representation of value is not copied and consumed by multiple sources that require it. The digital banking and credit card industries had dealt with a similar set of problems in which digital ledgers recording payments would need to be reconciled or communicated to multiple parties to ensure that digital representations of units of value were kept in sync with deposits. The existing solution to this problem had always been centralized trust authorities which held a legal obligation to maintain authoritative digital records and would handle discrepancies by introducing time delays for compliance checks and manual mechanisms to handle disputes and inconsistencies.

The mechanism described in the bitcoin whitepaper proposed a novel solution for the double-spend problem, which did not require a central trust authority. Instead, it relied on a computer program known as a *consensus algorithm* and clever use of a digital signature scheme to maintain a consistent record of a ledger database across multiple computers without needing an authoritative central source of trust. A digital signature is a technique in cryptography where a user uses a set of cryptographic keys (a public and a private key) to sign a piece of data to verify the integrity and origin of the data. The public key can be shared with the world and authenticated by associating it with another identity. The private key is kept secret and is used to generate digital signatures, which only the user who possesses the private key would be able to generate. This technique was extensively studied and widely used in existing internet infrastructure such as SSL, which protects not only online banking and other secure services but also the majority of websites.

A consensus algorithm is a kind of computer program in which multiple computers use a set of steps to write a shared set of data (such as a database) so that all users can access a consistent view of the data from any computer. Consensus algorithms are part of the branch distributed systems field in computer science. This field concerns itself with different approaches to building consensus algorithms, techniques of sequencing read and writes to shared data stores. All consensus algorithms are constrained by a fundamental result known as the CAP theorem, which states that any algorithm may have at most two out of three properties: Consistency, Availability, and Partition Tolerance.

- *Consistency* - Readers of data from the service see the same data at any given point of time
- *Availability* - All readers can retrieve the data you stored in a system even if a subset of the service goes down.

- *Partition Tolerance* - No set of failures less than total network failure result in the system responding to queries incorrectly.

The bitcoin network chooses the availability and partition tolerance properties of this triplet.

Moreover, the bitcoin algorithm took a particularly interesting approach to consensus by attempting to create a censorship-resistant network where no participant is privileged. The consensus process was *eventually consistent* and tied the addition of new transactions to the solution of a computational problem in which computers that participated in the consensus algorithm would need to spend a given amount of computational work to attempt to confirm the writes. This approach, known as *proof of work* created what is known as a random sortition operation in which a network participant would be selected randomly and probabilistically based on how much computational power (called *hashrate*) was performed to attempt consensus.

Because there is no central authority, and because it takes computational work—and thus an expense—to record transactions an incentive mechanism is required to reward those who sustain the network integrity. Therefore the bitcoin architecture created a computational game mechanic in which the computers in this network (called *miners*) competed to perform consensus actions and successfully confirming a block of transactions gave a fixed reward to the first "player" to commit a set of transactions. The rules of the game were defined by the shared software that all participants ran, which defined the network protocol. The critical ideas encoded in the protocol are the predetermined release schedule, fixed supply, and support for those protocol changes that have support off a majority of participants.

One of the core algorithms used in most blockchains is a hash function. A hash function is a classic cryptography algorithm in which data is repeatedly scrambled in a process that is difficult to reverse and produces a unique fingerprint of the data unique to the given input. The output of this function is an inordinately large number which is often encoded in the hexadecimal (base-16 number system).

Hello World

d2a84f4b8b650937ec8f73cd8be2c74add5a911ba64df27458ed8229da804a26

Minor changes to the input of a hash function alter the output. For instance, if the Hello World statement instead has a lowercase "w" the output changes drastically:

```
Hello world
```
1894a19c85ba153acbf743ac4e43fc004c891604b26f8c69e1e83ea2afc7c48f

The hash function's output follows some well-studied statistical distributions, and the probability of an output prefixed by a fixed number of zeros can be predicted to occur within a certain amount of hashes. This process allows the difficulty mechanism of obtaining a particular output to be scaled and gives rise to the adjustable puzzle that miners are forced to solve to perform block confirmation. This mechanism allows the difficulty of bitcoin mining to be artificially adjusted proportionally to the rewards.

This consensus algorithm's underlying data kept in sync a specific constructed data structure known as a *blockchain*. The blockchain is a ledger data structure that holds an authoritative record of all proposed spend activities of a digital numerical unit of value. A bitcoin is thereby a decimal value whose spend activities were enforced by the consensus algorithms and could be transmitted to other accounts, recorded on the blockchain, and mapped to addresses corresponding to public cryptographic keys. This design created a distributed digital ledger that recorded debits which could be continuously updated over time as the bitcoins were created and spent.

The *censorship resistance* of this algorithm was the critical improvement over existing eCash systems which previously had a single legal point of failure, in that the central register or central node would have to be stored in a single server that could be targeted by governments and law enforcement. In this trustless peer-to-peer (P2P) model—the same mechanism that powered Napster and BitTorrent—all computers participated in the network, and removing any one node would not degrade the availability of the whole network. Just as previous P2P networks had routed around intellectual property laws, bitcoin routed around money transmitter laws.

On January 3rd, 2009, the first block in the bitcoin blockchain, also known as the genesis block, was created. It contained a simple message in The Times concerning the bank bailouts during the subprime mortgage crisis:

```
The Times
03/Jan/2009
Chancellor on brink of second bailout for banks
```

The early history of bitcoin saw the technology primarily used as Nakamoto intended, namely as an anonymous global digital payment network. Early-adopter technologists used Bitcoin as an anonymous way to pay for goods and services and as a tip system for authors of online content. One of the first notable exchanges was two pizzas in exchange for 10,000 bitcoins ($40 at the time) on March 22nd, 2010. The first evidence of a price bubble followed in June 2011, when the exchange value for one bitcoin moved from $30 down to $2 in December 2011 after a prominent bitcoin exchange website hack. In 2013 the technology began to receive mainstream attention from the press, and this era represents the philosophical transition of the technology from use as a hypothetical digital currency into an asset for investment. The rapid price movement was at the time uncorrelated with traditional assets and proved an attractive investment for a class of traders looking for new speculative opportunities. After this point, the single defining feature of bitcoin no longer became its utility for anonymous payments but for its price action as a speculative investment.

The original author (or authors) of the technology withdrew from participation in the network and any communication; as other software developers and companies took up development. This new era marks a rapid expansion of a cottage industry of startups and early adopters who would build exchanges, mining equipment, and a marketing network to proselytize the virtues of this new technology. The culture around the extreme volatility of the asset created a series of memes within the subculture of HODL (a portmanteau of the term "holding," standing for "hold on for dear life"), which encourages investors to hold the asset regardless of price movement. This investment philosophy became central to the cryptocurrency sector and was a statement of faith in the asset class. The implicit promise of bitcoin and any cryptocurrency in this era is that if of easy money for nothing and; the idea that if you invest early, you can get rich when the value "goes to the moon." Effectively a digital form of the classic get-rich-quick scheme for the internet era. This marked the start of a new crypto era, the Grifter Era.

2.2 The Grifter Era

In addition to bitcoin, a series of similar technologies based on the same ideas emerged in the 2011-2013 era. The first movers were Litecoin, Namecoin, Peercoin, and a parody token known as Dogecoin based on an internet meme. These projects (called *altcoins*) were built on the bitcoin model but tweaked the implementation of the protocol to allow for different network behaviors and incorporated different economic models. As of August 2018, the number of launched cryptocurrency projects exceeded 1600. In 2015 a significant extension to the bitcoin model called the ethereum blockchain was launched with the aim to build a "world computer" in which programmable logic could be expressed on the blockchain instead of only simple asset transfers. This project would become the second-most traded token and would popularize the notion of smart contracts. In addition to fully visible transaction models of previous tokens, chains such as Monero and ZCash would incorporate privacy-enhancing features into the design, allowing participants to have blinded transactions that would obscure the endpoint details for illicit transactions with no public audit record.

Unlike in the original bitcoin paper, the idea of "one computer, one vote" was supplanted by the economic reality that large groups of computers could more efficiently compute the hashes required to confirm blocks and thus reap financial rewards from the network. Early entrepreneurs realized that they could gain an advantage over traditional server farms if they built faster and more specialized hardware to compute these hashes. These entrepreneurs began to build ASICs (Application Specific Integrated Circuit), custom hardware circuits that could do the computations required for the bitcoin network more efficiently than traditional CPUs offered by companies like Intel and AMD. This economic circumstance led to a technical arms race in which dedicated hardware became required to mine bitcoin, and larger groups would build clusters of computers that would pool the rewards acquired by mining together. These *mining pools* became a centralized and very lucrative business for early investors. An example is, the Chinese company BitMain, which began to centralize most of the computational resources, resulting in 70% of all bitcoin mining being concentrated in mainland China by 2019.

The underutilization of coal-fired power production and Chinese capital restrictions on renminbi outflows offered a unique opportunity for enterprising Chinese citizens to move capital outside of the mainland beyond government controls. In 2018 the Chinese government officially declared cryptocurrency mining an undesirable activity. The same year, Bloomberg reported $50 billion of capital flight from the Chinese state using the Tether cryptocurrency[2].

In 2017 a new trend emerged when market participants realized that secondary tokens could be launched on top of the ethereum blockchain. This trend gave rise to a controversial new market for ICO (Initial Coin Offerings), offerings of digital tokens to fund project development. In September 2017, an ICO named Kik raised $100 million within several days. Over the next year, many other ventures would raise unconventionally high amounts of money for early-stage ventures. Between January and June 2018, over $7 billion was raised to fund ICO projects. Most of these projects failed within a very short period and exhausted their funds to pursue business models that would prove intractable and economically unviable. Many, moreover, turned out to be fraudulent or thinly veiled *exit scams* in which the entrepreneurs simply abscond with the crypto assets raised and never build the product claimed in the prospectus. These cases are being litigated to this day.

The Grifter Era period also saw the introduction of stablecoins such as Tether, aiming to be a stable cryptoasset with its price allegedly pegged to the US dollar and theoretically backed by a reserve of other assets. This is followed by a 2019 period of market volatility and market consolidation of cryptocurrencies, during which many unfounded ideas fell off and left a handful of 20 projects which would dominate trading volume and developer mindshare.

In 2021 China outright banned all domestic banks and payment companies from touching cryptoassets and banned all mining pools in the country. At the same time, the United States continued to be hit by an onslaught of cyberterrorism and ransomware attacks that began to attack core national infrastructure and the country's energy grids.

Historical Market Manias

"The four most expensive words in investing are: 'This time it's different.' "

– John Templeton

While the mania surrounding cryptocurrency may seem like a purely contemporary phenomenon, there are a great many parallels to crypto manias in the history of finance, where irrational exuberance and greed have regularly and with increasing frequency infected the minds of otherwise rational people. Capitalism invariably and with enormous predictability falls sick to a form of madness. These manic episodes are periods where markets seem to defy gravity and only trend upwards; eras where new financial products offer seemingly limitless possibilities. The glowing aura of the promise of a "new economy" warps common sense and reason to the point of absurdity. The American economist Burton Malkiel wrote of these bubbles in his book A *Random Walk Down Wall Street*:

> A bubble starts when any group of stocks, in this case those associated with the excitement of the Internet, begin to rise. The updraft encourages more people to buy the stocks, which causes more TV and print coverage, which causes even more people to buy, which creates big profits for early Internet stockholders. The successful investors tell you at cocktail parties how easy it is to get rich, which causes the stocks to rise further, which pulls in larger and larger groups of investors. But the whole mechanism is a kind of Ponzi scheme where more and more credulous investors must be found

to buy the stock from the earlier investors. Eventually, one runs out of greater fools.

In 1978 the economist Charles P. Kindleberger published his seminal book *Manias, Panics, and Crashes*, a now-classic text on market manias that outlines what would become known as the Minsky-Kindleberger model[15,26] of speculative bubbles. Here, Kindleberger outlines six phases of bubbles:

1. *Expansion* - Investors are enamored with the promise of new technology, a new economy often accompanied by a period of low-interest rates.

2. *Euphoria* - Investors rush into the new investment, throwing caution to the wind and feeling that this event is a once-in-a-lifetime opportunity.

3. *Distress* - The market peaks as some early insiders decide to withdraw. These events spark controversy, reflection, and uncertainty about the previously-assumed "new paradigm."

4. *Revulsion* - As money flows out of the investment, scandals, bankruptcies, and liquidations occur.

5. *Crisis* - The realization there is not enough money for everyone, and insiders begin strategically selling.

6. *Contagion* - The knowledge of the crisis becomes widespread. This crisis becomes self-fulfilling and self-reinforcing, leading to the speculative bubble's collapse.

In most bubbles[9], there is a shift in public sentiment, known as the *Minsky moment*[19]: when sentiment shifts, euphoria gives way to fear, and the market risk catches up with buyers financing their positions based on debt. In many manias, a large bulk of the inflow results from buyers taking on debt to buy the asset, assuming they will be able to pay off their debt if the underlying asset continues to appreciate in value. However, these investors are the most exposed to risk in fluctuations of the underlying asset. Any short-term downturn in the asset prices may cause them to exit their positions as they cannot pay the interest on their debt. Minksy's work shows that the amount of debt financing in an asset bubble is highly predictive of the stability of the asset. While the warning signs and patterns are extraordinarily predictable, history tells us that each new generation has to learn for themselves the hard lesson that markets can only defy gravity for so long before reality reasserts itself.

The relationship between bubbles and fraud is historically linked. Mass delusions do not sustain themselves, and there are always opportunists and operators who choose to partake in the mania and, by doing so, reinforce and maintain the inflow of dumb money used to inflate it further. Charles Mackay's famous book accurately chronicles the historical manias and popular delusions of the 1700s. However, Mackay's heavy-handed moralizing of the madness of crowds reflects a somewhat antiquated attitude that manias are "done by others." The economist Ken Galbraith[7] gave a much more holistic interpretation of the manias as arising primarily from a lack of public sense-making and institutions willing to condemn the intellectual incoherence of popular delusions:

> The euphoric episode is protected and sustained by the will of those who are involved, in order to justify the circumstances that are making them rich. And it is equally protected by the will to ignore, exorcise, or condemn those who express doubts.

It is not surprising that in eras of populist uprisings, anti-democratic sentiment, distrust of public sense-making institutions, and when combined with low-interest rates and growing economic inequity, we almost invariably are faced with breeding ground for manias to grow and infect the public consciousness. The 18th-century British economist Walter Bagehot wrote of manias in his book *Lombard Street: A Description of the Money Market*, which describes the reality-distortion field for the possibility of easy wealth that infuses bubbles. Economic absurdities will be humored long past the public revelation of their inherent contradictions.

> The good times too of high price almost always engender much fraud. All people are most credulous when they are most happy; and when much money has just been made, when some people are really making it, when most people think they are making it, there is a happy opportunity for ingenious mendacity. Almost everything will be believed for a little while, and long before discovery the worst and most adroit deceivers are geographically or legally

beyond the reach of punishment. But the harm they have done diffuses harm, for it weakens credit still farther.

Speculative assets are often built around soft cults of personality around a charismatic individual, usually, a CEO or financier, who investors feel embodies the spirit of the new economy. These are figures like George Hudson in the Railway Mania, Kenenth Lay in the Enron scandal, Adam Neumann in the Venture Bubble, and Elon Musk in the cryptocurrency bubble; all these men speak to some underlying circumstance and opportunity that resonates with the zeitgeist and allows them to channel enormous amounts of capital into investments that in otherwise-rational eras would be seen as patently insane. At the heights of the market euphoria, these men often exhibit irrationality and begin to deify themselves, thinking their business to be above the law and their actions infused with cosmic significance, all with their worst character flaws manifesting in their increasingly bizarre antics. A man's character is his destiny, and the fate of these men is usually in ruin.

While waves of speculation and bubbles always coincide, we have nearly six hundred years of recorded history chronicling their initial conditions, internal structure, and aftermath, by which we can rational analyze many contemporary bubbles. Among past manias, there have always both productive and unproductive bubbles. Productive bubbles correspond with rapid advances in technology or the discovery of new commodities. While unproductive bubbles generally correspond to rapid advances in financial engineering or the proliferation of contagious mass delusions.

3.1 SOUTH SEA BUBBLE OF 1720

In 1711 Great Britain found itself in a dire financial position due[20], in part, to long sustained wars against the French and Spanish powers. The chancellor of the exchequer, Robert Harley, found that the state owed £9,000,000, the equivalent today to £1.8 billion when adjusted for inflation.

An entrepreneur with a somewhat dubious past, John Blunt devised a scheme with Robert Harley to address the government's debt problem. They constructed an empty company, called the South Sea Company, that would acquire all of the government's debt. The government would pay a 6% interest rate on this consolidated debt in exchange. In a mass restructuring of the debt, the company negotiated with the creditors to swap their debt for shares in the South Sea Company. These shares would pay out dividends to shareholders from the interest generated and represent fractional ownership in a government-backed monopoly where the South Sea Company would have sole rights to trade in South America. At the time, British companies like the East India Company were extremely lucrative ventures built on the back of the British empire, and to many of these creditors, the debt-equity swap was an enticing investment.

However, at the time, the Spanish Empire controlled the South American seas, with whom Britain had previously been at war leading to fraught Spanish-British relations. The South Sea Company negotiated a contract to trade enslaved people in the Americas; however, the tensions between the Spanish and British limited the amount of trade the two empires could engage in commercially. The South Sea Company grew to a massive scale and became systemically crucial to the British economy, given the amount of public money and shareholders attached to the venture. The company's original founders were exited from the directorship. Slowly, the company was captured by the state, where the Prince of Wales, George II, was installed as governor of the South Sea Company only to be succeeded by the King of England George I. The company became dominated by cronyism, and the King quickly installed his other Whig politicians from the government as managers in the company to secure his influence over the enterprise.

By 1718 the British and the Spanish returned to war, and the contractual relationship between the South Sea Company and the Government of Spain soured. The company was effectively a non-economic enterprise; its entire business consolidated government debt into financial products wholly detached from any productive enterprise to pay out dividends. Nevertheless, the company's stock price rose due to speculation in the enterprise detached from its underlying business fundamentals. The company created additional financial engineering on top of the already tenuous business model, whereby it would issue loans to shareholders to buy the company's own stock, thus inflating the share price and creating circular debt.

Just as during other manias, many entrepreneurs became aware of the precarious nature of the company's finances; however, seeing money be made on these complicated financial structures, their reaction was to create similarly fraudulent enterprises. Many other joint-stock companies were founded on similarly extravagant and often fraudulent claims about new ventures out of equally convoluted financial structures. These types of companies were described in the British press as an "undertaking of great advantage, but nobody to know what it is." Nevertheless, as is the perceptual story throughout the history of financial manias, the credulous multitudes piled into these schemes hoping to make a quick buck, utterly unaware of the enterprise they were investing in or what it entailed.

The hype in the South Sea Company continued to grow until it reached an all-time high of almost £1000 per share. However, by the end of 1720, the fear of missing out was quickly supplanted by fear as the market realized that the enterprise was almost entirely a fraudulent Potemkin village, which sparked a rapid sell-off of the stock. The stock price of the South Sea Company collapsed by 85%, a fall from which it never recovered. Many investors were financially ruined, and the implosion severely damaged the national economy of Britain.

At the same time, the British government passed The Bubble Act 1720, which forbade the creation of joint-stock companies except by royal charter in an effort to clamp down on the vast amount of purely-speculative enterprises that had arisen as copycats of the South Sea Company. The ensemble of the South Sea Company and its surrounding fraudulent enterprises would becomes known by historians as the South Sea Bubble and marked the first mainstream usage of *bubble* as a term of art in economics.

The Anglo-Irish writer and satirist Johnathan Swift published a humorous piece recalling the event entitled *A South-Sea Ballad, Or, Merry Remarks Upon Exchange-Alley Bubbles.* He satirized the fictitious financial "castles in the sky" that lead to the company's ruin as follows:

> *While some build castles in the air,*
> *Directors build them in the seas;*
> *Subscribers plainly see them there,*
> *For fools will see as wise men please.*

To this day, the South Sea Bubbles remains the canonical historical bubble[18] studied as an almost perfect example of criminogenic environments that give rise to fraud. The confluence of the corruption of government, financialization of non-productive enterprises, complicated financial engineering, and irrational exuberance are now the textbook hallmarks of bubbles. The South Sea Bubble took even the most clever scholars and capitalists of the day. Even the renowned physicist Sir Issac Newton, a man whose genius few in history rival, lost £20,000 on the South Sea Bubble, the equivalent of losing £4.3 million today. Newton wrote of the incident:

> I can calculate the motions of the heavenly bodies, but not the madness of people.

The South Sea Bubble presents the most explicit historical parallel to the cryptocurrency bubble[3]. Every aspect of the South Sea Company mirrors a nearly identical element of the crypto fraud we see today, from the lack of the pretense to productive activity to complex financial obfuscation and regulatory capture.

3.2 MISSISSIPPI BUBBLE OF 1720

At the same time, across the English Channel, the French were also being seduced by their own speculative mania. In France, the wars waged by Louis XIV had left the country completely devastated, both economically and financially. There was a vast shortage of gold, and the government was in a dire position with its debts. Seeing an opportunity, John Law[10] started a private bank called Banque Générale Privée, which began to issue paper notes that customers could redeem for gold in the now-common practice of maintaining fractional reserves for the notes. Each French livre note was only backed by a fraction of the note's face value, effectively replacing gold coinage with paper credit issued by the bank. Law believed that paper money was strictly superior to physical coinage because the supply of the paper could be controlled by the issuer and could then denominate transactions for shares in dividend-paying joint ventures, similar to the South Sea Company's idea. The paper notes and the bank were so successful that Law was given a charter for the Banque Royale and was given custody of all French national debt by the monarchy.

On the back of this success, John Law turned his eyes to using the advent of paper money to create a new joint venture to mirror the success of the East India Company and the South Sea Company in England. Law was granted a royal charter to establish the Mississippi Company to colonize the recently established Mississippi Valley in the Americas, then occupied by French settlers. Law consolidated the colonization efforts into a single entity and issued shares, denominated in notes issued by his own Banque Royale, sold to the general public in an initial offering of 500 livres per share.

On the back of an aggressive marketing campaign by Law and the captured aristocracy, the public was taken by a speculative frenzy of investing in the new Mississippi Company shares. Their price soon ballooned to 15,000 livres per share. The promises of easy money were seductive, and all classes of French society piled into what would later become known as the Mississippi Bubble.

As is the common theme of bubbles, the fundamental reality of the investment compared to its perceived value was not commensurate. In fact, Mississippi was little more than unsettled swampland at the time and was nowhere close to being a profitable colony. However, in France, the reality of this situation was not public knowledge the speculative mania proceeded utterly detached from the economic reality across the ocean. The bubble would be sustained by the simple fact that Law, who controlled the printing of money at Banque Royale, could simply expand credit by printing money at will and use this credit to pay out profits in the Mississippi Company thereby creating the illusion of growth.

There was only enough gold to match one-fifth of the paper money in circulation, and since the bank notes legally guaranteed redemption in gold, this situation exposed Banque Royale to the risk of a bank run. Following several large withdrawals of Mississippi shares into gold, the bank experienced gold reserve shortages and the public quickly lost confidence in the value of the shares. The speculative mania came to a rapid end as the bank experienced several crises following the runs and was forced to devalue the notes below their face value. Both entities collapsed shortly after that, and Law was forced to flee France, both destitute and villainized by the public. The French philosopher Voltaire reported on John Law and the madness that gripped the country:

They say that everyone who was comfortably off is now in misery
and everyone who was impoverished revels in opulence. Is this reality? Is this a chimera? Has half the nation found the philosopher's
stone in the paper mills? Is Law a god, a rogue, or a quack, who
poisons himself with the drugs he administers to all the world

And yet, nearly all the characteristics of the Mississippi bubble are ever-present
in today's stablecoin enterprises who solicit investments in their empty ventures
through derivative dollars of unknown leverage, much in the same way that John
Law did. The times have changed, the language has changed, but the grift has
remained the same.

3.3 Railway Mania of the 1840s

In the 1840s, Britain was at the height of the industrial revolution, and char-
acteristically low-interest rates spurred a burgeoning middle class to find productive investments in the economy. The Bubble Act, which had been implemented during the South Sea Bubble, was repealed, and once again, public
money flowed into joint-stock companies again as the middle class began to see
superior returns than widely available government bonds. Early railway companies were seen as a reasonably safe investment; they seemingly offered an honest
business model of laying track and charging fares. Existing railroad companies
were performing exceptionally well on the market, were largely profitable, and
paid higher dividends than many other stocks at the time.

With the Bubble Act overturned, there was no limit on new venture formation. Responding to a legitimate need for more infrastructure to transport
goods across the rapidly industrializing British state, opportunistic businessmen
created railway ventures left and right. These companies merely had to submit
proposals to Parliament to acquire land to lay track. However, as is common
in the case of manias, members of Parliament themselves were captured by the
fact that they were also investors in the companies they were set to regulate, and
generally rubber-stamped such railway approvals with little regard for the financial viability of the new lines. These companies saw a vast increase in their stock
price as the public, seeing an opportunity for profit, piled into railroad stocks

inflating their prices far in excess of the underlying business fundamentals.

At the start of 1840, Britain had barely constructed railways between London and Wales, but a mere twelve years later, over 6,600 miles of track had been laid during the massive building spree. However, the value of the railways' stocks was untethered to the economic realities of how much profit these ventures could generate. As railways opened and competed with one another, the market reached a point where there was a diminishing return on opening new lines. The capacity for outsized returns vanished as the market stabilized. Many members of the general public had invested their entire life savings in these ventures and found themselves subsequently wiped out.

3.4 WILDCAT BANKING OF THE 1800S

In the 1800s, the United States was firmly founded as an independent country. It had however, not yet instituted a national currency, letting its citizens instead use whatever currency they pleased. People used the small amounts of gold coinage officially issued by the mint; still, the lack of availability of these currencies and the lack of banknotes meant that these few "official" currencies of the United States were in short supply relative to the need for a widespread medium of exchange[12]. The dominant means to conduct commerce in the Americas was instead instead the currencies of foreign nations and private banknotes. These notes were all printed independently, and some bore the face of American presidents just as the US dollar does today, while others bore the faces of executives of the banks that issued them—one banknote even bore the face of Santa Claus. These banks and their associated era became known as the *wildcat banking era*[4,25].

In principle, the note acted as a form of scrip that customers could redeem at the local bank for its face value at a fixed amount of gold or silver. However, the note was only legally redeemable at the bank that printed it. The notes could, in principle, be used for commerce both locally in the jurisdiction the bank served and in limited capacity nationally as the individual notes could be exchanged at variable rates for other banks' private notes. The Bank of Indiana might hypothetically use a note with a face value of five private dollars, which the Bank of Kentucky might optionally honor in exchange for four of its private dollars and vice versa.

At the height of the wildcat banking era in 1859, there were over 8000 types of banknotes and coinage. This vast network of arbitrage opportunities meant that shopkeepers and exchangers had to keep up-to-date records of domestic currencies, much like foreign exchange works today[27].

The out-of-control private money printing, just as in France with the Mississippi Bubble, created a criminogenic environment ripe for fraud. Banks purposefully printed notes vastly in excess of their reserves of gold. Unlike today's system of bank reserve requirements, banks were not prohibited from creating massively leveraged notes against very few hard assets. Banks' reserves were monitored only by a patchwork of state-by-state laws and local commissioners, and banks often gamed the system and moved gold between banks to create the illusion of solvency. Bank runs and total bank defaults were not uncommon occurrences. The public trust in these banks was so low that their coinage was often melted down because the value of even the copper and zinc in the coin was intrinsically worth more than its face value. The wildcat system was rife with fraud, as one Michigan bank commissioner noted in 1839:

> A law which was established upon principles well digested and approved, and hedged round with so much care and guarded with so many provisions ... became by the base dishonesty and gross cupidity of a few, who had the control of the specie of the country, nothing less than a machine of fraud.

In 1861, the American Civil War broke out, and the Union states of the North opted to issue their own national currency, which was usable by the government as a universal means to pay for war expenses. The greenback note bore the now-standard legal claim:

> This Note is a Legal Tender for all debts public and private except Duties on Imports and Interest on the Public Debt; and is receivable in payment of all loans made to the United States.

The greenbacks were, at the time, seen as an emergency measure and temporary stopgap by which to expedite commerce during the war. However, by pure market forces rather than by legal decree, the public simply found the national notes far superior to their private counterparts. The public's ability to rely on the faith and credit of the United States Treasury to pay its debts was far less risky than depending on an unseen private company in some distant state.

These private banks started to finance the federal government's Civil War effort. As part of the legal right to issue war bonds, the banks would fall under the remit of the new National Bank Act of 1863, which gave the federal government the right to oversee banking activities by issuing national banking charters. These chartered banks had uniform capital and reserve requirements and suffered penalties for transactions done in the bank's private money. The Bank Act economically disincentivized private money and pushed the country to organically harmonize its currency under a single national uniform dollar that the United States still uses today.

Nevertheless, the lessons of wildcat banking are still a stark reminder today about the failures of experiments in private money. When the public allows private accountable entities access to a money printer, they usually use it as a "machine of fraud" just as much today as they did back in 1839. The wildcat era marked an era of unnecessary friction in commerce, rampant fraud, and a breakdown of trust in the financial system. The history lesson from the wildcat banking era is that bank deposits cannot reliably act as money without bank regulation and supervision and some form of government insurance. Bank runs and defaults are not only common with private money—they are inevitable and financial markets are subject to undue and completely unnecessary shocks when large blocks of assets and contracts denominated in those assets suddenly become valueless. This phenomenon, in turn, puts more pressure on the courts[6] to clean up the financial messes, which they are most often unable to do adequately. Finally, this turns into a vicious cycle that erodes more trust in public institutions. A developed economy needs a sovereign currency backed by the full faith and reserve of a single issuer, of which the state is the most qualified and natural entity. Putting faith in a free market for thousands of types of private money is always doomed to failure. The wildcat banking era is an important lesson to learn from the past, given the recent fringe efforts to return to a digital variant of private money with stablecoins and cryptoassets[13,11,28].

3.5 THE MARKET CRASH OF 1929

Throughout the 1920s, the American economy saw a period of rapid growth, with a 9-year bull market culminating in an all-time high on September 3, 1929. It was an era marked by easy credit and increasing prosperity, consumerism, and a liberalizing way of life. It was the era chronicled in the *Great Gatsby* by F. Scott Fitzgerald, who wrote:

> The pace was faster, the shows were broader, the buildings were higher, the morals were looser, and the liquor was cheaper.

The Liberty Loan Act of 1917 granted the United States federal government the capacity to issue war bonds, known as the Liberty Bond, to fund Allied Efforts in World War I. The United States emerged from the war victorious, and the bonds were retired. The buying of bonds was seen as a patriotic duty and gave many Americans their first taste of buying government-backed securities, a concept which had previously been seen as abstract and purely the purview of wealthy capitalists.

In the wake of the war recovery, the Federal Reserve kept interest rates exceptionally low to encourage productive investment in European allies' post-war economies. With periods of low-interest rates, money was cheap. The public was able to take out increasingly more significant positions on margin to speculate on financial assets in the flourishing securities markets that would become the hallmark of the Roaring 20s. In 1928 President Herbert Hoover would claim the country was so prosperous that it was on the verge of eliminating poverty altogether, the characteristic glowing aura of a "new economy" that always coincides with bubbles.

> We in America today are nearer to the final triumph over poverty than ever before in the history of any land. [...] We shall soon, with the help of God, be in sight of the day when poverty will be banished from this nation.

As is characteristic of euphoric episodes, charlatans and hucksters rushed in to exploit the public. Now infamous characters like Charles Ponzi[30,1], whose namesake the Ponzi scheme is based, began running his fraudulent investment scheme in 1920. Similarly, many fraudulent brokers known as *bucket shops*[17] emerged, that offered clients the ability to place positions on publicly traded stocks. These buckets shops would provide clients with unusually discounted shares with extremely large margin positions. In these margin schemes, often at 100 times leverage, every $1 in cash would allegedly permit the client to purchase $100 in stock. However, the bucket shop would take the money from the customer without actually executing the trade on the market. This allowed bucket shops to act effectively act as a casino, paper trading the positions and paying out clients' withdrawals from other clients' deposits while collecting interest on margin positions and liquidating clients on the frequent margin calls induced by highly leveraged positions. The business model of the 1920s buckets shops mirrors that of crypto exchanges today.

In 1929 approximately 60% of all credit was invested in American equities. Large banks in New York offered new investment vehicles to the public to pool money into managed trusts. These trusts, which many buyers bought on margin, used their holdings to take leveraged positions in other trusts creating chains of geometrically-increasing debt, which increased both the possible returns and risk of the entire edifice. The public began to discuss the market as part of everyday conversation, and newspapers printed financial advice and hot stock tips. John F. Kennedy's father, Joseph P. Kennedy Sr., was quoted, perhaps apocryphally, saying, "If shoeshine boys are giving stock tips, then it's time to get out of the market." His reservation contrasted with the irrational exuberance of American economist Irving Fisher who infamously declared that stock prices have reached "what looks like a permanently high plateau."

However, a sequence of corporate scandals and bearish analyst opinions soon after shook public trust in the markets, and through a sequence of staggered crashes, the markets began to unwind. Between 1929 and 1932, stocks lost 90% of their value, and $500 billion was wiped off the markets. The shocks in the Americas markets spread across the pond to the London Stock Exchange. The market shocks quickly shook the European economy[21] as well, which according to many historians was because of due to their intertwined and inflexible dependence on the gold standard. The autumn of 1929 signaled the beginning of the Great Depression with stock market shocks causing over 10,000 American banks to fail, leaving Americans with no access to their savings and no recourse.

In the aftermath of the crisis, the United States federal government put into place a series of reforms to prevent the extreme risk and opaque structures that had contributed to financial instability and a breakdown in public trust. The Percoa Commission investigation into the market collapse found evidence that many of the transactions leading up to the market collapse resulted from fraudulent claims by sellers of investments and their failure to disclose pertinent information to buyers. The act also held sellers of securities and directors of companies liable for misselling and misrepresentation of company information. Lawmakers folded these findings into what would become the Securities Act of 1933 and which set in place the Securities and Exchange Commission to oversee the registration and regulation of investment contracts in the United States. This post-regulatory era marked a series of even greater bull markets, and the postwar market recovered to new all-time highs as consumer confidence in markets was refreshed in light of the success of the market reforms of the New Deal.

3.6 ALBANIAN PYRAMID SCHEMES OF THE 1990S

In 1991 Albania moved from a communist system directly into a free market economy, with very few institutions to protect or regulate the new market. It was the pure libertarian economy most crypto acolytes dream of, a greenfield scammers paradise where anything goes with little to no government oversight.

In this environment, several significant development "funds" emerged that promised to take retail investment and use the funds to invest in other developing enterprises and infrastructure in the nation. They enticed investors with promises of large yields with low risk and the public lept into these schemes without much due diligence.

From an accounting perspective, all of these funds were insolvent from the start. The liabilities exceed assets since the scheme has no income other than bringing in new investors. It required constant recruiting and promotion to sustain the illusion. As in any pyramid scheme, investments were solicited from the public on the pretense (implicit or explicit) of offering high returns on their investment. Still, the secret sauce that makes the pyramid scheme work time and time again is that returns are paid to the early investors out of the funds received from those who invest later. The lack of returns is then obscured by restricting access to redemptions and by opaque accounting and corporate structure.[29]

Later investors are drawn in by cherry-picking anecdotes and stories about the returns of a small group of early investors while ignoring the macro cash flows of the entire scheme. Eventually, when late investors try to get their money out of exchanges or brokers, they discover the truth about the scheme being insolvent. The scheme operators usually flee with the remaining funds, and it all quickly collapses, leaving a wake of victims behind.

In Albania, many of these schemes were outright run by government officials that promised to serve as rudimentary financial service providers in a developing economy that lacked many of the services found elsewhere in Europe. This scheme reached its zenith in 1997 when two-thirds of the country's population invested in them, and over 10% of the national GDP was invested or locked into these pyramid schemes. Before their end, the schemes promised exorbitant 40%/monthlhy returns to draw in the last few victims.[14]

The corrupt government stayed silent about the scams throughout this era, further fueling the myth that the pyramid schemes were legitimate. In the end, the schemes were revealed to be nothing but thinly veiled pyramid schemes that kept soliciting more and more public money until finally collapsing. The leaders of the scams absconded with the last money that remained and fled the country. The victims of the scams started to riot and petitioned the government to intervene to recover their money. These protests triggered violent unrest and claimed an estimated 2000 lives. Ten of these schemes were wiped out overnight, the economy collapsed, and not long after, the government fell. Albania descended into a state of anarchy and civil war.

The story of Albania is an omen about what can happen when a public obsessed with quick riches not tied to actual economic activity chases schemes that are simply economically impossible. Speculative manias left to grow unchecked always end badly. They become systemic to economies at a certain scale when more money is locked up in the bubble than sustaining productive enterprise.

The moral of the story is that a competent government, strong regulation, and a financially literate public are the only forces that can calm the public frenzy before large pyramid schemes damage economies and markets. People who are personally invested in pyramid schemes will fight tooth and nail to legitimize it. They want to believe. They **need** to believe. After all, the con artists behind the schemes are not selling facts, they are selling emotion which naive investors will channel to post hoc rationalize nearly anything that promises free money.

The history of Albania from 1996 to 1997 provides an uncanny historical parallel to understand the extent of damage that widespread investments in pyramid schemes can bring to a country. Widespread and unchecked investment fraud hurts innocent people, destroys lives, poses a systemic risk to economies, and can collapse entire nation-states. Albania's pyramid schemes are a grim warning about a possible future of the speculative crypto bubble if it is allowed to grow unchecked.

3.7 ENRON SCANDAL (1985 - 2007)

In 1985 the Houston Natural Gas company and Internorth Ince merged into a newly formed company, Enron. It would emerge as a powerful player in the American energy markets as a massively diversified company with plays in the financialization of energy products and the underlying natural gas market.

The company's business increased throughout the 1990s and quickly became the darling of Wall Street analysts for its seemingly unbounded growth potential and solid fundamentals. Enron showed consistent year-on-year revenue growth, a strong balance sheet, and extremely low debt to equity for a company of its size. At its height, the total market capitalization of Enron exceeded $60 billion, which was a glowing 70 times its earnings.

However, beneath the rosy exterior, the company was vastly misrepresenting its fundamentals to investors through byzantine accounting tricks and loopholes. In reality, the company was masking a massive amount of debt that was discharged from the parent company into a series of special purpose vehicles (SPVs) as a sin bin for the company's financial problems. The SPVs were kept off the books of the main public company, which gave the appearance of better company performance than was reflected in their quarterly financials. In a massive scandal, the company's auditing from Arthur Anderson likely deliberately omitted the existence of the SPVs from its audits of the company's financials and, after the fact, attempted to cover-up these ommisisons The company was tried and convinced of obstruction of justice and never recovered, after which the company's assets were sold off in pieces in a fire sale.

Fortune magazine journalist Bethany McLean uncovered parts of the scam in a now-famous article *Is Enron overpriced?* where she dares to ask radical questions such as "How exactly does Enron make its money?". Bethany would then go on to author the best-selling book *Enron: The Smartest Guys In The Room*, in which she quotes an Enron employee about the company's now-infamous creative accounting practices:

> Say you have a dog, but you need to create a duck on the financial statements. Fortunately, there are specific accounting rules for what constitutes a duck: yellow feet, white covering, orange beak. So you take the dog and paint its feet yellow and its fur white and you paste an orange plastic beak on its nose, and then you say to your accountants, 'This is a duck! Don't you agree that it's a duck?' And the accountants say, 'Yes, according to the rules, this is a duck.' Everybody knows that it's a dog, not a duck, but that doesn't matter, because you've met the rules for calling it a duck.

While Enron did engage in small amounts of illegal activity, much of what the company did was entirely legal and by the books. Enron was one of the first examples of so-called *legal fraud* in which many of the individual actions were considered legal, despite, the cumulative result being one of a clear objective to deceive.

3.8 Beanie Babies (1995 - 2000)

In the 1990s, a craze for collectible children's toys gripped the United States and caused a widespread speculative mania. The so-called Beanie Babies were small stuffed plush animals filled with plastic pellets. They were initially developed by Ty Inc, an American toy manufacturer, and distributed to boutique hobbyist shops and while initially marketed to children. However they quickly became adult collection items as people started to treat them as speculative commodities. The rise of sites like eBay gave rise to substantial secondary markets in which rare Beanie Babies would trade at 10-fold multiples of their retail value. At the time of eBay's initial public offering, roughly 25% of their auction transactions involved Beanie Baby sales resulting in these simple plush toys having an outsized influence on shaping the dot-com bubble. The confluence of these events generated a speculative mania in which Beanie Babies were traded as a form of a speculative commodity in which the primary demand for the toys was no longer as playthings but to flip them to a greater fool at a higher price than was initially paid. At the height of the mania, some especially rare or limited Beanie Babies sold for more than $20,000 - $30,000 on secondary markets.

The whole gimmick behind the Beanie craze was that the distributors understood both human psychology and behavioral economics combined with the novel appeal of creating artificial scarcity on speculative products. Collectors often have a completionist mentality and feel compelled to collect all available toys in the wider collection; by creating variable scarcity amongst the toys, the company could force customers to buy bulk quantities of plush toys simply to have the chance to get the rare items needed to complete their collections. Buyers of Beanie Babies could never find the whole collection in one store, and the artificially limited supply meant it always appeared that the products were selling out. By limiting the distribution channels, creating the toys as part of a broader collection and simultaneously creating variable artificial scarcity within the collection, the company bootstrapped a collectible item seemingly based on a small children's toy which had very little intrinsic value unto itself—Not unlike the crypto market for non-fungible tokens (NFTs) today.

By 2000 the speculative mania for Beanie Babies had died down. The prices of the toys reverted or below to their retail value as the collective delusion that plush children's toys were a path to vast wealth became increasingly seen as absurd in public consciousness. The company also began to retire specific lines of the toys, self-deal in its own product, and engaged in a series of questionable practices that seemingly presented as market manipulation that offended the speculators of the toys, who felt that they were being manipulated for the benefit of insiders. The company's actions alienated its fanbase, and the illusion of value and easy wealth faded.

Collectibles based on contemporary fads have historically never formed the basis for a solid investment. One generation's obsession with tulips gives way to another generation's obsession with a stamp collection, which gives way to another generation's Pokemon cards, and the cycle of cultural deprecation continues. These items, while nostalgic for some, have never been an outperforming long-term investment due to their performance as an asset being intrinsically linked to their cultural relevance, which invariably fades with time. Thus, all but the most important of these cultural artifacts almost invariably have a negative expected return as an investment. The creation of artificial scarcity as a commercial enterprise only serves to decrease the cultural significance of the artifacts, as their value is derived not from present cultural relevance but the expectation of short-term profits derived from speculation. Beanie Babies are the perfect example of a flash-in-the-pan mania that had little cultural relevance after their artificial scarcity and irrational demand became untethered. The illusion of momentum sustains bubbles based on artificial scarcity, and momentum based on non-economic enterprises is ultimately unsustainable on long-time scales.

3.9 THE DOT-COM BUBBLE (1995 - 2001)

The most recent bubble in living memory was is the dot-com bubble in the 1990s. It all started with the early internet, called ARPANET, which was created directly to address the need to network together specific government computer systems at the height of the Cold War between the United States and the Soviet Union. It was the information backbone for academics at national government labs and universities to share information relating to defense projects. Soon after, the uses of the technology beyond the defense sector became apparent, and the scope and reach of the internet expanded to commercial enterprises. In 1989, British computer scientist Tim Berners-Lee created the hypertext protocol for sharing linked documents, which would become the surface interface for interacting with the internet and give rise to the modern world wide web and the browser interface we see today.

Shortly after that, the use of the web for private commercial applications exploded. The era saw the rise of Google, eBay, PayPal, and Amazon coupled with

a vast Cambrian explosion of both technologies and new business models. Seeing the opportunity to make easy money, a wave of entrepreneurs launched so-
called dot-com companies, which attempted to capitalize on the internet hype to
sell everything from dog food to virtual currencies. For every Google, there were
a hundred flops based on unsound economics and little more than technobabble
and hot air.

Companies such as pets.com, which sold pet supplies online, became em-
blematic of the era's excesses. They spent fortunes on user acquisition while
simultaneously taking a loss on nearly every sale as the company spent lavishly
on super bowl advertisements featuring their corporate mascot, a talking sock
puppet espousing the virtues of buying dog food online. The company went
public on NASDAQ in February 2000 while still being an utterly unprofitable
enterprise, an event which is often regarded as the peak of the dot-com mania.
It would be defunct only nine months later.

At the peak of the bubble between 2000 to 2001, hundreds of internet-related
companies went public globally, only to see most of the market capitalization
quickly evaporate as both geopolitical shocks of the September 11 attacks and
the economic realities of the vastly unsustainable business models asserted themselves. By 2002, $5 trillion in market capitalization had been wiped off the mar-
kets, marking the dot-com bubble's definitive end.

3.10 The Subprime Mortgage Crisis (2003 - 2008)

American markets were in a precarious situation following the accounting scandals of the 1990s and the dot-com bust of the early 2000s. The stock market
was widely seen as too risky, while the bond market was underperforming. Investors had considerable hunger for products that promised high returns with
low risks, and the banks responded to demand by creating a vastly more sophisticated debt market in the form of mortgage-backed securities (MBS). These
mortgage-backed securities were financial assets that pooled similar risk debt
obligations for mortgages into pools and then packaged this pool into a security that speculators could trade. The interest and principal payments from the
underlying borrower or homebuyer would pass through the pool to the current

MBS holder. The underlying property collateralized the mortgage itself, so in the event of a default, the owner of the MBS could repossess the property via a legal process known as *foreclosure*.

By 2003 the equities markets began to turn around, and the mania of the dot-com bubble and geopolitical shocks of September 11 subsided. The Federal Reserve slashed interest rates, creating a glut of easy credit. Still wary of the stock market after the dot-com bubble, the public instead looked towards the real estate market as their preferred asset class. Easy access to credit, limited supply in real estate, and increased demand created a growing housing market that seemed to perpetually trend upwards perpetually. A cottage industry of house-flipping speculation and real estate investment advertisements permeated public life. Average Americans were encouraged to use their homes as their personal "piggy banks" and even take out multiple loans to purchase multiple homes.

Increased financial engineering by the banks created all manner of derivative products on top of the mortgage-backed securities. Products known as *collateralized debt obligations*, or CDOs, packaged fixed income products such as mortgage-backed securities and corporate bonds into a structure where the buyers would be sequentially paid from the underlying cash flows of the assets based on their underlying assessed risk of default on these assets. The CDOs were then packaged into even more complicated derivatives known as synthetic CDOs.

At the time, buyers of CDOs believed the underlying mortgages to be a very low risk because the value of the collateral underlying the loans was rising due to the housing bubble. In the case of default, the underlying assets could therefore be repossessed and paid out to investors independent of the underlying cash flows of the mortgage. These synthetic CDOs were widely believed to be so sufficiently hedged that they were essentially risk-free investments. Internal literature declared that Wall Street had finally cracked the problem of building a financial perpetual motion machine, the vanguard of a "new economy".

Spurred by low-interest rates and investors chasing unsustainable yield, the markets had an insatiable demand for more mortgage-backed securities in ever-increasing quantities and at any risk level. Mortgage providers would originate loans to nearly anyone with a pulse. Individuals with no credit history, no income, and no collateral could take out so-called NINJA loans, which blatantly stood for: no income, no job, and no assets. People with almost no capacity to repay their mortgages were offered these products to purchase houses they would never have otherwise been able to afford. Many of these products were an intentionally predatory form of lending. The loan would have a low intro rate for the first few years and then quickly balloon into unaffordable monthly payments. Some mortgage lenders even offered mortgages with unheard-of terms of 50 years, allowing buyers to finance houses half a century in advance. In the decade of real estate euphoria, the amount of mortgage-derived credit increased from $900 billion to $62 trillion.

At the same time, the credit rating agencies tasked with assessing the credit risk of the buyers and, by proxy, the credit risk of the composite CDO products, overwhelmingly failed to evaluate the risk of these products. Financial products subject to high default risk were given the highest triple-A rating possible, thus misrepresenting the risk to buyers of the financial products. Credit rating agencies fundamentally had a conflict of interest since the sellers of the securities paid their costs. The internal pressures for increased profits incentivized the credit agencies to misrepresent mortgage-backed securities regardless of the risk of such products. There was a moral hazard induced by the fact that sellers of the MBS products were incentivized by the upside of selling more products, wholly detached from the underlying default risk of said products.

It should come as no surprise that this housing boom was unsustainable, and soon the gap between consumer income and debt began to widen. Throughout the 2000s, there was very little increase in median consumer income. At the same time, the housing bubble meant that individuals were taking out increasingly larger loans that their stagnant salaries would never allow them to repay. By September 2008, the housing market had its first downturn in many years, and most housing prices declined 20% from their 2006 peak. This downturn propagated through the many credit derivatives as wave after wave of defaults propagated through the composite products.

The subprime mortgages, rated inaccurately by the credit agencies, were deeply embedded inside many mortgage-backed securities sold en-masse by the banks. On August 6, 2007, the 10th largest retail mortgage lender, American Home

Mortgage, filed for bankruptcy. Soon after, BNP Paribas suspended withdrawals of three of its investment funds, while across the pond in Britain, Northern Rock experienced the first bank run in British history for 100 years. Wave after wave of bankruptcies rocked the American economy as financial institutions of all sizes faced the stark reality of defaults on nearly incalculable amounts of debt.

The shocks soon after propagated throughout the entire American and European financial system, leading to the catastrophic collapse of United States investment banks Lehman Brothers and Bear Stearns. On October 1, 2008, the United States Senate passed the Emergency Economic Stabilization Act of 2008, which issued a taxpayer-backed package to bail out the remaining institutions lest the United States face economic collapse[8,2]. By 2009 the global financial system had reached the brink, and recessions ensued in what would become the worst economic crisis of the 21st century. A confluence of greed, moral hazard, and reckless financialization created a house of cards of staggering complexity that few could understand or assess the risk of, except in the wake of catastrophic collapse, for which the public bore the brunt of the costs[23,5].

3.11 VENTURE CAPITAL BUBBLE (2010 - PRESENT)

Although most of this chapter was concerned with historical market bubbles, by most definitions, we are currently living in the midst of a long-running venture capital bubble that has been proceeding since the early 2000s.

Venture capital funds are investment vehicles that take high-risk positions in early ventures, often tech companies, in exchange for an equity stake in the company. Venture funds source their money from high net worth individuals, pension funds, or sovereign wealth funds (called limited partners or LPs). Pooled into the venture fund it is then invested in a diversified portfolio of many early companies. Almost all portfolio companies are likely to fail. Yet, if sufficiently diversified, the fund will return money to its LPs on the back of the success of one or two portfolio companies that generate vastly outsized returns.

Venture capital is a highly competitive space in the American economy. The booms and busts of the technology sector on the back of the dot-com bubble have created an extraordinarily loose and liquid market in capital for tech companies. The early 2000s saw the rise of the mobile app economy, ushering in a new era of social media and cloud computing business. The defining feature of these purely digital products their extremely low operating costs, low customer acquisition costs, and the possibility for parabolic returns on customers. For venture capital, this meant that small $100,000 checks into early companies would sometimes generate returns in the millions on the back of comparatively small amounts of seed capital. This rate of return, rarely seen in other markets, has created an environment in which there is an outsized incentive to find "the next big thing" in tech because the upside is so vast.

Although some prominent funds have seen parabolic returns, this success is not evenly distributed across the entire sector. For a fund to be successful, it must have a return that is three times its initial investment, the so-called "venture rate of return" is the benchmark for most venture funds. However, there simply are not enough new companies to satiate all these funds' hunger for new deals, and even fewer high-quality, high-growth companies that could grow into successful companies. This dynamic creates an environment in which there is a vast amount of idle capital (called *dry powder*) sitting around unallocated to new ventures. Since the fund's mandate is to make new investments, what inevitably ends up happening is that the criterion for high-quality companies becomes exceptionally loose. Instead, the incentives for high-growth take precedence. The name of the game these days is growth at any cost.

This investment thesis led to the 2010s being marked by many of the fastest-growing companies of all time. Companies such as WeWork and Uber practiced a business model known as blitzscaling, using the deep pockets of the venture backers to corner the market and figure out how to be profitable on the back of a near-monopoly. While these companies did achieve scale, they became mired in controversy and scandals as a direct result of their predatory and unsustainable business model. Although both WeWork and Uber went public, neither company was able to become profitable and is now trading at fractions of their inflated private valuations.

Nevertheless, the abundance of easy access to capital has meant that a new crop of companies now raises vast sums of money to build solutions to non-problems on the back of empty promises to their investors of parabolic returns. Strangely enough, in an environment with an abundance of capital with nowhere to go, many venture investors suspend disbelief and invest anyways. For example, the now infamous Theranos raised $700 million at a $10 billion valuation on the promise of a new blood testing machine that had no revenue, no customers, and was built on fraud and faulty science. Theranos is a perfect example of the fraud triangle (see Frauds & Scams) enabled by venture capitalists who simply felt no need to do due diligence on the product and claims made by its 19-year-old Stanford dropout founder. The company Juicero similarly became the laughing stock of Silicon Valley when it raised $118 million at a $449 million valuation, only to reveal the company's revolutionary technology was a seemingly overly complicated and useless device that would squeeze a pre-blended bag of juice into a cup, of which the same task could be better done by gently squeezing the bag by hand. Several of the largest and most sophisticated investors in Silicon Valley, including Google Ventures and Kleiner Perkins, had invested money into Juicero with seemingly little regard for the absurdity of the business.

The rise of social media also gave way to a new form of business model based purely on spectacle and hype. In 2017 a New York-based entrepreneur named Billy McFarland attempted to launch a music festival in the Bahamas. However, his knowledge of the logistics of running such a festival was minimal. The festival quickly devolved into a Lord of the Flies-like event as thousands of young party-goers descended on the island only to find a lack of essential services such as toilets, food, and water. For months McFarland had hyped the festival on social media and created an appearance of the event completely detached from the fundamental mechanisms of actually putting on the festival. Both the employees of the company and McFarland himself engaged in an irrational form of directed reasoning, blinded by their own incompetence, and were incapable of separating the spectacle of social media from reality.

As with many other bubbles throughout history, much of the irrationality in the venture bubble stems from a herd mentality toward investing. With a scarcity of deals to go around, venture capitalists often stampede to get into hot deals, and investors will offer extremely favorable terms to entrepreneurs in order to secure their position in the funding round. These circumstances often mean an expedited capital call and a complete lack of due diligence for fear of losing the position to another fund. This cutthroat environment creates a context in which pressure, opportunity, and rationalization—all three edges of the Fraud Triangle—are present, leading to highly criminogenic and irrational environment. The Venture Bubble bears witness to the uncomfortable truth that the madness of crowds is not purely a spectacle of the unwashed masses, and investors can indiscriminately behave like lemmings at any level of sophistication.

3.12 The Crypto Bubble (2016 - Present)

To say cryptocurrencies are an economic bubble is partially inaccurate: the term "bubble bath" is perhaps a more apt description of the phenomenon. Crypto is not a single bubble but an ever-growing set of economic bubbles that inflate and pop, giving rise to a new bath of bubbles before anyone has had time to recover from or remember the last wave of frauds. It is a symptom of our collective societal stupor that the writer William Gibson accurately describes as "the endless digital Now, a state of atemporality enabled by our increasingly efficient communal prosthetic memory." Keeping track of the increasing deluge of crypto frauds and flash-in-the-pan bubbles is beyond any sane person's cognitive capacity.

However, the entirety of crypto is almost universally recognized as an economic bubble. In the opinion of eight Nobel Prize laureates, bitcoin is, in their words, an obvious economic bubble. The 2017 Economics Nobel prize winner Joseph Stiglitz condemned bitcoin, stating:

> Bitcoin is successful only because of its potential for circumvention and lack of oversight. [...] It seems to me it ought to be outlawed

Unlike past economic bubbles such as the Dot-com bubble of the early 2000s or the Railway Mania of the 1840s there is no productive economic activity, crypto is a speculative bubble itself built purely on self-referential speculation. Suppose crypto is to be regarded as an alternative financial system, as its advocates so boldly claim, in which case, it is an entirely insular financial system and self-referential market that trades within its boundaries, undermining its claim. Rather than being harmonious with existing infrastructure, crypto is overwhelmingly parasitic to the external financial system, sucking in capital and offering no efficiency or better solutions to existing problems.

The simple undoing of this idea of a new financial system is that there is no economy in crypto; because it can never function as a currency. Nothing is priced in crypto. No commerce is done in crypto. No developed economy recognizes crypto as legal tender or collects taxes on it. The price of crypto simply oscillates randomly, subject to constant market manipulation and public sentiments of greed and fear, detached from any activity other than speculation. Crypto is a pure casino investment wrapped in grandiose delusions. As an investment, it is almost definitionally a bubble because crypto tokens have no fundamentals, no income, and correspond to no underlying economic activity.

As surreal and vacuous as the crypto bubble might appear to the modern observer, the history of markets is fraught with uncannily similar events that all draw on the same extraordinary delusions of easy money detached from any effort and attached to a persistent belief that somehow this time is different[24]. Perhaps not surprisingly, people are not always economically rational actors. Human psychology is subject to all manner of biases and exuberance that manifest in extremely bizarre modes in individuals, and in aggregate, in markets. In his famous book on historical financial manias, *Extraordinary Popular Delusions and the Madness of Crowds*, the Scottish author Charles Mackay expressed an observation that was just as true in the 18th century as in the 21st century:

> Men, it has been well said, think in herds; it will be seen that they go mad in herds, while they only recover their senses slowly, and one by one.

Cryptocurrency synthesizes many aspects of other historical manias yet wraps the absurdity of the grift in a new package of techno-solutionism and libertarian politics. Yet the underlying means of grifting remains the same throughout the ages. Each historical case study in this chapter has a lesson to teach us about the cryptocurrency bubble:

1. *The South Sea Bubble* - The financialization of non-economic enterprises and use of financial engineering for obfuscation
2. *The Mississippi Bubble* - Conflicts of interest arise when society

allows an unaccountable money printer for private enterprises.

3.   *The Railway Manias* - A glut of cash that flows into even pro-
     ductive investments will create Potemkin villages of compa-
     nies based on activity that simply creates the illusion of pro-
     ductivity to drive investment inflows.

4.   *The Enron Scandal* - The destructiveness of creative accounting
     and lack of reliable audits to ensure against fraud.

5.   *The Dot-Com Bubble* - New technology can create new busi-
     ness models, but those business models are not wholly unteth-
     ered to the base reality of having to be profitable.

6.   *Beanie Babies* - Artificially scarce commodities can induce spec-
     ulative manias by exploiting weaknesses in human psychology
     and via manipulated markets.

7.   *Subprime Mortgage Bubble* - Financial environments with loose
     regulation are fraught with moral hazards and conflicts of in-
     terest that can create systemic catastrophes when combined
     with opaque financialization.

8.   *Venture Capital Bubble* - The indiscriminate nature of market
     manias and their ability to capture institutional and sophisti-
     cated investors in non-economic and fraudulent enterprises.

9.   *Cryptocurrency Bubble* - The financialization of narrative and
     populism can be used to spawn pathological financial assets
     which can be sustained for long periods based on the cultural
     relevance of their narrative to attract more greater fools into a
     scheme.

It is not surprising that manias like this occur in times of historically low-
interest rates as we see today. When money is cheap it inevitably chases ever-
increasingly more bizarre things to generate yield out of desperation. However,
some manias, like the Railway Manias and the Dot-Com Bubble, left remnants
in the wake that became the foundation for a paradigm shift[22] in the economy.
Others like the South Sea Bubble, the Mississippi Bubble, and the Beanie Baby
Bubble left nothing but bagholders. Participating in bubbles can be rational and

justified if and only if there is real intrinsic value and utility created independent of pure speculation[16]. There is no way to financialize hot air or non-economic hype, and it never ends well for those who try.

While history may not repeat itself it does rhyme. Many new manias are simply an attempt to avoid the regulation meant to clean up the fraud of the last mania, and crypto is the amalgamation of centuries worth of fraud packed into a particularly virulent narrative package. Financial scandals and bubbles are inevitable, and yet they have a very predictable pattern and character that remains invariant through the ages; follow where the dumb money on the street is flowing, and you will find all manner of scum and villainy repeating exactly the same scams of the past wrapped in a new too-good-to-be-truth pitch for a new generation.

Unfortunately, the history of fraud and market manias is often overlooked in our history curricula. It falls upon very specialized historians to write the history of these events, and yet, they are not widely known to the general public. Studying the manias of the past is the best way to innoculate yourself against future mania and popular delusions. History has many brutal lessons about what happens on the other side of bubbles based on collective delusions and fraud[24]. But rest assured, this time is different, just like last time.

Economic Problems

"Money, again, has often been a cause of the delusion of multitudes. Sober nations have all at once become desperate gamblers, and risked almost their existence upon the turn of a piece of paper... Men, it has been well said, think in herds; it will be seen that they go mad in herds, while they only recover their senses slowly, and one by one."

– Charles Mackay, *Extraordinary Popular Delusions and the Madness of Crowds*

The ideas of cryptocurrencies are based on economic absurdities that outright contradict two hundred years of economic thought. To unpack the absurdity of cryptocurrencies, we first have to understand the two major narratives about the purpose of cryptocurrencies:

- Crypto as a form of money
- Crypto as an investment

The assumption that both of these narratives simultaneously hold is known as the *crypto paradox*[7]. The more attractive a crypto token is as an investment, the less useful it is as money. Moreover, conversely, if a token were to become useful as money, it would lose its use as an asset offering high expected returns.

Money must be **stable** so that we can save it today and spend it tomorrow. Moreover, investments are inherently **risky**; we are taking a risk and hopefully being compensated with a commensurate reward. We don't want our money to be risky or our investments to be stable. Nevertheless the promoters of crypto like to rely on both stories, usually whichever is rhetorically opportune—but they cannot both be true and on their own. And, independently, neither story stands up to intellectual scrutiny.

In fact, the very term cryptocurrency is a misnomer and misleading[13,23]. Indeed, academics now instead use the word *cryptoassets* to separate the false conception that cryptocurrencies are related to monetary instruments. Nevertheless, the term has entered the public lexicon, and in this text, we will adopt its colloquial use despite the confusion in terminology.

4.1 FAILURE AS MONEY

The fundamental concern at the heart of economics is known as the *economic problem*. The economic problem is the inescapable issue of scarcity and how best to produce and distribute these scarce resources. At its core, economics is the study of systems to make the best use of limited or scarce resources in the presence of a desire for consumption that exceeds supply. The creation of money is a tool that forms the substrate for a society's collective solution to the economic problem. Money is thereby the means by which markets can discover the price of goods through an equilibrium for the supply and demand in terms of a universal value metric in which the price is denominated[19,10].

The Scottish philosopher and early pioneer of economic thought Adam Smith supposed that civilization operated on a quid-pro-quo *barter system* in which goods were exchanged directly for other goods before the advent of money. In barter, sheep could be exchanged for wheat at an exchange rate relative to the supply and demand of the two commodities and independent of an exogenous measure value. However, most modern scholars reject the barter model as having no historical grounding. The late anthropologist David Graeber argues that early societies instead created complex debt systems within their tribes and that credit systems in the ancient world were ubiquitous and far preceded the invention of money and coinage. Graeber further argues that barter and money were reserved for low-trust environments or inter-civilization exchanges where the counterparty's creditworthiness could not be determined or enforced.

Thus money, credit, and trust are an inexorably linked throughout human history, and as civilization has evolved towards modern high-trust liberal democracies, so too have the money and credit systems evolved in their sophistication. By corollary, money is an inherently political structure since its creation originates in trust, and its distribution is linked to a society's thinking about the interplay of scarcity and the value of labor. Decisions regarding whether money is produced, how it is distributed, and who receives it are questions that are inexorably linked to the values of the lives of people who interact with it. In other words, there cannot be apolitical money[8], just as there is no such thing as water that is not wet.

The history of the technology of money is also one of incremental evolution. Civilization has evolved from trading in wheat[9], to trading in gold, to trading in notes backed by gold, to trading notes backed by nothing, and finally to trading in bytes backed by notes. Each step along this process carried a shifting set of concerns and compromises and ultimately shifted the custodianship of our money supply to different entities in our civilization. The role of money has a descriptive definition as having three core properties:

- **A medium of exchange** - Money can be used to facilitate transactions between parties who agree on it for exchange for goods and services.
- **A unit of account** - Money can be used to track gains and losses across multiple transactions, and the result is aggregated across these transactions. It can be represented as a single numerical value and used to compare the value of other goods.
- **A store of value** - Money provides a means to store value from the present for reliable use in future transactions. The movement of its value has a low variance over long periods.

These properties present a "moneyness" spectrum[18] on which currencies can fall on the end of either good money or bad money. Currencies such as the US dollar are optimal forms of money because they fulfill all three definitions very well on long-time scales. In contrast, historical currencies like units of grain used in early Mesopotamia are suboptimal money since they are inconvenient as a medium of exchange and means of deferred payment due to transport costs, storage concerns, and eventual spoilage.

Amongst these three points, the most essential property of money is that it is a stable store of value against a basket of commodities that consumers buy most often. The amount of money used to buy a coffee in the morning should not differ drastically from the amount used to buy a coffee tomorrow. In developed economies, complex measurement procedures called consumer price indexes are used to measure the relative change of the value of a currency against a standard basket of household goods to measure the efficacy of a managed monetary system.

Historical monetary systems were forms of commodity-based money, in which notes represented a legal claim against the commodity which could, at least in principle, be redeemed at the government treasury. Up until August 15, 1971, the United States was on a gold standard[1], and the government maintained that $35 could be redeemed for an ounce of gold. However, starting with the United Kingdom in 1931, most advanced economies exited their commodity-based money systems in favor of *fiat money*, a system where the government issued notes are backed not by the commodity but by three ideas:

- The full faith and credit of the issuing government. The assertion that the government cannot default on its debts.
- The artificial demand for the currency is in the form of taxation since all citizens must obtain the currency to extinguish their obligations to the state.
- The recognition of the currency under the rule of law as a means to denominate contracts and private debt and the state's monopoly of justice can be used to enforce said contracts and debt.

In practice, the legitimacy of a national currency comes from both a collective social contract about the rule of law and its utility to fulfill the properties of money, price stability, and capacity to spur economic growth. Financial historian Adam Tooze said of the dollar fiat system:

> [The dollar] is backed by "nothing" other than the trifling matter of tens of trillions of dollars in private credit, the rule of law, and the power of the state itself inserted into a state system. In other words, the entire structure of global macrofinance.

The defining feature of fiat money is that it has a variable supply. In theory, the issuer fully controls the money supply and can expand or contract the money supply by adjusting deposit terms of commercial banks, quantitative easing, or modifying interest rates. These activities are the primary mechanisms by which price stability and inflation targeting are implemented. However, despite the dynamic money supply, there is a great deal of confusion concerning the fact that the central banks cannot and do not simply "print money" on demand.

A dynamic money supply is a core principle of Keynesian economics and forms the basis for all modern managed monetary systems. Keynesianism refers to a school of economic thought advanced by the British economist John Maynard Keynes in the early 20th century. In his 1936 work *The General Theory of Employment, Interest and Money,* Interest and Money, Keynes outlined a set of macroeconomic theories and models of how aggregate demand has strong explanatory power for modeling economic output and inflation. Keynes' work, together with the post-war neoclassic school pioneered by Kenneth Arrow and others, gave rise to the mainline branch of modern economics that focuses on quantitative and empirical models to explain market phenomena.

A defining feature of Keynesian thought is that in the presence of market shocks and business cycles, economies do not naturally stabilize themselves very quickly and thus require active intervention that boosts short-term demand in the economy. Keynesians argue that wages and employment are slower to respond to the market's needs and require central banks and governmental intervention to smooth over economic turbulence and mitigate recessions. Federal Reserve chairman William McChesney Martin once famously said that the role of the central bank is to "take away the punch bowl just as the party gets going," indicating the need for intervention to tighten easy access to credit once the economy recovers from recession. This school of thought largely influences the modern fiscal interventionist policies of central banks like the Federal Reserve and the European Central Bank in their policies after these economies moved off commodity-based gold standards.[1,21,12,4]

In modern advanced economies based on Keynesian ideas, most money takes the form of digital bank deposits. These bank deposits are created by commercial banks whenever they make loans. Whenever a bank makes a loan, it simultaneously creates a matching deposit in the borrower's bank account, and this process creates new money. While commercial banks can create[17] money from debt, they cannot do so without limits but are instead constrained by their own profitability, regulation, and the policies of the central bank.

The central bank is effectively the bank for commercial banks. It is a government established entity that acts to facilitate the exchange of money between licensed banking institutions. In many economies, the central bank is a quasi-governmental institution that maintains a monopoly on its role by the consent of democratic approval while functioning much like a corporation at arm's length from the government. To prevent conflicts of interest, the central bank usually does not receive its budget directly from the government. Instead, its income comes primarily from the interest on government securities that it acquires through the open market.

In the United States model, the central bank chair is a government appointee by the federal government and approved by the Senate for a four-year term. However, a strict separation between the government and the central bank ensures its independence. In the American model, the president can hire and fire the central bank chairman, but the government cannot directly set central bank policy or directly control interest rates. The firewall between the people who metaphorically "create the money" and "spend the money" is an essential part of the central banking model and as we have seen in cases in other countries where this firewall has been broken down, the result is almost invariably nationwide financial ruin.

Central banking is thus a hub and spoke model, in which the central bank is, as the namesake implies, the hub that connects all other commercial banks. The central bank maintains a ledger with other banks as its creditors, and these balances thus reflect the total balances of deposits held by the commercial banks on behalf of their customers. Commercial banks operate in a fractional reserve model where the total reserves held at any one point in time are strictly less than the total value of all deposits. Commercial banks engage in lending and investing activities with customer money to facilitate economically and socially productive enterprises in their communities. However, the central bank determines the specific minimum amount of reserves. Every day, during the course of regular banking business, a bank will service its customers, engage in lending, and balance its deposits and withdrawals; all of these services result in changing the bank's balance sheet, which may fall above or below the required reserve balance. To maintain reserve requirements, banks will issue short-term loans to each other at a fixed rate set by the central bank or directly from the central bank. The inter-bank interest rate is therefore the primary lever that the central bank uses to mediate the rate and flow of money in the economy, with everything downstream in the economy dependent on it.

> **The central bank does not print money or fix the amount of money in supply. Instead, it controls the mechanisms by which money can be created through commercial lending.**

Monetary policy acts as the ultimate limit on money creation and is guided by the central bank's policy to achieve specific goals in the economy. If the price of goods and services rises disproportionately to the currency's purchasing power, this results in inflation. Conversely, when prices decrease disproportionately to purchasing power, this results in deflation. While economists debate about the causes of inflation, an excess of either inflation or deflation is seen as a hindrance to in a healthy economy.

Under deflationary pressure, prices fall, so it is always rational for individuals to hoard rather than spend money as much as possible, as it will be worth more tomorrow than it is today. This self-reinforcing process takes more money out of the supply, risking deeper deflationary spirals that threaten economic productivity — if no one wants to buy anything, the market cannot fund economically and socially productive activities. Left unchecked, this type of deflationary cycle is enormously destructive to society.

In contrast, while in environments with inflationary pressure, prices rise rapidly. This leads to individuals who exchange their labor and time for money to see the value of their labor decrease relative to the goods and services they need to live. Economic environments of extreme inflation or deflation are not desirable, and both scenarios have led to the collapse of governments and regime change in countries such as Yugoslavia, the Weimar Republic, Hungary, and Zimbabwe. Both hyperinflation and deflationary spirals are antithetical to capital formation and a productive economy, and as such, the central bank's monetary policy is aimed at avoiding these two situations. Most mainstream economists believe that a small amount of predictable inflation, often 2%, is seen as a desirable target since it discourages hoarding and encourages productive investments.

However, bitcoin is, by its very design, a deflationary asset. The distribution of bitcoin is subject to an algorithm in which its future supply is both finite and fixed at 21 million bitcoins. The amount of bitcoin in circulation increases slowly as new blocks are mined, but there will never be more than the fixed cap allows. Considering the number of tokens irrecoverably lost to technical failures, lost keys, dust transactions, and the death of key holders, the number of tokens viable to transact in must strictly and monotonically go down over time. Supposing that demand remains constant or increases, a decrease in supply will drive the price upwards, thus creating deflationary spirals. A rational economic actor should therefore never spend their bitcoin since it may increase in value in the future, which is antithetical to the purpose of money.

In addition, without any nation-state[14] recognizing cryptocurrencies as its sole legal tender, there is no demand for the currency to pay one's taxes. The demand for a cryptocurrency is only based on either criminality or speculation. Since there is no underlying asset or intrinsic value of the currency, its demand is purely from a form of recursive speculation: a bet on what the next fool will pay for it, who in turn bets on what the next fool will pay for it. An indefinite and infinitely recursive version of the silly line of reasoning "I think that you think that I think..." with no basis in any actual economic activity.

Artificially scarce deflationary assets can never form the basis for a modern economy because the basis for all economic growth is the capacity to issue and service debt. Loans denominated in stable currencies are the very foundation of the economy, in everything from home mortgages, to business loans and corporate bonds, all the way up to sovereign debt issued by nation-states themselves. Loans allow individuals to access the future value of money today to be put towards socially and economically productive activities, such as buying a home to start a family or to found a business. The US dollar has the deepest and most liquid debt markets mainly because the dollar has a relatively predictable inflation rate on a long time scale, and its monetary parameters remain predictable up to the scale of decades. Thus the risk of servicing loans is readily quantifiable, and banks can build entire portfolios of loans to their communities out of their reserves.

Trying to construct the same form of loan denominated in bitcoin is impossible[11]. Since the value of the supply of the deflationary asset is fixed, and its price is subject to unpredictable and extreme deflationary spirals, it is nearly impossible to calculate the present risk of the loan in terms of its future cash flows. If the asset's value unpredictably increases in the future, the interest paid on the loan may not be sufficient to cover the loan's future market value. The activity of lending, denominated in a hyper volatile deflationary asset, is thus fraught with extreme risk compared to the predictability of fiat systems.

Even removing the deflationary cap, as some other cryptocurrencies aim to do, we are still left with intractable problems that the supply of the alleged currency must be determined by a preset algorithm which a priori determines the distribution of the currency ahead of time, thus detached from market conditions. Unlike in the fiat system, where the market conditions for debt products organically determine the supply of money in circulation relative to demand, a cryptocurrency must determine both supply and demand prescribed in unchangeable computer code. This would be like if the United States Federal Reserve decided what the monetary policy of the United States would be from their armchair in 1973 and into the future, regardless of any future market conditions, pandemics, or recessions. This is simply not possible, as we are not prescient enough to predict such long-term cycles of history, and monetary policy must be an organic process that balances supply and demand given present economic conditions in conjunction with future forecasts.

The Greek economist Yanis Varoufakis wrote of this failure of the bitcoin model in his interview *Crypto, the Left, and Techno-Feudalism*[24]:

> The problem with Bitcoin is not just its fixed supply. It is the presumption that the rate of change of the money supply can be predicted and foreshadowed within any algorithm. That the money supply can be de-politicised. So, it is not a question of how sophisticated and complex the algorithm is. It is, rather, that a purely political, unknowable, process can never, ever, be captured by an algorithm. It cannot and, therefore, it should not.

The core fallacy at the heart of the economic problem of bitcoin as money is the fixed supply, the deflationary construction, and the supposition that a neutral and apolitical algorithm could replace a central bank.

> **Speculative cryptoassets cannot perform the function of money and are instead speculative assets with no fundamental value.**

The economic problems of cryptocurrencies as money are intractable and cannot be solved; no amount of new technology or software could ever fix the inescapable truth that commodity-based money is a rubbish foundation on which to build productive enterprises or run an economy[6]. Combined with the technical issues of scalability (see: Technical Shortcomings), hyper volatility, and unsuitability as a store of value (see: Digital Gold), cryptocurrencies are an extremely suboptimal form of money. In other words, cryptocurrency is not used as a medium of exchange because it cannot scale and is simply unfit for this use case[20,5,6].

4.2 FAILURE AS AN INVESTMENT

Allegedly, in the absence of cryptocurrency having the properties of money, we should consider the economics of investing in it as we would other assets. However, when we try to determine what cryptocurrencies, or cryptoassets, would offer investors, we arrive at a different set of contradictions than in our analysis of them as currencies. Assets are either tangible assets that are intrinsically useful or financial assets that produces a yield that does not purely depend on price appreciation.

A tangible asset has a use value; for example, real estate provides a place to inhabit, a cow can be turned into a steak, and gold bricks can be smelted down to be used in jewelry and electronics. These assets' value is derived from a fundamental human need, and their demand is organically created from this value.

Financial assets, however, have no tangible existence: they are a useful legal construct. A financial asset is a non-physical asset whose value is derived from contractual claims on income, legal rights, an underlying currency or commodity, or risk transfer between counterparties. Examples of financial assets are stocks, bonds, patents, and derivatives.

Player Y

		A	B
	A	$(1,-1)$	$(-1,1)$
Player X	B	$(-1,1)$	$(1,-1)$

Crypto assets are not money, they have no tangible existence, no use value, and no intrinsic value. However, we can analyze them as financial assets using the standard tools of economics. To do this, let us consider the two properties of a financial asset:

- A financial asset's source of income and where the money associated with an asset originates.
- The payout structure of the financial asset. What legal or market forces determine which stakeholders receive income associated with the asset, and on what terms.

In the mathematical formalism of economics, we study the markets for financial assets in terms of simplified economic models called *games*, which give us insights into the payout structures that give rise to markets.

A *zero-sum game* is a specific class of game where any one player's gain is equal to the other player's loss on any given play of the game. We model the game as a *payoff matrix* where the outcomes of the participants are given rows and columns (see A and B below). A two-person zero-sum game is thus a game where the pair of payoffs for each entry of the payoff matrix sum to zero.

A coin flipping game is an example of a zero-sum game, where two players, A and B, simultaneously place a coin onto the table. A player's payoff depends on whether the coins match or not. If both coins land heads or tails, Player A wins and keeps Player B's coin. If they do not match, Player B wins and keeps Player A's coin.

A *positive-sum game* is a term that refers to situations in which the total of gains and losses across all participants is greater than zero. Conversely, a *negative-sum game* is a game where the gains and losses across all participants sum is less than zero, and played iteratively with increasing participants, the number of losers increases monotonically. Since investing in bitcoin is a closed system, the possible realized returns can only be paid out from funds paid in by other players buying in.

A cryptoasset is fundamentally different in kind from traditional instruments such as stocks, bonds, or physical commodities because it has absolutely no future income other than the money provided by the investors themselves. Stocks are a stake in a company with tangible assets, intellectual property, and employees that give voting rights over the company's core functioning. An individual stock tracks the economic growth of an underlying business in terms of its future profit and losses. Through dividends, stock buybacks, or mergers and acquisition events, these profits are paid to shareholders. Similarly, bonds are debt instruments that carry the legal obligation of redemption with interest.

Crypto assets are completely non-productive assets; they have no source of income and cannot generate a yield from any underlying economic activity. The only money paid out to investors is from other investors; thus, investing in cryptoassets is a zero-sum game from first principles. If one investor bought low and sold high, another investor bought high and sold low, with the payouts across all market participants sum to zero. Crypto assets are a closed loop of real money, which can change hands, but no more money is available than was put in. Just as a game of libertarian musical chairs in which nothing of value is created, and participants run around in a circle trying to screw each other before the music stops. This model goes by the name of a *greater fool* asset in which the only purpose of an investment is simply sell it off to a greater fool than one's self at a price for more than one paid for it.[2]

However, there is a net drain of the total wealth from the closed-loop of a cryptoasset. These take the form of transaction costs, market fees, and miners minting new coins increasing the supply and cashing them out. Coins are sold by miners to pay for their power and operating expenses to maintain their equipment. As of 2020, the current market outflow was a drain of $3.84 billion per year or around $10.54 million per day. This outflow transforms investing in cryptoassets from being a zero-sum game into a negative-sum game as—the payouts across all market participants sum to a negative value. There will be some winners in a negative-sum game, but most participants will lose money. The only net winners for extended periods are the cryptocurrency interactions and market makers who capture the outflow from the closed system.

To understand negative-sum investing, imagine a game of poker. Some strangers meet up to play poker at a casino. They each bring a pile of chips representing money and play against each other in rounds of a game of chance. The total amount of chips the players bring to the table is the total amount that any one player could hypothetically win. As the rounds are played, the chips will change hands between players but no new chips will be introduced onto the table. In addition for every round, the casino will take a percentage of chips for facilitating the game; these chips are taken off the table. Playing many rounds simply results in the casino extracting more and more wealth from the players, and thus the game of poker is negative-sum, and if were considered an "investment," it would have a negative expected return.

Investing in cryptocurrencies has the same game-theoretical mechanics as investing in other negative-sum games such as lotteries, casino gambling, pyramid schemes, Ponzi funds, and multi-level marketing schemes. Is it possible that some participants will make money speculating on cryptocurrencies? Absolutely. Some participants also make money from multi-level marketing and playing roulette in Vegas, but overwhelmingly most do not. In negative-sum investment activities, the inescapable mathematical fact is that more money goes in than comes out.

> Investing in cryptocurrencies is a negative-sum game with more losers than winners and, as an investment, it has a negative expected return.

The reporting bias between winners and losers of this rigged game ultimately means that we will likely never hear about the majority of losers compared to the minority of winners. Few will advertise their bitcoin losses on social media because of the shame and embarrassment associated with losses. This knowledge gap divides cryptocurrency traders into two classes. Those that do not understand the underlying statistics and counterparty risk of cryptoassets believe that the price going up means they are inevitably going to realize a return. Moreover, those who understand the underlying market dynamics are simply predators hoping to extract money from the fools. The entire structure of the cryptocurrency market is predatory and depends on an influx of *dumb money* and low-information speculators whose behavior is economically indistinguishable from gambling.[22,15]

> **Speculation drives cryptocurrency price formation. People buy cryptocurrency because they believe they can sell it at a higher price later, in dollars.**

Many economists and policymakers have likened cryptoassets to either Ponzi schemes or pyramid schemes, given the predatory nature of investing in cryptoassets. Crypto assets are not a Ponzi scheme in the traditional legal definition. Nevertheless, they bear all the same payout and economic structure of one except for the minor differentiation of a central operator to make explicit promises of returns. Some people have come up with all manner of other proposed terms of art for what negative-sum crypto investments might be called:

- Decentralized Ponzi scheme
- Headless Ponzi scheme
- Open Ponzi scheme
- Nakamoto scheme
- Snowball scheme
- Neo-Ponzi scheme

The story is much the same as the classical Ponzi scheme. Crypto schemes make claims of fantastic investment returns independent of economic activity. Nonetheless, crypto schemes achieve the same result through anonymous internet promoters who are not bound to a single legal entity such as Bernie Madoff's fraudulent fund.

> **Bitcoin and other cryptocurrencies are a negative-sum game with more losers than winners, and as an investment has a negative expected return.**

The economics of cryptocurrency is fundamentally unsound and intellectually incoherent[3]. There is no solution to the crypto paradox: the more attractive a crypto token is as an investment, the less useful it is as money—and neither story makes any sense because the story of crypto is just a retelling of the same story as historical financial scams[16]: money for nothing out of nothing, just get in early and do not ask where it comes from.

Technical Problems

"The structure of software systems tend to reflect the structure of
the organization that produce them."

– Douglas Crockford

The success of an emerging technology is not an inevitability, and not all
technical innovation is unqualifiedly good. The software industry's history is like
any other engineering discipline: full of dead ends, false starts, and wrong turns.
While software is unconstrained by many traditional factors, it is ultimately
constrained by the economics of its applications and the limitations of computer
science.

The fundamental technical shortcomings of cryptocurrency stem from four
major categories: scalability, privacy, security, recentralization, and incompatibility with existing infrastructure and legal structures.

5.1 SCALABILITY

In computer science *scalability* refers to a class of engineering problems regarding if a specific system can handle the load of users required of it when many
users require it to function simultaneously. However regarding this problem,
the technological program of bitcoin carries the specific seed of its own destruction by virtue of being tied to a political ideology. This ideology opposes any
technical centralization, and this single fact limits the technical avenues the technology could pursue in scaling. As noted in the second chapter on the culture
of cryptocurrency, bitcoin is inherently an anarchist project with an anti-state

mentality that runs deep within its development community. This ideology informed the initial development of bitcoin to pursue censorship resistance as a core feature at any cost, including performance and transaction throughput. This design choice comes attached to a terrible set of engineering trade-offs that introduce several intractable problems to scalability.

By design, the bitcoin network should allegedly be immune to payment interdiction or law enforcement that wishes to restrict funds' movement. This guiding principle is the central proposition any proposed scaling solutions must conform to to be considered acceptable in the cryptocurrency community, but it is also its technical undoing.

> **The bitcoin network cannot handle the volume of transactions that traditional payment systems can**

The bitcoin scalability problem arises from the consensus model it uses to confirm blocks of pending transactions. In the consensus model, the batches of committed transactions are limited in size and frequency, and tied to a proof of work model in which miners must perform bulk computations to confirm and commit the block to the global chain. The protocol constrains a bitcoin block to be no more than 1MB in size and a single block is committed only every 10 minutes. For comparison, the size of an average 3-minute song encoded in the MP3 file format is roughly 3.5MB. Doing the arithmetic on the throughput results in the shockingly low figure that the bitcoin network is only able to do 3-7 transactions per second. By comparison the Visa payment network can handle 65,000 transactions per second.

The transaction throughput of bitcoin is very low by traditional database standards. It is a common marketing tactic in the database industry to inflate benchmarks or use synthetic workloads that advertise inflated write speeds for databases. Nevertheless, there are mature and open source databases such as Microsoft SQL Server, Postgres, and Redis for which we can gather very accurate information about their write throughputs. Postgres is a classical relational SQL database and is capable of 200 to 300 updates per second, or 12,000 transactions per minute. Redis is a key-value store that can perform 110,000 writes per second or 6 million transactions per minute. However, since all core banking solutions use traditional databases as their storage engine, these numbers represent a baseline figure throughput that should be stated for base comparison[7].

An appropriate comparison would be the Visa credit card network, whose self-reported figures are 3,526 transactions per second. Most credit card transactions can be confirmed in less than a minute, and the network handles $11 trillion of exchange yearly. Credit cards and contactless payments are examples of a success story[3] for digital finance that have become a transparent part of everyday life that most of us take for granted. The comparison between bitcoin and Visa is not perfect, as Visa can achieve this level of transaction throughput by centralizing transaction handling through its own servers that has taken thirty years of building services to handle this kind of load. The slow part of transaction handling is always compliance, ensuring parties are solvent, and detecting patterns of fraudulent activity. However, for the advocates proposing that bitcoin can handle retail transaction loads on a global scale, this is the definitive benchmark that must be reached for technical parity.

Building these payment processing systems can be viewed through a lens of compromise between three factors: scalability, decentralization, and security. The design choices of bitcoin favor decentralization and security while making a sacrifice in scalability. The database infrastructure behind standard money transmitter services is designed to be scalable and secure.

The scalability issues of the bitcoin protocol are universally recognized, and there have been many proposed solutions that alter the protocol itself[6]. Bitcoin development is a collaboration between three spheres of influence: the exchanges who onboard users and issue the bulk of transactions, the core developers who maintain the official clients and define the protocol in software, and the miners who purchase the physical hardware and mine blocks. The economic incentives of all of these groups are different, and a change to the protocol would shift the profit centers for each of the groups. For example, while the exchanges would be interested in larger block sizes (i.e., more transactions), the miners (who prioritize fee-per-byte) would have to purchase new hardware and receive less in mining rewards for more computational work and thus incur significant electricity cost. This stalemate of incentives has led to mass technical sclerosis of the base protocol and a situation in which core developers are afraid of major changes to the protocol for fear of upsetting the economic order they are profiting from.

It is a common joke in software development that the answer to any difficult technical problem is simply to add another level of indirection to the problem. This leads us to our new problem: the *lightning network*. Since the base protocol is unscalable, the seemingly natural solution to adapting this network is to add yet another network on top of the bitcoin network. The proposed design of this system would batch settlements between peers into bidirectional state channels. These state channels are managed by a smart contract but must be monitored by the two parties on both ends to efficiently close the channel when a batch of transactions is finalized. This design opens a small but non-zero time window for fraud in a system in which one party will broadcast an old state to the contract and can extract the remaining bitcoin locked in the contract before the other party has finalized the transaction. The proposed solution is either a central registry in which lightning network participants would suffer reputational damage for this kind of fraudulent transaction or yet another level of indirection known as a watchtower contract. That watchtower is another smart contract that monitors the first contracts looking for mismatches between the main network and the channel states.

The lightning network itself introduces a whole new set of attack vectors for double spends and frauds as outlined in many cybersecurity papers such as the *Flood and Loot* attack[5]. This attack effectively allows attackers to make specific bulk attacks on state channels to drain users' funds. The lightning network is an experimental and untested approach to scaling, with progress on this scaling approach having stagnated since 2018. According to self-reported lightning network statistics, less than 0.001% of circulating bitcoin were being managed by the network, and transaction volume has remained relatively flat after 2019. No merchants operate with the lightning network for payments and as of today it is nothing more than a prototype. There is little evidence supporting this scaling model even works without introducing implicit custodial requirements, novel attack vectors, or new mechanisms for fraud. The perpetual narrative around the lightning network is that it has always been 18 months away from adoption. A narrative that is updated every 18 months it fails to deliver. In software parlance, the term *vapourware* is used to describe software perpetually in the works of being developed but never materializing into a usable form. The bitcoin lightning network is pure vapourware[13].

Outside of the bitcoin network, there are similar problems in other cryptocurrencies. The bitcoin meme of technical indirection through Layer 2 solutions have been translated to other systems and their development philosophies. This perspective views the base protocol as being only a settlement layer for larger bulk transfers between parties, and those smaller individual payments should be handled by secondary systems with different transaction throughputs and consistency guarantees. The ethereum network has taken a different set of economic incentives in its initial design. At the time of writing, this network is still only capable of roughly 15 transactions per second. There is a proposed drastic protocol upgrade to this network known as ethereum 2.0 which includes a fundamental shift in the consensus algorithm. This project has been in development for five years and has consistently failed to meet all its launch deadlines, and it remains unclear when or if this new network will launch. Since this new network would alter the economics of mining the protocol, it is unclear if there will be community consensus between miners and developers that the protocol will go live or whether they will see the same economic stalemate and sclerosis that the bitcoin ecosystem observes. The ethereum 2.0 upgrade is unlikely to ever complete because of the broken incentives related to its development and roll-out.

> **Because of slow transaction speeds, cryptocurrencies are almost impossible to use for legitimate commercial transactions.**

The broader cryptocurrency community has seen a zoo of alternative proposed scaling solutions, these proposals going by technical names such as sidechains, sharding, DAG networks, zero-knowledge rollups and a variety of proprietary solutions which make miraculous transaction throughput claims. However, the tested Nakamoto consensus remains the dominant technology. At the time of writing, there is little empirical evidence for the viability of new scaling solutions as evidenced by live deployments with active users. Central to the cryptocurrency ideology is a belief that this technical problem must be tractable, and for many users, it is a matter of faith that a future decentralized network can scale to

Visa levels while maintaining censorship resistance and avoiding centralization.

However, the inescapable technical reality is that every possible consensus algorithm used to synchronize the public ledger between participants are all deeply flawed on one of several dimensions: they are either centralized and plutocratic, wasteful, or are an extraneous complexity added purely for regulatory avoidance[1].

A consensus system that maps wasted computational energy to a financial return, both in electronic waste and through carbon emissions from burning fossil fuels to run mining data centers, is Proof of Work. Proof of work coins such as bitcoin is an environmental disaster that burns entire states' worth of energy and is already escalating climate change, vast amounts of e-waste, and disruption to silicon supply chains (see Environmental Problems). The economies of scale of running mining operations also inevitably result in centralized mining pools, which results in a contradiction that leads to recentralization[11,10,14].

The alternate consensus model *proof of stake* is less energy-intensive; however its staking model is necessarily deflationary, it is not decentralized, and thus results in inevitably plutocratic governance which makes the entire structure have a nearly identical payout structure to that of a pyramid scheme that enriches the already wealthy. This results in a contradiction that again leads to recentralization, which undermines the alleged aim of a decentralized project. The externalities of the proof of stake system at scale would exacerbate inequality and encourage extraction from and defrauding of small shareholders[12].

Any Paxos derivative, PBFT, or *proof of authority* systems are based on a quorum model of pre-chosen validators. In this setup, even if they are permissionless in accepting public transactions, the validation and ordering of these transactions is inherently centralized by a small pool of privileged actors and thus likewise involves recentralization. Any other theoretical proposed system that is not quorum-based and requires no consumption of time/space/hardware/stake resources would be vulnerable to Sybil attacks[11] which would be unsuitable for the security model of a permissionless network.

The fundamental reality is that cryptocurrency currently does not scale and cannot adapt itself to fit the existing realities of how the world transacts. The technology can never scale securely without becoming a centralized system that undermines its very existence[8,13].

5.2 PRIVACY

Bitcoin wallet addresses are a unique global addressing system derived from the use of hash functions. In a nutshell, a bitcoin wallet address is generated from an elliptic curve private key which is a unique number generated randomly when a bitcoin wallet is created. This number is inconceivably large by everyday standards and will have hundreds of digits. If generated by a proper random number generator, the probability of that specific set of digits ever being generated again during the universe's lifetime is infinitesimally small. This number satisfies the necessary properties of a secret value that the user holds private and uses to control access to their funds. There are 2^{160} total possible addresses in the bitcoin protocol. An example wallet address:

```
1A1zP1eP5QGefi2DMPTfTL5SLmv7DivfNa
```

The public address generated associated with a wallet is encoded in a format where uppercase and lowercase letters stand for numerical values. This sequence of letters and numbers uniquely identifies the endpoint for other users to send funds to and can be shared publicly either in textual format or in a graphical format such as a QR code without containing any information about the user. From base assumptions, the number is essentially anonymous.

In the traditional banking system, a coding known as IBAN (International Bank Account Number) is the standard numbering system used to identify accounts and associated financial institutions. When issuing an international wire transfer, a bank account will ask for the receiving IBAN as part of the transfer. This number is then mapped internally to the account holder's account and is stored within the bank's core banking software and routing system.

A bitcoin address is, however, not fully anonymous. The bitcoin ledger itself is a fully public list of transactions that have ever occurred since the network's inception. It contains the very first transactions allegedly by Satoshi as well as the most recent transactions conducted in the last 10 minutes. The full provenance of a bitcoin can be traced back to its creation and through every address it passed through.

This feature means that while accounts are anonymous, the global transaction data can be used to infer specific properties about when, with whom, and in what amounts an address is transacting. This kind of information is traditionally called metadata. For instance, metadata about your text messaging habits may not contain the direct messages you send. However, given a sufficiently large sample size, it is possible to deduce a person's social network, their life partner, and coworkers from the frequency and timing of messages. Likewise, a great deal of information can be deduced from tracing the provenance of a bitcoin address, and thus bitcoin addresses are not entirely anonymous but partially anonymous or *pseudonymous*[9].

The tracking and tracing of bitcoin involved in criminal activities has emerged as a standard practice in law enforcement and emerging companies such as ChainAnalysis have been able to deduce quite a bit of implied information simply from public information. Unlike with bank accounts, law enforcement does not require a subpoena of public information for an ongoing investigation. Notoriously many users of darknet services such as the Silk Road were caught because of a misunderstanding about the transparency of the bitcoin ledger used by these actors.

Acquiring bitcoin has always had a bootstrapping problem for new users. In the early days of the protocol, one could use a home computer to mine small amounts by devoting spare CPU cycles to generate small amounts. However, for the last decade, this has been economically unviable. These days, the traditional onramp is to go through a domestic exchange or one of the offshore services. In the case of exchanges domiciled in the United States or in Europe, the onboarding process for accounts requires the account holder to present a government-issued identification and proof of address. This process is similar to opening a bank account and provides a mechanism for the institution to contact you and alert law enforcement of any suspicious or criminal activity associated with the account opened. This is a legal requirement known as *Know Your Customer* or *KYC* is the legal requirement to maintain an audit log of the account holder's personal information and account activity.

Since the exchanges themselves operate accounts with massive inflows and outflows of transactions, their wallet accounts are massive hubs of activity that can easily be observed in the global ledger. If the exchanges are operating in a compliant manner, every transaction they process should internally be mapped to metadata about the account holders and their respective information. If an account was associated with criminal activity, law enforcement could subpoena the exchange and demand the information required to trace the account back to an individual. This information chasing through account metadata is the mechanism by which money laundering and wire fraud cases can be prosecuted.

This is in contrast to how the traditional banking system works, where bank secrecy laws are a central part of the obligation between a bank and its customers. Banks cannot use the transaction flows of their customers as part of their investments or share this information with other parties unless required by the courts. Bank transactions are required to be secure, private, and generally confidential information. When a wire transfer is issued by a company whose corporate account is at HSBC in London to Morgan Stanely in New York City, the metadata contained within that transaction could contain commercially sensitive information. For example, if a British company is sending large amounts of funds to a newly created American division, it may indicate the intent for the company to expand into the American market. There are cases where the constellation of transactions between known entities could be used to deduce confidential information about the parties. However, this fact poses an existential question about the efficacy of cryptocurrency networks as an international payment system if pseudonymous accounts leak information.

A retail bank account held by individuals is usually a simple structure that periodically collects deposits from an employer and frequent small debits for everyday activities such as groceries, rent, and buying coffee. Corporate banking, especially for large multinational corporations, can be quite complex and span a significant number of accounts and institutions.

In contrast, a corporation that wants to transact in cryptocurrency would have to address the fundamental issue that inflows and outflows from their accounts are commercially sensitive information. The amount of money that a corporation pays in payroll correlates with staffing and their operating expenses in specific regions and divisions in the company. The accounts receivable correlates with invoices it collects, its commercial interactions with its clients, and its lines of business. Public metadata of any of these transactions is private information, in fact it is usually some of the most protected information inside a corporation that is only shared with auditors and its direct banking relationships. Both of these parties are professionally and legally bound by confidentiality. A company electing to transact in cryptocurrency would leak confidential information like a sieve by choosing this public mode of payment.

The technical answer that one might propose to this problem is that the corporate should create a network of wallets and shuffle the payments between the wallets in random amounts and times to obscure the provenance of funds[15]. This solution is needlessly complicated for a traditional corporate treasurer who should not perform this level of financial obfuscation and needless overhead for their normal daily activities. This solution is also indistinguishable from the money laundering process used by criminals. For cryptocurrency to pose any value to the commercial banking sector, this question requires a good answer.

If we step back, this conundrum begs a more profound question: Why are we making what was once a non-problem into a complex problem? Since banking was invented in Florence in the 13th century, the privacy problem has been solved. A mixed-visibility network with some access to authorities and privacy otherwise works very well. What does cryptocurrency offer except creating new problems[16]?

5.3 Security

The standard advice around the custodianship of cryptocurrency is that one should "be your own bank" and "if you do not hold your keys, they are not your coins". These idioms are related to the fact that cryptocurrency is a bearer instrument, and if you hold the private keys to a set of funds, you are effectively in control of the assets, just as if you physically hold euros or dollars in a wallet. A problem arises when these funds are held by an exchange account which holds funds before they are withdrawn. These exchanges are not banks, they are not legally bound to hold deposits, and they are most likely not located in the customer's jurisdiction. Most cryptocurrency exchanges provide no legal recourse for lost funds, and the funds held are not insured under any deposit insurance scheme.

> **Lost private keys for account have resulted in 20% of the supply of bitcoins being irretrievably lost.**

In addition, these exchanges are some of the most targeted entities on the planet for hackers. In 2019, twelve major exchanges were hacked and the equivalent of $292 million was stolen in these attacks. Over time and in conjunction with bubble economics, these events have only increased in severity and frequency.

While some best practices can mitigate this risk, the fundamental design of bitcoin-style systems is that the end-user is responsible for their own keys and wallets by safeguarding their cryptographic secrets. This can be done through several strategies. So-called cold wallets are wallet keys stored in physical objects such as paper and not connected to electronic devices. Other systems such as hardware wallets allow users to secure and encrypt their keys on a dedicated hardware device.

Cybersecurity is one of our era's biggest problems, and companies with significant information security budgets and dedicated teams regularly fail. A system that requires every depositor to have the same level of security as a chief information security officer and constantly be aware of threat vectors and potential attacks on key storage is an enormous cognitive overhead. At face value, this seems like an unnecessary burden on an average user who simply wants to hold funds and be protected against fraud in their daily transactions. The ask of individuals to supply their own banking institution-level information security is highly unreasonable.

In the course of human life, many situations occur which require third parties to be able to access or reset our accounts. If you forget a PIN code or lose a credit card, there is a simple mechanism to retrieve your funds by going to a banking branch and proving your identity. In a more extreme case of an untimely death, a person's funds will be passed along to their spouse or children through inheritance and wills. The successors can petition the bank for access to the funds by presenting a death certificate and gaining control of the deceased accounts.

Being one's own bank makes both cases either impossible or needlessly complex. The human mind is fragile and subject to decay, mental disorders, and memory loss. If you forget the passwords to your hardware wallet or if it is physically destroyed, you lose access to your accounts. These events have already occurred to even some of the most sophisticated investors. An elaborate setup of data backups could mitigate this, safety deposit boxes or multiparty wallet setups, but such technical solutions are an unnecessary complexity burden for most users.

There are many news stories of ransom, kidnapping, and murder of crypto asset holders who attempted to safeguard their wallets personally. In cybersecurity, the term rubber-hose cryptanalysis satirically refers to extracting cryptographic secrets from a person by coercion or torture. A digital attack vector is unnecessary if criminals could extract the keys by kidnapping and torturing the owner and then laundering the funds from anywhere in the world.

Of course, the natural solution to this would simply be that most users should not be their own bank; instead, they should use a "cryptobank" which holds their funds and provides them access. However, this is ultimately just recreating the same centralized authority system which cryptocurrency advocates attempted to replace. Providing cryptocurrency security for the masses either introduces more social problems that thee technology has no answer to or results in a re-centralization that undermines its own ideological goals. After all, we already have centralized banks and existing payment systems that work just fine.

5.4 COMPLIANCE

The fundamental reality of international commerce is that money management has been vital to a nation's sovereignty and its ability to manage its economic growth and security. The movement, storage, and handling of money are regulated, and most countries have laws on the international movement of funds. Showing up at an airport in Berlin with undeclared cash above €10,000 will land one in quite a bit of trouble. If the value proposition of cryptocurrency is international money movement or extranational stores of value, then the technology will have to conform to existing regulations at entry points and exit points.

As a point of reference, it is helpful to consider how money transfers currently work. Nations with advanced economies have a domestic settlement system that allows banks within a regulatory regime to transfer funds between entities quickly. The United Kingdom has FasterPayments, Australia has BPAY, and the United States has CHIPS (Clearing House Interbank Payments System). These systems act as netting engines between the banks where trades are netted against each other instead of the total amount of all trades being cleared on every transaction. A trade goes through two steps. The first is *clearing* which is the confirmation of information between the payer and payee, and the second is *settlement*, which is the actual transfer of funds. For financial institutions to transfer funds, they will have what is called a *Vostro account* of the other bank, which records the funds held by the current bank on behalf of the other. Conversely, the other bank will have its Nostro account, which is an account held by the other bank which holds the current bank's money. Transfers between the banks will be debited and credited in their respective Vostro accounts, thus allowing them to transfer money.

International wire transfers are done on the SWIFT (Society for Worldwide Interbank Financial Telecommunication) network[2], which forms the messaging systems by which banks communicate messages about international transfers. The SWIFT network does not move money itself but simply is a messaging protocol for institutions to communicate the intent of transfers to happen. In addition, banks can only work directly with overseas banks with whom they hold an account, this is known as a *correspondent account*. If a bank does not have a correspondent banking relationship, it will have to route the wire through a third-party bank. This process entails having a Vostro account of a foreign bank or going through a chain of correspondent banks that do.

Every step along this chain incurs compliance checks with domestic laws and often involves multiple human and technical touchpoints inside and outside of the organization to complete the wire transfer. Along this process, each party involved in the transaction is legally required to carry out anti-money laundering (AML) and sanctions checks to ensure that the transfer complies with domestic laws and international treaties. First when these checks are complete can the transfer be completed and the money credited to the target account. The fees associated with these transfers are deducted from the total amount and represent the operational costs of performing all of these compliance checks along the way.

> **Cryptocurrency is purposefully built to evade regulation and make compliance impossible and is thus incompatible with cryptocurrency existing under the rule of law.**

The bottleneck along this process is never the technical transmission of the messages. Just as any modern electronic messaging system, they are almost instantaneous. Any human touchpoint will be subject to the bank's operating hours and days on which they are open for business, which is often only business hours and workdays.

Regular financial services companies such as Wise (previously known as TransferWise) have invented alternative solutions to international payments for small amounts that customers send often. Since most retail transactions are small (less than $5000 per day), Wise's internal system matches users attempting to send small amounts in one currency block with corresponding users sending amounts in the opposite currency block. Wise uses these pools of funds to net out aggregate transactions via local bank transfers.

The inability to move money from a country is ultimately one of domestic internal infrastructure development and external international relations, rather than technical limitations. Moreover, the proposed use case for cryptocurrency as a mode of international remittances is fundamentally limited because of a lack of a coherent compliance story. Even if we were to use cryptocurrency as a hypothetical international settlement medium, this system has not removed financial institutions from the equation. The system's entry and exit points would have to perform the same checks of outgoing and incoming money flow required by many international agreements.

In this hypothetical scenario, we have simply shifted the custodial, compliance, and identity management responsibilities to a different centralized entity that performs precisely the same activities and ultimately is subject to the same legal liabilities. In this setup, instead of settling in a national currency pair, there are now two currency pairs with a useless and volatile intermediary step in between. Using cryptocurrency for remittance has not disintermediated anything-it has simply shifted the intermediaries and introduced another level of indirection for no apparent reason.

A system that aimed to replace the existing international transfers would be subject to a similar set of rules regarding international transfers and capital controls, and it is naive to think that hundreds of treaties would be renegotiated on behalf of digital currencies. This wishful thinking is at the heart of the absurdity of crypto; the belief that somehow because something is on a peer-to-peer network[10], it is somehow exempt from the rules of being in a society.

Of course, like all cryptocurrency arguments, the counterargument is ideological: compliance is a non-issue because nation-states should not exist and should not have capital controls. This ideological goal is inexorably embedded in the design of cryptocurrency, making it an unscalable and untenable technology for any real-world application where sanctions, laws, and compliance are an inescapable part of doing business in financial services[4].

Valuation Problems

Any discussion of cryptocurrency ultimately trends towards the central question we would ask of any financial product: What should a crypto token be worth?

Warren Buffett has presented the opinion that most investment professionals arrive at when applying conventional financial valuation models to the question of cryptoassets:

> Cryptocurrencies basically have no value and they don't produce anything. They don't reproduce, they can't mail you a check, they can't do anything, and what you hope is that somebody else comes along and pays you more money for them later on, but then that person's got the problem. In terms of value: zero.

However there are many types of value we can discuss that correspond to different types of assets. Some include:

1. *Market value* - The price an asset is traded at in a public market.
2. *Fundamental value* - The price of an asset derived from an analysis based upon the present value of estimated future cash flows.
3. *Exchange value* - The proportion in which one commodity is exchanged for other commodities.
4. *Present value* - Present value is the current value of a future sum of a stream of cash flows given a specified rate of return.

5. *Sign value* - Sign value denotes and describes the intangible value according to an object because of the prestige or social status that it imparts upon the possessor.

6. *Use value* - Use value is a feature of an asset that can satisfy some human requirement, want, or need.

7. *Terminal value* - Terminal value is the value of an asset beyond the forecasted period when future cash flows can be estimated.

6.1 ASSET CLASSIFICATION

We must bracket our discussion based on a context-specific description of the underlying asset when discussing abstractions such as value. The process by which we rationally value a Picasso painting or an Apple stock is inherently incommensurate, as one is a piece of art and the other is a financial asset based on the cash flows of a corporation. We cannot compare financial apples to oranges.

Thus, to even begin to analyze the question of the value of cryptoassets, we need to determine what type of asset a crypto token is. There is no single narrative for what crypto is. However, we can examine the bulk behavior of people involved with the asset and find comparables for it within existing markets. While the original intent of cryptoassets might have been as a cash-like asset for use in a digital payment system, this is overwhelmingly not the use observed today. Discussions about crypto are often deeply confusing because of the mode switches between referring to it as a currency, a commodity, and a speculative asset in the same context, sometimes even in the same sentence. Often, this mode-switching is an intentional intellectual bait and switch; a form of sophistry to confuse and misdirect.

Transactions on speculative crypto tokens such as bitcoin and ethereum are considerably more expensive than credit card networks and wire services. Moreover, as we know they do not scale to national level transactions volumes, and lack the most basic consumer payments protections found in nearly every traditional payment system. No economy trades in crypto, no large-scale commerce is completed in the currency, and no goods or services are denominated in crypto because of its hyper volatility. Crypto payments are uniformly worse than any other payment mechanism except perhaps for illegal purchases. Let us therefore consider these aspects separately through a number of different theories.

6.2 The Theory of the Greater Fool

Although the payments narrative has failed, the initial experiment and ambiguity around the technology generated paper profits for a sufficiently large enough number of insiders to cause them to pursue alternative narratives in hopes of enticing more retail investors to bail out the first failed scheme. In this new reimagined form, crypto tokens are presented as a speculative asset, and a means to generate short-term returns rather than technology with intrinsic utility.

We thereby arrive at the comparable of *commodities*. Commodities are economic goods used in commerce. The value of a commodity is derived exclusively from its use-value. Use value, sometimes referred to as intrinsic value, is a feature of an asset that can satisfy some human requirement, want, or need or serve a useful purpose. It is an asset whose demand is generated by organic economic activity rather than artificial demand or narrative.

Commodities can either be maintenance-free or require a maintenance fee to sustain their value as a commodity. Pork is an example of a perishable commodity; it has a finite time horizon and requires an ongoing cost of maintenance to sustain its value (i.e refrigeration) before it can be sold based on its use-value as food. Metals such as nickel or gold are effectively maintenance-free; after they are produced, they continue to exist on an infinite time horizon and require no upkeep to sustain their value. Every commodity has an intrinsic industrial or economic use, which generates a demand for its application.

Crypto tokens have no such use or organic demand and exist purely to speculate on detached from any pretense of use-value. Cryptoassets are speculative financial assets with neither use-value nor any other fundamental value, while not being monetary; and can therefore not be commodities or currencies. The demand for a crypto asset is not generated by any use-value but rather from narrative and the *greater fool theory*. A financial asset that behaves like a commodity—by virtue of a lack of underlying cashflows—but whose demand is derived purely from its self-referential exchange value or sign value, rather than use-value, is sometimes in academic literature referred to as a pseudo-commodity.

We can therefore conclude that crypto tokens are a pure speculative financial asset that presents as an exchange-traded investment. Its valuation rationally should then be assailable by the traditional quantitative finance models by treating it like any other securities contract. In security pricing models, the representative investor's expectation today of their expectation tomorrow of future payoffs must be equal to their expectation today of a future payoff. If today we an expect that we will expect the price to vary at some point in the future, then this variation must be incorporated into the price today. If we are trading a risky asset that will be liquidated at date $T + 1$ but is traded at dates 1 to T, wherein only realizable gains on the asset are a function of its income between dates 1 to T. In a security valuation model, the intrinsic value is the present value of all expected future net cash flows associated with the asset calculated via discounted cash flow valuation.

Unlike equities or derivatives contracts, a crypto token does not derive its value from underlying assets. Equities generate an income from exposure to the economic activity of a company, while derivatives represent a contractual or formulaic claim on some underlying asset. Therefore, a company's stock will naturally reflect the expectation of future earnings, which flow to the shareholders through dividends from these earnings or indirectly via stock buybacks or mergers. A company's stock provides exposure to the market that the company serves with its business activity and is a fractional legal claim on the accumulated assets of the company. This analysis makes cryptoassets extremely pathological in the space of financial assets since it has no underlying asset and represents no claim on literally anything.

By virtue of crypto being a closed system with a finite fixed supply of tokens issued, the trading of crypto tokens is necessarily a zero-sum game. Since a token generates no external income, any wins made by one participant speculating on a token are necessary losses from another participant. Since there is a net negative cash flow associated with the maintenance cost of mining and facilitating transactions, the zero-sum game transforms into a negative-sum game (see Economic Problems). The expected return in the limit of iterated trading of crypto is negative, and therefore an economic game is in the same category as games of chance in a casino in which a rational player should expect a negative payout.

A crypto token can only be modeled by a game of chance distilled into a tradable token, a pure momentum position based on recursive speculation and untethered to any fundamentals or economic activity. The nature of this type of game is that its value only goes up so long as the hype monotonically increases and the market can find increasingly greater and greater fools to buy its tokens, pushing the price higher. Therefore, investing in this scheme is inextricably linked to an irrational expectation that ever more fools will continue to believe in the scheme indefinitely in the future. All short-term gains are ultimately paid out from recruiting later investors into the scheme to pay out the paper wins of early investors. This type of scheme has a payout structure that, to a first approximation, is identical to a Ponzi scheme, albeit an *open Ponzi scheme*.

The statistician Nassim Taleb, author of *The Black Swan*, makes a salient observation regarding the underlying fragility of purely-narrative-driven financial assets and open Ponzi schemes in his *Bitcoin Black Paper*. Taleb describes how in the common analysis of games of chance, there is an event in some games known as an absorbing barrier, which is an event when a failure event at which no possible gains are realizable. Gambling in a casino has an absorbing barrier when the gambler exhausts his funds, and markets have an absorbing barrier when a company ceases to be solvent or becomes unavailable to trade. Traditional maintenance-free commodities (such as metals or gemstones) do not have an absorbing barrier globally because their value is tied to their physical existence. Since a crypto token is not a physical item, there is a non-zero chance of regulatory, sabotage, exit scams, or technical catastrophes that would cause the network's failure and destruction of all stored value. Cryptoassets such as bitcoin have an absorbing barrier associated with their technology failure whose probability must be non-zero unlike commodities with a physical existence.[3]

Since crypto token produces no income and is a negative-sum game with an absorbing barrier, the asset cannot be valued on its future cash flows because there is no yield generated. Trading an asset of this type can generate a return for individual holders based only on the greater fool theory; the value of a crypto token is then only what the next fool will pay for it. In simpler terms: the only purpose in buying it now is to find someone who will pay more for it in the future. It is an asset that needs to be traded ad infinitum to a greater and greater pool of fools, all of whom are willing to pay out early investors for more than they paid. The only allowable solutions under the discounted cash flow model are that the asset's market value must grow exponentially, without remission, and with total certainty requiring an infinite chain of future buyers. The terminal value is then contingent on an infinite sum of the present valuations in terms of an infinite chain of fools. Since human economic activity and existence are finite, this is not a realistic model, and as such, cryptoassets cannot have a non-zero fundamental value.

In the rational bubble model[1], the value paid by increasingly-greater fools must increase exponentially as a function of the discount rate and the probability of failure. If the asset does not sustain this growth or stabilizes, then the sales to the infinite chain of fools cannot overcome the cash outflows, and the yield of the entire scheme must become negative. Bubbles need to be fed, and bubbles cannot sustain themselves with stable inflows. Under the rational bubble model, a crypto asset can only be an "economic black hole" investment on long time scales requiring increasing capital to be fed to sustain its ultimately unstable and transient existence.

Since cryptoassets cannot technically function as a currency, they are speculative assets with no income, non-zero maintenance costs, negative-sum, and an absorbing barrier. By backward induction on its future expected value, we must say that its present value is zero, and its fundamental value must be zero. The market value of a crypto asset will fluctuate along with any number of allowed paths as it reverts to its fundamental value of zero. Any rational investor should regard it as presently worthless.

Crypto assets are quantitatively a completely irrational investment, and theoretically treating them as a sensible asset class necessitates irrational assumptions of infinities or introductions of absurdities that contradict all of established economic thought. We are thus left with the most obvious conclusion: crypto is a bubble much like tulips[2], Beanie Babies, and other non-productive curio that humans have manically speculated on in the past. It is a financial product whose only defining property is random price oscillations along a path that inevitably leads to its ruin.

Environmental Problems

"At present, we are stealing the future, selling it in the present, and calling it gross domestic product."

– Paul Hawken

The technical inefficiencies of cryptocurrencies are the mark of a technology that is over-extended and not fit for purpose. However, what is even more concerning is the environmental footprint these technologies introduce into the world. Bitcoin and currencies that use *proof of work* consensus scheme require massive energy consumption to maintain their networks. This feature is central to their operation and is the mechanism that allegedly "builds trust" in the network. No network participant has any privileged status except in the amount of energy they expend to maintain the consistency of the network itself. The amount of energy spent in this global block lottery results in an expected direct return per watt, which is statistically predictable. In a nutshell, the premise of mining is to prove how much power one can waste, and the more power one can waste, the more resources one receives in return. The system is fundamentally inefficient in its design[4,17,9].

The impacts of new technology have to be considered within a framework of environmental shortcomings since the stakes of our era are staggeringly dire. Climate change is happening now, the global temperature on earth is rising, and the polar ice caps are melting. In Greenland, the glaciers are receding six times faster than expected. Climate change is not an abstract phenomenon happening elsewhere; it is happening everywhere ever day, and technology plays an important part in the future of our planet.

7.1 WASTEFUL MINING

The bitcoin network automatically adjusts the difficulty of mining so that each block takes an average of 10 minutes to mine. If a miner performs a fixed number H of hashes every 10 minutes, each hash has a $1/H$ chance of mining a block. If a miner performs N hashes every minute, the number of blocks they can expect to find per minute follows a binomial distribution with maximum N and with probability $1/H$. We can then compute the expected value of the binomial distribution, calculated by multiplying the number of trials by the probability of success. The expected return is the expected value of computing a block times the block reward amount (currently 6.25 bitcoins). This expected return can be calculated as a single variable function: the number of hashes a miner can compute per second. This unit is dimensionalized in hashes/second and often denoted in megahashes (10^6 or Mhash/s), gigahashes (10^9 Ghash/s), or terrahashes (10^{12} Thash/s). At the time of writing, for a data center to consistently produce an expected return of 1 bitcoin per day would require approximately 140,000 Thash/s. These computations are spread over many racks of computing devices running in parallel[12].

Off-the-shelf computers can be used for building cryptocurrency mining rigs. However, the performance of these devices is suboptimal compared to dedicated mining hardware. A top-of-the-line CPU such as the Intel i9 processor can perform 5.2 Mhash/s with an expected return of 0.00000001 bitcoin per week or at the time of writing $0.00012 per week. Mining using standard CPUs found in most computers is generally infeasible. However, a single specialized *graphics processing unit* (GPU) such as an Nvidia GeForce RTX 2070 uses a model of execution with a great deal more parallelism, can have up to 42 Mhash/s, and has an expected return of 0.0051 bitcoin per month or $60.30 per month. One of these graphics cards retails between $500 and $1000 per device and consumes 214 watts of power.

As many people learned during the California gold rush, sometimes the most profitable activity is not the mining itself but selling picks and shovels to the miners. Globally there is a cottage industry of services and providers selling cryptocurrency mining wares, and this global trade has drastically driven up the price and lowered the supply of high-end graphics processing hardware. Cryptocurrency's volatility has led to the usual economics during speculative bubbles. Bitcoin has created a veritable arms race of mining equipment that attempts to optimize hashes per watt. This context makes a massive network of data centers worldwide, all clustered around areas of cheap[2,1] power where the input capital per watt can yield an optimal return on investment. Regions such as Siberia in Russia, Texas in the United States, and Xinjiang in China have seen upticks in cryptocurrency mining activity due to their geographic proximity to cheap fossil fuel power.

However, the environmental impact is that we are drawing more power from the grid, burning more fossil fuels to maintain this cryptocurrency network, and lining the pockets of cryptocurrency miners. For the bitcoin network, with only 5% of activity corresponding to economic transactions[13], this would result in a truly staggering amount of economic and environmental waste if we compute the volume of carbon emissions required to sustain this entire scheme. Each miner, in their short-term interest, has an incentive to waste more power to have more chance of earning the reward. However in aggregate the amount of power is used for almost no purpose, and the amount of waste is staggering.

Since the statistics involved in the proof of work system are readily quantifiable, it is possible to estimate the energy required to sustain the bitcoin network. Alex de Vries and others estimate that the bitcoin network consumes 87.1 TWh (terawatt hours) of electrical power annually as of September 30, 2019.[14]

This amount of wasted energy on bitcoin is comparable to the energy consumption of the entire nation of Argentina, a country of 50 million people. In his paper, de Vries also estimates that the network has doubled its electricity consumption between 2018 and 2019. This figure represents 43% of the current global data center electricity across the entire IT industry, as estimated by the International Energy Agency.[8]

> **Bitcoin consumes nation-state levels of energy to process a minuscule amount of transactions considerably slower than any other payment method.**

For a comparison with the traditional IT and banking sectors, the Visa network processed 111.2 billion transactions in 2016. An internal audit of the company reported its data centers 674,922 gigajoules, which during the course of the year amounts to 21.4 megawatts (10^6 watts). All of Google's data centers globally used an annual 5.7 terawatts (10^{12} watts). This includes operations which provide anyone on the internet with Google search and video streaming of YouTube.

The bitcoin network consumes more power than all the Amazon, Microsoft, Facebook, Netflix, Google, and Microsoft's data centers combined.

7.2 ENVIRONMENTAL HORRORS

The per transaction costs of bitcoin is an even more alarming statistic. The transaction statistics from aggregated chain data indicate the bitcoin network is performing 326,140 transactions per day or 119,041,100 transactions per year. The per transaction energy cost is 2077.54 kWh, or the equivalent to the power consumption of an average US household over 75.67 days. Comparatively, the Visa network can perform 100,000 transactions for 151 kWh, and a single transaction takes 0.002 kWh. [1]

The yearly carbon output of this energy consumption is quantifiable as a percentage of power derived from fossil fuel emissions, and the bitcoin network is estimated to emit 51.9 megatons of carbon dioxide annually. A single bitcoin transaction alone produces 270 kg of CO_2.[5,14]

On top of the carbon footprint and energy waste, every single data center running computer hardware to perform useless proof of work computations emits a steady stream of e-waste in discarded graphics cards, ASICs, and servers. Each of these chips contains an abundance of heavy metals and carcinogens such as lead, cadmium, mercury, and chromium that are dumped straight into the landfill after being discarded. The annual e-waste of the bitcoin network amounts to all the cell phones, laptops, tablets, and computers of every person in the Netherlands put together. A single transaction on the bitcoin network amounts to the amortized destruction of 2.29 iPhones.

The bitcoin network requires constant hardware replacement and produces a

---

[1]A time of writing the bitcoin network was performing 359,405 transactions per day.

continuous stream of waste from broken and exhausted components.[16] A substantial new change to the software protocol of a cryptocurrency network may invalidate the previous purchases and require a complete overhaul and repurchasing of all global mining hardware, specially for dedicated ASIC miners. The network produces 11,000,000 kg of electronic waste annually or 96 grams per transaction. This annual e-waste[7] is equivalent to several small countries and 482,456 people living at the German standard of 22.8 kg of e-waste per person per year. Moreover, approximately 98% of bitcoin mining equipment will become obsolete before returning any value[11].

Bitcoin is a single network among hundreds that use similarly wasteful proof-of-work models. It is challenging computation to estimate the global energy cost and CO2 emissions across the entire cryptocurrency sector, but the total sum of hundreds of proof-of-work currencies could conservatively be 50% on top of bitcoin energy requirements. Gallersdörfer et al. estimate that "bitcoin accounts for 2/3 of the total energy consumption, and understudied cryptocurrencies represent the remaining 1/3. Therefore, understudied currencies add nearly 50% on top of bitcoin's energy hunger." The entire cost in terms of health and climate damages caused by the continued operation of these services is an alarming number and is deserving of further study and estimation.[3,15]

Whether bitcoin has a legitimate claim on any of society's resources is a question that does not have a scientific answer, it is fundamentally an ethical question. There are many activities where humans burn massive amounts of fossil fuels for entertainment activities or activites that do not serve any productive purpose. For example, Americans burn 6.6 TWh annually for holiday lighting. The software industry must ask whether we should sustain a perpetually wasteful activity in perpetuity.

The answers to this fundamental question from outside of the tech industry have raised some alarming extrapolations from current trends. In an environmental study, Mora et al. estimate that *Bitcoin emissions alone could push global warming above 2 °C*[10], and Goodkind et al. suggest that[5]:

> Each \$1 of bitcoin value created was responsible for \$0.49 in health and climate damages in the US and \$0.37 in China

Climate change is a runaway phenomenon that may pose an existential threat to human civilization[6]. Today massive CO_2 emissions are a debit on the quality of life for future generations. The problem of cryptocurrency mining needs to be addressed within a framework that considers the quality of life for future generations and in terms of a cost-benefit analysis of running a network that is consuming nation-state levels of power and whose purpose is primarily speculative gambling.

Cryptocurrency Culture

"Our century will properly be called the century of the intellectual organization of political hatred"

– Julien Benda, *Treason of the Intellectuals*

The intellectual center of cryptocurrency culture is the premise to reinvent money from first principles independent of existing power structures. The cryptocurrency phenomenon can therefore be viewed as a political struggle over the fundamental question of "who should exercise power over money" in a world idealized by its acolytes. There is a great insight to learn about the movement from their manifestos: How a group describes their path to utopia gives a great deal of insight into their mind and values[21].

There are three ideological movements and distinct subcultures within the cryptocurrency movement that gives rise to the intersection that defines cryptocurrency culture or simply crypto culture. Accordingly, each of its facet is defined by reverence for a concept that it holds sacred and forms the basis for its conception of utopia. How these groups frame their advocacy for cryptocurrency is a normative process that exhibits their implicit prioritization. There is no complete ethnography[16,35] of cryptocurrency culture, nevertheless it still constants three distinct large subcultures[22]:

- **Cryptoanarchism** - A political movement that sees technology as the mechanism to dismantle the state.
- **Austrian economics** - An economic philosophy that believes in unconventional views about economics, money and its independence from state intervention.

- **Technolibertarianism** - A culture that believes in the inefficiency of institutions and the need to replace these with software.

Each of these cultures describes a different final state for the technology originating in these worldviews and different creative and destructive mechanisms by which to arrive at their stated goals[32]. Each crypto culture similarity recieves different response from those outside of cryptocurrency. Consider for example how the Nobel laureate and Keynesian economist Paul Krugman sees cryptocurrency as a destructive force and bluntly describes[37,36,38] the phenomenon as a speculative bubble:

> [Bitcon is] a bubble wrapped in techno-mysticism inside a cocoon of libertarian ideology.

While Steve Bannon, the Trump political campaign strategist reactionary populist leader, describes bitcoin in terms of a creative force to achieve his revolutionary ends:

> [Bitcoin is] disruptive populism. It takes control back from central authorities. It's revolutionary.

8.1 CRYPTOANARCHISM

Contemporary anarchism emerged after World War II as a counter-cultural movement that perceived the failure of governments to solve enduring social problems as endemic to the existence of the state itself. The problems of poverty, environmental destruction, wars, and gender inequality originated from the state's social contract[47] and its failures to address these problems. This movement flourished after the war and found sympathy in a broad mixture of philosophical, political, and literary sources.

Cryptoanarchism or *cyberanarchism* is a political ideology the aim of which is to achieve the protection of privacy, political freedom and economic freedom through the use of cryptography and crypto assets. It considers itself a reaction to the overreach of governments and the state into the private and financial lives of citizens and asserts the need for so-called total freedom[12,31]:

1. Total anonymity of individuals in digital spaces.

2. Total freedom of speech without censorship or moderation.

3. Total freedom to trade without regulation or protections.

In this tradition, early internet mailing lists developed an interpretation of anarchist ideas contemporaneously to the rapid technological evolution of the 1990s and the internet revolution. This movement came to be known as *cryptoanarchy* and is a political ideology that proposes that the internet and strong cryptography will ultimately diminish the sovereignty of nations and destroy the capacity of governments. The movement's founding documents are the 1988 *The Crypto Anarchist Manifesto* and *Cyphernomicon*[40], written by the early Intel engineer Tim May. The former piece begins with an allusion to Karl Marx[41]:

> A specter is haunting the modern world, the specter of crypto anarchy. Computer technology is on the verge of providing the ability for individuals and groups to communicate and interact with each other in a totally anonymous manner. [...] Arise, you have nothing to lose but your barbed wire fences!

The manifesto is a vehemently anti-state document and describes the political landscape of the 20th century as an escalating conflict between the internet and the state. The ideology sees the rise of the internet as supplanting the privileges of the state "to snoop, wiretap, eavesdrop, and control" its citizens. This diffusion of power from the state to the internet-enabled individual (called *cyberspace*) is the heart of its proposed conflict theory. Cryptography— the branch of computer science concerned with protecting and transmitting data privately—is then seen as the core mechanism of building out this conceptual cyberspace and ensuring its supremacy over the state:

> When you want to smash the State, everything looks like a hammer.
> Strong crypto is the "building material" for cyberspace

John Barlow, an American political activist and founder of the Electronic Frontier Foundation, is the author of a seminal essay entitled *Declaration of The Independence of Cyberspace*[8], which declares the domain of cyberspace to be a sovereign entity. The essay describes the premise that cyberspace is a distinct political entity and is outside the domain of other nation-states.

> Governments of the Industrial World, you weary giants of flesh

and steel, I come from Cyberspace, the new home of Mind. On behalf of the future, I ask you of the past to leave us alone. You are not welcome among us. You have no sovereignty where we gather.

- Declaration of The Independence of Cyberspace

The weak form of this ideology proposes a view of how to protect the individual against state surveillance. This document accurately predicted government overreach and the use of surveillance infrastructure on its populace, as later revealed by the Snowden leaks. We now live in an age where digital surveillance is pervasive, both by governments and corporations. In this conflict worldview, all the traditional institutions[17] have entered into a holy alliance to exorcize the specter of strong cryptography. The individual is seen as self-sovereign and thereby in conflict with the authoritarian state.

The extreme form of this ideology is a synthesis of anarchism with technology as the means to "smash the state." Cryptography and digital currencies are seen as vehicles to wrestle back the state's monopoly on violence by creating anonymous *assassination markets* in which financial incentives to assassinate politicians will inevitably destroy governments.

16.23.7. As things seem to be getting worse, vis-a-vis the creation of a police state in the U.S.–it may be a good thing that anonymous assassination markets will be possible. It may help to level the playing field, as the Feds have had their hit teams for many years (along with their safe houses, forged credentials, accommodation addresses, cut-outs, and other accouterments of the intelligence state).

This inflammatory document explored the implications of digital internet money, which is privately issued, anonymous, and allegedly can overturn central banks' power. Central to the ideology is also the belief that the core functions of the state inevitably will be replaced by software, with the technical supremacy of these functions will result in the irrelevancy and dissolution of the state.

Cryptoanarchism is adjacent to a less extreme political narrative known as technolibertarian, an extension of libertarianism that adopts an additional assumption of the "defense of the absolute freedom of the internet." Traditional libertarian ideology maintains that the role of government is strictly limited to protecting citizens from aggression, theft, breach of contract, fraud, and enforcing property laws. Instead of the complete destruction of the state[5,6], the technolibertarianism ideology seeks to minimize the role of government and presents the internet as a great liberating mechanism on which to build society. Software is thus seen as a force of liberation whose purpose is to dismantle bureaucracy. In this worldview, cryptography provides privacy[30,2] for the weak and enforces transparency for the powerful.[4] The ideology posited by subsequent books like *The Sovereign Individual* is an idealized future where code is seen as incorruptible and can be trusted[15] while people and institutions cannot[38,1].

Cryptocurrency is a technology built on and inseparable from right-wing philosophy.

Technolibertarianism remains a popular school of thought for many information technology professionals. This ideology is prevalent in the capital and software engineering culture, with two central modes of action: *disruption* and *decentralization*. Disruption involves dismantling existing institutions and power structures by undermining their mechanisms, while decentralization involves reconstructing these structures in a form for which power is subsequently diffused to many parties using network technologies. The term disruption has entered the mainstream lexicon and describes new ventures that attempt to undermine existing institutions and business models. The notion of decentralization is central to the blockchain philosophy. The technolibertarian perspective is that digital currencies are disrupting and decentralizing the bureaucratic institutions of banks and supplanting the sovereignty of nations to control the money supply.

This perspective of government disruption resonates with American ultraconservative political ideology, whose core tenet is that the state is intrinsically authoritarian and any form of government intervention breaches the individual's freedom. In this worldview, the state itself is the primary source of violence, theft, oppression, and all forms of coercion. Freedom and liberty are thus synonymous with "freedom from the state."[3]

A characteristic of anarchistic politics is the practice of living the movement as if the desired society already existed, and as is common in Silicon Valley culture to "fake it til' you make it". In this practice, one adapts their present behavior to embody the ideals of the future outcome before it occurs. This notion of prefigurative politics[33] is central to the cryptocurrency movement, and the idea to "live now in the future we are building" is a standard rhetorical device[10] in cryptocurrency marketing and rhetoric.[34]

Part of the contract of living in a democracy is giving up individual liberties to secure others' collective rights. However, within the cryptoanarchism world-view, technology has removed this compromise and instead freedom is "freedom from the collective." Technology and software do not offer an escape from government; they can only offer another competing governance system[7] with its own power dynamics and coercive institutions[20]. Technolibertarianism is, at its core, simply a preference for that system over democratic institutions.[14,27,44]

8.2 Technolibertarianism

Software developers are as vast and varied as any arbitrary sample of people, and little about the profession of writing software implies any particular cultural characteristics. Nevertheless, distinct subcultures within the software have shaped history and had an outsized influence on the craft of software itself.

The *hacker culture* is a term to describe a subculture and general mentality toward engineering that emphasizes demonstrations of technical aptitude and cleverness as well as a set of ethics around information sharing. This usage contrasts with the colloquial use of the word hacker to refer to actors who penetrate computer systems for criminal activity. This hacker philosophy traces its roots to the Massachusetts Institute of Technology and was contemporaneous to the early internet development. American journalist Steven Levy first canonized the hacker ethic in his 1984 book *Hackers: Heroes of the Computer Revolution*. Levy defines the five hacker values as sharing, openness, decentralization, free access to computers, and societal improvement. Additionally, proponents of the hacker ethic often espouse a distaste for authority and the belief that bureaucracies are inefficient or fundamentally flawed.

This set of principles and the early internet is an overarching faith in the transformative power of computers and a belief in meritocracy. The belief is that one's programming skills are the ultimate determination of one's value as a hacker and can and should be separated from identities such as age, sex, race, orientation, position, and qualification.

Simultaneous to the hacker culture was the rise of the free software movement arose that aimed to create free computer software independent of the corporate offerings of the day. The notion of freedom was a term of art that referred to the right "to copy the information and adapt it to one's own uses." This notion of freedom was jokingly defined as "free as in free speech, not as in free beer."

The free software movement was led by the MIT researcher Richard Stallman, and ultimately evolved into the GNU collaborative initiative to develop free software. This created a legal initiative to license software under a set of provisions known as the GNU General Public License (GPL), which ensured that software (and software derived from that software) remained available to inspect (open source) and available for public use. The defining feature of open source software is thus that anyone can freely inspect it and share it for others to understand its inner workings. The GNU movement was a highly influential political initiative and enormously transgressive for its time.

In 1991 the renowned software developer Linus Torvalds released the Linux kernel. The combination of the GNU software and the Linux kernel would form the GNU Linux (often shortened just as Linux) operating system. This operating became very influential in the history of computing.

The open-source movement thrived beyond the Linux operating system, and the sharing of code under permissive software licenses became the norm. Platforms such as GitHub allowed rapid collaboration on open source projects by participants from anywhere in the world.

At the same time, questions concerning digital assets and what ownership meant in a world of bytes instead of atoms were being explored. The technology to copy and disseminate files freely became available was effectively a solved problem by 2010. These technologies marked the move toward censorship-resistant platforms, where information could be shared resiliently against removal by external actors. The mantra "information wants to be free" was an expression of the hacker mentality that all people should be able to access any information they desire without constraints. Many software engineers began to believe that an ever-growing corpus of human knowledge cannot and should not be contained within any legal framework.

This era also saw many leaks of private government information and dumps of classified intelligence by activists such as Julian Assange, a cypherpunk[II] who started Wikileaks[18,28]. This organization successfully leaked sensitive military and intelligence information from whistleblowers within the United States government and was able to disseminate this information using censorship-resistant internet protocols.

Central to the contemporary developer mindset is that all technology has no moral character. The design of a device or structure is neither good nor bad, it simply depends on its use. In other terms, the tool is independent of the consequences of using it. The internet can disseminate mathematics lectures just as easily as it can disseminate hate speech. The overarching presupposition is that whether the design of the software has ethical intent or purpose is not even a well-formed question. According to this worldview, the question simply has no answer. The perspective of the universal amorality and absolute neutrality of technology is an extreme view commonly held by technologists but rare outside of the industry.

As the internet became more mainstream and intertwined with everyday human experience, the radicalism of the old hacker culture sublimated into a more moderate developer culture with a generation of software developers. In place of the anti-authoritarian proclivities of their predecessors, many software engineers have embraced a new order of economic growth and prosperity within the software engineering profession. The craftsmanship of software and hacker mentality faded into a new vision of market-oriented mentality which prioritized rapid iteration and customer experimentation.

Tech workers unhappy with this outcome that find their positions simply make them puppets of the corporate milieu without much sway over the corporate hierarchy or change to alter the course of the industry. Some tech workers even feel that their work has led to the overall degradation of civilization but cannot see an actionable path out.

The anti-authoritarianism of past hackers has faded into the learned helplessness of the current generation. The hacker culture's idealism of the internet's transformative power has itself transformed into a culture of corporate serfdom and subversive opportunism. Idealism and practical utopianism have become a parody, and the promise to "make the world a better place" has become a punchline to industry jokes.

A malaise has descended over Silicon Valley as an unexpected dystopia has unfolded in the wake of the hopeful disruption. In the absence of advancement in the field, many developers have retreated into technolibertarian fantasies that center around pipe-dream decentralized technologies as a panacea to the world's problems. While these dreams may not be realistic or internally consistent, they at least offer some kind of respite from the ambient nihilism of the tech hegemony. At least, these dreams are grasping at something, literally anything, that could be better than current route towards an undesirable tech-led neo-feudalism.

The cryptocurrency ecosystem derives its intellectual structure precisely from this escapist alternative fantasy world. A fantasy that presents a future vision in which decentralized code, artificial intelligence, and universal access to technology dissolve the coercive influence of the corrupt bureaucracies of modernity. The libertarian ideology has consumed the hacker notion of decentralization, transforming the egalitarian vision of progressive inclusion and access to an ideology in the service of centralized wealth creation, privilege, and the power of capital.[43]

8.3 Austrian Economics

Austrian economics is a heterodox perspective on economics that embraces a radical view on laissez-faire markets and non-interventionist government strategies in matters of the economy. It emerged from a series of debates in the London School of Economics in the 1920s on whether centrally managed communist economies could be well-managed enough that they would outpace the market economies of democratic capitalist states. Austrian economics had already gained some prominence in the late-19th and early-20th centuries from the studies of philosophers and economists Ludwig von Mises, Friedrich von Hayek, and Murray Rothbard.

The school of Austrian economics differs from orthodox economics in its methodology. Instead of proceeding from an empirical framework of observations and measurements, Austrian economics is a presuppositional framework that attempts to create a model to describe all human economic activity by purely deductive reasoning. The framework presupposes core axioms of human behavior, which form the philosophical foundation of the theory. The central tenet, called the action axiom, is the synthetic a priori statement "human action is purposeful."

Grounded in the action axiom the Austrian view attempts to describe a framework for rational choices in the presence and ranking of human desires, resource scarcity, time preference for resources, and the synthesis of activities that give rise to economizing behavior. The Austrians call this line of reasoning *praxeology*, a pure axiomatic-deductive system that its founder Mises claims can be knowable and derived independent of experience, in the same way that mathematics can be known.

> [Economic] statements and propositions are not derived from experience. They are, like those of logic and mathematics, a priori. They are not subject to verification and falsification on the ground of experience and facts. They are both logically and temporally antecedent to any comprehension of historical facts. They are a necessary requirement of any intellectual grasp of historical events.

> — Ludwig von Mises, *Human Action: A Treatise on Economics*

Mainstream economics arises out of the empiricism philosophy in which all knowledge is derived from experience, where true beliefs derive their justification from measurements, observations, and coherence to scientific models which make falsifiable claims. In contrast, Austrian economists believe that knowledge is difficult to obtain in social sciences, some truths that are knowable, and it is possible to posit models that can be falsified. Mises further asserts that no economic truths are knowable empirically and that praxeology is the only method for deriving economic knowledge[25,26].

> No laboratory experiments can be performed with regard to human action. We are never in a position to observe the change in one ele-

ment only, all other conditions of the event remaining unchanged [...] The information conveyed by historical experience cannot be used as building material for the construction of theories and the prediction of future events [...] Neither experimental verification nor experimental falsification of a general proposition is possible in its field.

Ludwig von Mises - Human Action: A Treatise on Economics

The Austrian framework is unconventional in the larger realm of scholarship and is not widely taught in universities. Its presuppositional nature makes it more akin to philosophy than mainstream economics, which proceeds from explicit models and predictions that can be derived from data and which are falsifiable. However, some of the individual ideas from Austrian economics have found integration in mainstream schools of thought.

The Austrian school diverges drastically from the other schools its view of the role of the government should play managing the economy. Most other economic schools see the government as playing an essential interventionist role in managing the economy and money supply, especially in times of recessions and shocks. However, Austrian economists see a minimal case for a government role in managing the market economy. Hayek proposed replacing central-banking controls with a free-market setting to set interest rates from within the private sector. In this view, central banks, regulation, and market intervention contain logical contradictions which achieve the same effect as central economic planning. Hayek further claims these policies empower the state over the individual and disrupt the ability of the market to transmit information and achieve price information, thus leading to harmful cycles of instability.

In the Austrian perspective, centralized market intervention turns economic influence into political power and financial rewards based on non-public information. This process considered to be worse than centrally planned economies as it does not allow for accurate price formation of assets and ultimately leads society into a loss of freedoms, a rise of tyranny, and a state of serfdom. For many hardline Austrians, all other views are lumped under the amorphous term "Marxism" if they involve divergence from the complete free-market orthodoxy. In this worldview, intervention is inherently undemocratic in that it allows a select few individuals to exert undue power over the lives of the rest of a nation and beyond. Hayek argued that fascism is itself inexorably linked to central economic planning and called this a state of "serfdom"[24,25].

The central political call of some Austrian economics is to set up a system that is immune by construction to government meddling. Menger and Mises argue that the gold standard is the mechanism that can form the basis for sound money and argue strongly against the modern fiat central bank system. Acccording to these two scholars the fiat system of money is unstable and will inevitably self-destruct as it is based on unsound economics that contain logical contradictions[29].

Many of these contradictions stem from an analysis of inflation, that is the rate of increase in prices for goods and services relative to the current purchasing power. Many Austrians prescribe what is known as the *monetarist theory*. This idea is that inflation is not rooted in economic reasons within the economy but rather only arises from central banks' activities. While it is true that if we double the number of dollars in circulation, then the classical interpretation is that this dollar will purchase half as much. Uncontrolled expansion of the money supply can potentially be a source of inflation, but it is not necessarily the source of all inflation.[23] The sophistry and confusion are where the monetarist theory devolves into a right-wing conspiracy theory, which is the redefinition of the word inflation to mean any event which introduces new money into circulation. According to these heterodox economic ideas, inflation has pejorative connotations and is seen as a completely undesirable force. In contrast, most mainstream economists view low inflation ($< 2\%$) as a desirable feature of a managed economy as it discourages hoarding and encourages investing in productive assets.

One of the fundamental flaws of Austrian economics is the mistaken belief that inflation only results from expansion of the money supply.

The intellectual edifice built by the Austrians to argue for commodity-based money was a convenient framework for early bitcoin advocates to adopt[49]. The roots of the movement within libertarianism meant that advocates for gold could see sufficient similarities in the artificial scarcity mechanism of cryptocurrencies.

Just as the gold supply on Earth is limited, the number of bitcoins is similarly constrained by a fixed supply. In the bitcoin neo-metallism worldview, the decentralized nature of cryptocurrency is theoretically immune to intervention and driven purely by market forces thus fullfilling the Austrian notion of a basis for so-called "sound money" or "hard money."

A *gold standard* is a commodity-based currency regime in which money can be exchanged for gold at a fixed price. In 1699 Sir Isaac Newton was made the Master of the Mint, and after the accession of Queen Anne in 1702, England was under a bimetallic regime with silver and gold backing the British pound. Issac Newton set an exchange rate of 21 silver shillings to 1 pound sterling and quickly discovered that there were difficulties in balancing market rates and the standard exchange rate. Eventually, with gold prices remaining relatively stable while silver prices were volatile, England switched to a full gold standard marking the beginning of the longest-running international gold standard.

The heterodox economists that argue for a gold standard and sound money are fundamentally pushing for a scenario in which the fixed price of gold constrains governments, institutions, and people. They argue that this limits government power by restricting the ability of governments to print money at will. The main argument against a gold standard is that the supply of gold is relatively fixed; thus, an economy that is growing can rapidly outpace the money supply and, as a result, create economic contractions and periodic deflationary pressure. Under deflationary pressure, prices fall, so it is always rational for individuals to hoard rather than spend money as much as possible, as it will be worth more tomorrow than it is today. This self-reinforcing process takes more money out of the supply, risking deeper deflationary spirals that threaten economic productivity—if no one wants to buy anything, the market cannot fund economically and socially productive activities. Left unchecked, this type of deflationary cycle is enormously destructive to economies.

When money is fixed to the price of gold instead of the price of goods and services, fluctuations in the price of goods replace gold's market price. Between nations, those running external trade deficits face increasing deflationary pressure. Central banks cannot have too little gold in reserves, but they can never have enough. This inescapable fact creates a massive imbalance between nations' financial stability[48].

Historians and economists often cite the gold standard as the reason for the Great Depression spreading from the United States to the rest of the world setting the stage for the start of the Second World War. Fed Chairman Ben Bernanke said of the gold standard[13]:

> The gold standard-based explanation of the Depression is in most respects compelling. The length and depth of the deflation during the late 1920s and early 1930s strongly suggest a monetary origin, and the close correspondence (across both space and time) between deflation and nations' adherence to the gold standard shows the power of that system to transmit contractionary monetary shocks.

Modern economists widely regarded commodity-based money as a terrible idea and a barbarous relic best relegated to the ash heap of history.[50] The United States National Bureau of Economic Research has shown that there were 15 business cycles between 1800 to 1933. During the gold standard era, recessions would occur every 3½ years, while since 1972 (after the abolishment of the gold standard), there have been about eight recessions occurring roughly every six years. Booms and busts are natural, but governments have the tools to mitigate the volatility and frequency of these cycles under a modern fiat system[42].

Nevertheless, after nearly a century of the success of fiat money, the conspiratorial side of the Austrian movement still views the fiat banking system as a plot to acquire the gold of citizens and replace it with a system of illusory value. In their worldview, only gold is seen as the asset of any real persistent value, and the last forty years are seen as a massive conspiracy for the wealthy to "acquire our gold." This perspective is not mainstream, nevertheless, it is common in certain ultra-conservative American political circles[9]. Recently, however, the bitcoin movement has been seen often adopt this same narrative with one difference: instead of gold it is that the "government is trying to steal our bitcoins at all costs."

Curiously, although cryptocurrency advocates are rather keen on embracing Austrian economics, the same can not be said the other way around. Within the contemporary Austrian discourse, bitcoin and cryptocurrencies are often seen as untenable pipe dreams, and they argue strongly against the notion of bitcoin as sound money. The blog for the Mises Institute, an Austrian advocacy group, offers their counter perspective:

> Some experts maintain that bitcoin will displace the existent fiat money and will usher in a new era of free banking, which will finally put to rest the menace of inflation. Unfortunately, this is a pipe dream. Electronic money will not replace fiat paper money. The belief that it can stems from a failure to understand the nature and function of money and how it emerges on the market.
>
> — "The Bitcoin Money Myth", mises.org

Nevertheless, cryptocurrency advocates have repackaged the Austrian arguments and rebased them with bitcoin or other cryptocurrencies as their center. Trade books central to the bitcoin movement (such as *The Bitcoin Standard*) proceed from an exclusively Austrian perspective to posit the notion of bitcoin as a basis for a new global reserve currency to displace the US dollar and an alleged improvement on gold.

The presuppositional nature of the Austrian framework effectively places it outside the realm of reason, forming the basis of integration into what the industry calls *cryptoeconomics*. The libertarian ideology and incommensurability of praxeology with other economic schools make the bitcoin philosophy nearly impossible to debate in conventional terms since it redefines terminology and contradicts most orthodox economic assumptions. Most debates about bitcoin in mainstream economics will therefore simply reduce to debates about the legitimacy of the nation-state itself[39] and the axioms of praxeology. The veracity of cryptoeconomics conveniently requires no evidence, testing, or falsification; it is simply a matter of faith in its underlying assumptions. For many, the incoherence of this intellectual edifice is irrelevant, as Austrian economics simply serves as a pseudointellectual posthoc rationalization[45] for crypto investing and resonates with their existing political ideology.

8.4 FINANCIAL NIHILISM

While the ideologies and ideas around crypto vary, the most common worldview held by most crypto investors is simply a complete lack of any worldview. In normal philosophy, this perspective is called nihilism: the belief that all values are baseless and that nothing can be known or communicated. Philosophical nihilism is associated with extreme pessimism and a radical skepticism that condemns all of existence; a belief in nothing and the lack of any purpose other than an impulse to destroy. Financial nihilism is a "philosophy" on investing and markets where value does not exist or is inherently unknowable. The claims of this ideology stem from an underlying belief that markets have no purpose and cannot or do not exist for capital formation because of an underlying belief that capitalism or markets simply can not work. With regards to crypto, this vacuous ideology posits that there is no reason or purpose to anything involving cryptocurrency and that the sole purpose of the entire enterprise is simply to make the "number go up" as a means to demonstrate the absurdity of all financial structures.

In contrast to the previous ideologies, financial nihilism posits no utopian, political, economic, or social enterprise to cryptocurrency other than to personally realize financial gains by encouraging others to invest in the same tokens one is invested in to drive up the price. All is permitted, and the legality or ethics of any actions which drive the price up are inconsequential or meaningless to analyze as they have no moral or economic structure. The goal is simply "number go up," and any means justify the ends[19].

Thus, cryptocurrency is often seen as an absurdist joke or "trolling" of the financial system either to illustrate the folly of existing institutions or as a political statement about the inherent emptiness of human existence in a hypercapitalist society. This mindset stems from a low-information worldview in which traditional financial instruments such as stocks and bonds are simply another form of a meme, a narrative[46] with an equally empty intellectual structure.

The political economy of the crypto movement is as varied as the people involved; their ideologies have become a nexus of convenience around which heterodox ideas[51] and thinkers of various stripes have rallied to make quick money and spread their ideas. As a result, the crypto movement has spread the seeds of extremely fringe right-wing ideas to a crowd that would not otherwise be exposed to heterodox ideas about economics and monetary policy.

Ethical Problems

"Basically, I exploited the phenomenon of the technician's often blind devotion to his task. Because of what seems to be the moral neutrality of technology, these people were without any scruples about their activities. The more technical the world imposed on us by the war, the more dangerous was this indifference of the technician to the direct consequences of his anonymous activities."

– Albert Speer, *Inside the Third Reich*

We sometimes think that technology is essentially neutral. That it can have good or bad effects. Although it is essential who controls or wields it, a tool is just a tool with no moral character. As the cliché goes, a hammer is just a hammer. Guns don't kill people; people kill people. However, the reality of the world is that humans build technologies and technical artifacts carry the intent[34] of their creators, along with their political imaginaries, into the world.

Slot machines are a technology, yet it is a technology that is purpose-built for financial exploitation. In many ways, cryptocurrency carries the same moral character as slot machines. Cryptocurrencies are purpose-built for avoiding regulation and facilitating illicit financing, effectively enabling a dark network for payments in which illegal transactions external to the technology can be achieved within the system. There are several major categories into which the inescapable harm of cryptocurrencies falls.

9.1 SELLING SNAKE OIL

Retail investors who choose to purchase cryptocurrency assets are exposed to various risks from four distinct categories: suitability of the investments for the consumer, presentation of the prospectus to consumers, operational concerns from infrastructure, and legal protections in the event of fraud. Retail investors who choose to invest in crypto products are exposed to market risk, platform risk, and counterparty risk far more than traditional markets and likely have no legal recourse to regulators or ombudspersons in the case where their products evaporate into nothing due to fraud or error.

Retail investors who chose to invest in cryptocurrencies overwhelming cite the pursuit of "easy money and wealth," "an investment to retire on," and "fear of missing out"[3] as the driving factors behind their investment. The presentation and touting of cryptocurrency investments are widespread and largely unregulated. For many retail investors, social media influencers and unconventional trade press drive the initial informal presentation of the investment opportunity. These influences come from decentralized sources and can be disparate from those offering the investment[9,26,20].

The presentation of these whitepapers and prospectuses is not regulated or governed by advertising codes. More often than not, these prospectuses are entirely untethered to the fundamentals of the investment, making wild and unsubstantiated claims the consumer may not be able to assess. The use of technical and obscurantist language, known as techno-obscurantism, often confuses consumers and is used to defraud potential investors. The prospectuses for cryptocurrency assets overwhelmingly overstate the potential for returns and underestimate the volatility and potential for loss. Promises of 350% to 1000% returns for early investors are often routinely cited as motivation for initial investment.[18]

Retail investors who choose to enter the cryptocurrency market are often forced to use a series of unregulated offshore exchanges which serve as on-ramps to enter the cryptocurrency market. Many of the crypto exchanges are set in jurisdictions on the FATF blocklist and use a network of correspondent banks in Eastern Europe and Asia to collect funds from customers. These funds are allegedly held by the exchange, uninsured, and with no guarantee of returns or ability to withdraw funds. Since these entities are outside of the customer's jurisdiction, there is little, if any, legal or regulatory protection in the event of fraud or loss.[16]

The operational risk of engaging with these exchanges is unusually high. The risk of hacking on these exchanges is considerable, and historically this has resulted in either the dissolution of the exchange or a complete loss of all customer funds. In 2018 the number of customer funds lost was $1.7 billion, while in 2019, this figure increased to $4.4 billion. The exchanges' unregulated and unsophisticated cybersecurity precautions pose a significant risk to retail investors.[4,9,31]

A 2019 whitepaper by Panos and Karkkainen analyzes the risk perception of cryptocurrencies based on demographics and concludes[26]:

> It is conducive to shedding light to the demand side of cryptocurrencies and suggests that a large part of the cryptocurrency market comprises unsophisticated investors with lower financial literacy skills. These investors are likely to overestimate the reward prospects in cryptocurrencies and underestimate the risk involved in related investment.

Cryptocurrencies disproportionately victimize vulnerable people. The overwhelming risk is too unsophisticated, and low-information investors are persuaded to put their savings into volatile cryptocurrency assets by spurious promises of fantastic price increases. Cryptocurrency takes a demographic that may otherwise have gambling problems[22]. It legitimates their addiction by wrapping it up in a veneer of technical legitimacy, presenting it as a simulacrum of trading actual financial products. Online gambling might be socially frowned upon, however, gambling on cryptocurrency exchanges is not yet widely seen as antisocial or risk-seeking behavior.

Day-trading cryptocurrencies can negatively affect the mental health[30] of individuals involved in this activity. The stress and anxiety associated with attaching one's life savings and well-being to an unnaturally volatile market can be both exhilarating and exhausting. The mental energy required to maintain a portfolio exposed to this level of risk requires a great deal of time, focus, and discipline that many retail investors lack and that in the long term may have a deleterious effect on mental well-being.

9.2 Illicit Activity

The primary uses of cryptocurrency predominantly fall into six categories:

- Speculation
- Ransomware
- Money laundering
- Evasion of sanctions
- Evasion of capital controls
- Purchasing of illicit products

Cryptocurrency speculation is the dominant mechanism that creates market liquidity that provides cover for the final five activities[13]:

Retail investors who invest in cryptocurrency assets may be inadvertently exposed or complicit in criminal activity by engaging with these markets. Exchanges notoriously exist in legal gray areas and are relegated to the fringes of the financial system because of their general non-compliance with most regulations. Foley et al. estimate that "approximately one-quarter of all users (25%) and close to one-half of bitcoin transactions (44%) are associated with illegal activity".[11]

The confluence of violent drug gangs and hackers is significant in cryptocurrency. In Latin America, these two groups have combined their influence, skills, and resources to achieve common goals in laundering funds. Many Caribbean island nations have loose KYC/AML laws and are a hub for global money-laundering efforts.[7,6,35]

Laundering money through cryptocurrency is efficient and accessible even for unsophisticated actors. There are many mechanisms and open-source software tools for obscuring the provenance of funds. These off-the-shelf software packages create complex chains of new wallets that can move funds between the accounts to cover their origin and beneficiary. These processes are known as *peel chains*. Through this technique, a single account starts with the total amount to be laundered, and then this balance is split ("peeled") to a fixed set of several one-time wallet addresses. This process is repeated hundreds or thousands of times until the funds are split across many wallets. These wallets thereafter dump their funds into a single address that aggregates the obscured funds from the original origin wallet but with their provenance obscured. Sophisticated versions of this technique may also randomize the times and amounts transferred between the peels to create the illusion of economic transactions instead of blatant money laundering.[29,32]

Even more sophisticated launders use a technique known as *chain hopping* in which value in one cryptocurrency is swapped in a trade with the equivalent value in another cryptocurrency and then swapped back. This technique further obscures the origin of funds commonly using privacy coins such as Monero and ZCash.[23]

In addition, self-service laundromats such as tornado.cash provide automated money laundering services on the ethereum blockchain and require no technical expertise. These services are used to launder funds stolen from ransomware attacks using chain hopping techniques.

Across the ecosystem, we even see companies set up explicitly to clean tainted crypto funds and turn them into clean money for criminals to abscond with to jurisdiction areas with loose money controls. A money-laundering firm known as Crypto Capital served as a payment processor for the Bitfinex exchange to deposit funds to purchase the popular Tether stablecoin. Polish officials found the company's Polish correspondent banking relationship was a front for a Colombian drug cartel. The founders were arrested in Europe and convicted of money laundering.

On the opposite side of the globe, Japanese organized crime has also had its hand in using cryptocurrency as a vehicle to clean its funds tied to criminal activity. $270 million was laundered through Japanese cryptocurrency exchanges by individuals involved with the Yakuza crime syndicate. Japanese authorities have cited several businesses for their failure to comply with domestic money laundering laws.

Terrorist organizations also require a steady cash flow to remain afloat, just as organized crime does. Traditionally terrorist[10] organizations use the *hawala system* of laundering money. Money is moved between hawala brokers who exchange information about deposits between sender and receiver through coded verbal exchanges between the brokers. The system relies on the honor of the brokers who maintain counterparty risk for the transfer of funds. According to the FATF report, cryptocurrency has replaced a major part of this system as a medium of exchange for terrorist organizations. In 2020 the United States seized a $2 million store in 300 cryptocurrency accounts controlled by the al-Qassam Brigades and the Islamic State of Iraq and the Levant.[27]

In 2018 United States intelligence showed that the North Korean government had stolen $100 million of cryptocurrency from exchanges in South Korea. Nation-state actors were alleged to have been involved in 35 cyberattacks on cryptocurrency exchanges in 17 other countries and may have stolen as much as $2 billion. United States sanctions make moving money in and out of the country difficult via conventional payment rails. The state's acquisition of cryptocurrency assets allowed it to fulfill payments for its sanctioned coal and petroleum exports in violation of United Nations sanctions. The North Korean state has created a network of foreign brokers who use their seemingly legitimate accounts at exchanges in China, Japan, and South Korea to facilitate transactions from the cryptocurrency stolen in attacks to pay for the state's expenses abroad in defiance of sanctions. United Nation sources cite the company's use of cryptocurrency mining to fund both its nuclear and military programs.[24]

The United States Justice Department has reported that North Korea operates a covert branch of its government known as *Room 39* that maintains a foreign currency slush fund for the Kim family. Since North Korea has been shut out of the global banking system, the agents of Room 39 have become particularly adept at using South Korean exchanges and decentralized exchanges to launder money.

In a civil action brought by the United States Justice Department, the government indicates the technical sophistication of these actors [1] in laundering crypto assets (primarily Algorand, Steller, and Tether) valued at over $2 million in defiance of United States sanctions:

> According to that Member State stolen funds following one attack
> in 2018 were transferred through at least 5,000 separate transactions
> and further routed to multiple countries before eventual conversion
> to fiat currency, making it highly difficult to track the funds.

---

[1]United States of America vs 280 Virtual Currency Accounts, Civil Action No. 20-2396

In 2019 an early developer on the ethereum project was arrested by the FBI for allegedly providing technical instructions to the North Korean on the technical mechanisms to launder money through the ethereum network between North Korea and South Korea.

The crimes associated with cryptocurrency and money laundering are not victimless. These are crimes that facilitate taking human lives and serve to protect the criminals who are giving orders from prosecution. Cryptocurrency exchanges are the central mechanism for criminals to perform business, evade detection, and make a profit far more straightforward than dealing with traditional banks, thus emboldening the criminal sector and encouraging more illicit activity.

9.3 THE UNBANKED

The marketing of cryptocurrency typically invokes the notion that the technology serves as a vehicle of financial inclusion for the masses and is aligned with the interests of the rhetorical "little man." An infamous New York Times op-ed in 2014 openly discussed the merits of bitcoin to address the problem of citizens without access to bank accounts, customarily referred to as the *unbanked*.

> And even in the United States, a long-recognized problem is the extremely high fees that the unbanked—people without conventional bank accounts—pay for even basic financial services. Bitcoin can be used to go straight at that problem, by making it easy to offer extremely low-fee services to people outside of the traditional financial system.

> — The New York Times, *Why Bitcoin Matters*

However, the reality on the ground could not be further from this fantasy. Given the public audibility of bitcoin accounts, it is readily quantifiable to answer how much of the simulated wealth of the ecosystem is tied to individual accounts. The statistics show a profound inequality, vastly above any real-world country. The top 2.8 percent of wallet addresses control 95 percent of the supply of bitcoin[8]. This figure is, however, difficult to interpret because exchanges will hold the balances in their accounts on behalf of individuals. The most in-depth analysis was performed by Kondor et al. in their investigation *"Do the rich get richer? An empirical analysis of the bitcoin transaction network"*[19]:

> [...] we find that the wealth of already rich nodes increases faster than the wealth of nodes with low balance; furthermore, we find positive correlation between the wealth and the degree of a node.

An abundance of studies and statistical evidence leads us to believe that bitcoin investments are simply a means for the already wealthy to become wealthier. This observation mirrors the exogenous statistic that those with crypto wealth are already rich outside of crypto. Wealth in the cryptocurrency world is inexorably correlated to wealth in the real economy, early adoption, and education. Access to technology, internet connectivity, and capital to invest in early technology is a state of high privilege that is not accessible to most of the world. While there is not an abundance of data on the demographics of cryptocurrency holders; if the investor base follows the demographics of the technology sector[5], then most holders are male. A system that primarily rewards early male investors in developed countries with easy access to capital is hardly a progressive cause for the unbanked.

The notion that cryptocurrency could serve any purpose in helping the unbanked is absurd, given its unsuitability as both a medium of exchange and its hyper volatility. An average citizen in a developing country (with an annual income of less than $1,035) is more likely to lose a significant portion of their savings even attempting to transact in bitcoin simply due to hyper volatility and exchange costs. Bitcoin is merely a rubbish currency, and those who labor under the pretense that it could function as money will ultimately get financially burned. In 2020, for example, the bitcoin price went from $8,500 to $4,500 occurred in twelve hours.[12] This situation would be a nightmare scenario for a family in the global south that tried to hold their already small savings in this asset.

Vision statements about the blockchain community's unbanked and global development rhetoric carry the political ambition of imposing tech-centric solutions for an often non-tech community. This phenomenon is a form of authoritarian paternalism wherein the cryptocurrency community—primarily situated in North America and Europe—believes itself best suited to decide the development of disenfranchised populations continents away. In their world-view, their theoretical African person in an imagined African village becomes a marketing device for their desires to advance cryptocurrency adoption for their own ends—likely to enrich themselves[15,25,28]

9.4 MMM PONZI SCHEME

At the end of the Soviet Era, a Russian Ponzi scheme arose out of the chaos and opportunism of the collapsing regime. The scheme was known as MMM and was formed by the initial letter of the surnames of its founders: Sergei Mavrodi, Vyacheslav Mavrodi, and Olga Melnikova. The company was founded in the 1980s and changed its presentation during its duration to present many different ways of drawing in new inflows of money. In the initial form of their venture, MMM started by importing computers and electronics in Russia; however, this was quickly shut down by the government due to being a front for tax evasion.

Infamously, in 1994, MMM pitched a financial scheme for the "ordinary Russian man" to be given the opportunity to catch up with the newly established oligarch class. The fictional TV character Lenia Golubkov was portrayed as the Russian everyman who was crushed by his low wages and used the MMM scheme to generate income. MMM created a narrative around Lenia, an excavator operator, with an advertisement series related to the struggles of the ordinary Russian working man who did not even receive their wages regularly. In one advertisement of the series, Lenia buys his wife boots, a coat, and later a car merely by investing his wages into MMM's shares.

This scheme was particularly well-suited for its time, as this was an era where Russian oligarchs aggressively accumulated what was once previously public property under the Soviet regime. During this period, Russian people were given government vouchers as part of their share of the national wealth, i.e., equal pieces of institutions, factories, and companies, which they could acquire translated stake in the privatized enterprises. However, most people in Russian society lacked the financial knowledge of what the vouchers meant and quickly exchanged them.

Mavrodi claimed to use the funds generated from the scheme to return to the people what was seized by the oligarch class, effectively wrapping the project in a supposed Russian Robin Hood narrative. The advertising for the scheme was compelling and resonated with the general public, therefore generating massive public interest in this supposedly egalitarian get-rich-quick scheme. With this momentum and his popularity, the points of sale where the public could buy into MMM increased exponentially. These outlets allegedly sold shares in a joint-stock company which was an obscured Ponzi scheme. To perpetuate the Ponzi scheme, the perpetrators distributed paper shares to buyers, which resembled stock certificates or banknotes, and created the illusion of legitimate ownership in a joint enterprise. Notably, at no point did the scheme intentionally advertise itself as a joint enterprise in any economic activity; it seemingly generated money from nowhere. In an interview, Mavrodi himself describes the scheme plainly and in no uncertain terms:

> MMM is a financial pyramid, as it has been written on the site hundreds of times. Everyone is being warned honestly, plainly, and openly that it's a financial pyramid. Where does the money come from? The money comes from the previous at the expense of the subsequent. That is all—there are no other sources of income—only this one.

MMM is a perfect example of an "open Ponzi scheme." At its height, the scheme promised insane returns of up to 3000% annually simply by paying out old investors from new investors. Moreover, in 1994 Russia was experiencing hyperinflation of 412.67%, and so for many desperate individuals, investment schemes that promised any returns did not seem all that risky compared to simply holding cash.

The Russian Ministry of Finance eventually caught onto the scheme, and the ministry shut it down for the sale of illegal securities. Ironically, some of the early winners of the scheme regarded Mavrodi as a folk hero and simply dit not care that the scheme was an outright Ponzi, not all that dissimilar from the arguments used to advocate for cryptocurrencies today.[17]

Even though the principal founder Mavrodi faced prosecutions, busts, and imprisonment, he continued his Ponzi schemes until his death in 2008. The scam mutated and lived on in many new forms, and new MMM organizations popped up across Africa. Including a multi-level marketing structure based on the Ethereum blockchain with the cryptocurrency shamelessly called Mavro. Mavrodi's tale is the age-old story of the rise of fraudulent opportunists in periods of economic chaos and political unrest. The MMM scheme preyed on the same universal human sentiments as cryptocurrency is doing today, fear of missing out, greed, and a chance to make easy money in a period of desperation.

While the MMM scam had been mainly strangled out of existence by traditional financial controls, it found new life on the ethereum blockchain and now continues to target its victims in undeveloped African, Asian, and Latin American countries. As of July 2020, 10% of ethereum's total global transactions were related to inflows into the MMM Ponzi scheme.[2]

Cryptocurrency is not standing on some moral pillar, nor is it acting as some technological Robin Hood. Instead it is simply removing all the processes protecting both sides of transactions and distributing those trust mechanisms to those parties. Bitcoin ATM operators are now forced to step in to prevent the vulnerable from scams where banks would have generally served as the safeguard. Instead of protecting the vulnerable against fraud, cryptocurrency now pushes this obligation on individuals themselves.

The central ethical problems of cryptocurrency is simply that it redistributes risk to the vulnerable[1,14] and allows the wealthy to extract from low-information investors under the false promise of technological progress[33] and financial liberation[21]. Cryptocurrency investments are a regressive tax on the poor and financially illiterate, which comes attached to both a terrible opportunity cost and societal cost from its externalities.

The Cult of Crypto

"You don't get rich writing science fiction. If you want to get rich, you start a religion."

– L. Ron Hubbard

Cryptoassets are inherently negative-sum and, as such, consistently hemorrhage money. Sustaining the scheme therefore requires increasing the pool of greater fools which in turn requires more than just a value proposition: it requires a self-organizing high control group that recruits and maintains the inflow of money from its followers. Cryptocurrency economics needs active investors to hold their positions and onboard more investors[5]. The system's structure further requires new users to consistently pump more money into the scheme to counter the negative-sum economics. If numerous people simultaneously lose faith in the asset and decide to liquidate their positions, this would result in a run that would collapse the entire structure on which any of these investments rest. There is nothing under these investments except a collective delusion that "number go up."

The high control group that has organically emerged to sustain this scheme is a new kind of emergent internet phenomenon that exhibits many of the same phenomena as a traditional religious cult. This kind of movement is broadly one that provides three ideological frames:

1. A framework for making meaning of the world.

2. A mechanism for group control of the practitioners.

3. A mechanism for self-control.

L. Ron Hubbard's classical term of *new religious movement* does not fully encapsulate the recent decentralized phenomenon of internet-based high control groups. We lack a proper term of art to describe these movements. However, some sociologists have coined the new term *conspiracy cult* as a more appropriate description of the contemporary phenomenon in the internet age.

10.1 THE GOLDEN CALF

Non-theistic religious movements like Scientology are the closest to the cryptocurrency phenomenon. Scientology is a self-help business hiding behind the front a bizarre theology found in the science fiction writings of its founder L. Ron Hubbard. Hubbard was transparent about the intent of his religion and was regularly quoted as saying the entire enterprise was a cash grab and tax avoidance scheme. Nevertheless, the movement he created persists to this very day.

At face value, the Scientology movement presents to its followers a doctrine on self-improvement with a set of prescriptions on actions and behavior that will reveal the true nature of reality. These scriptures and training are defined by a set of Operating Levels that the followers must purchase from the church in ever-increasing amounts of money to reach some form of alleged enlightenment. Scientology encourages existing members to proselytize Scientology to others by paying commissions to those who recruit new members, much in the same way pyramid schemes operate. Other countries have banned such enterprises for socially corrosive or tax evasion. For example, the German courts have declared that Scientology operates as a for-profit business masquerading as a religion for tax avoidance purposes.

The cryptocurrency movement shares many aspects of economically-based new religious movements such as Scientology. Crypto is fundamentally a belief system built around apocalypticism, the promise of utopia[14] for the faithful, and a process for discrediting external critics and banishing heretical insiders.[13]

There is an almost zealous disdain for mainstream Keynesian economics and what is perceived as the central banking-led political establishment. The ideology perceives the "other" or the "oppressor" as central banks, the Federal Reserve, financial regulators, and other traditional financial institutions. These conspiracy theories embrace fringe economic views and propositions that the

Federal Reserve is engaged in a systematic conspiracy to rob the public via inflation and Keynesian monetary policy.

A key differentiating factor of the crypto ideology is that it lacks a central
doctrine issued by a single charismatic leader; it is a self-organizing high control group built from individuals on the internet who feed a shared collective
together. An organic movement it has arisen, evolved, and adapted to be a more
viral doctrine of maintaining faith[15] in a perceived future financial revolution
in which the faithful view themselves as central. The inevitability of cryptocurrency's future is dogma that is sacred and cannot be questioned.

This narrative of central banking conspiracies is a particularly virulent form
of conspiracy theory because, in part, it is rooted in, and perhaps rightly so,
distrust[2,8] of financial institutions in the wake of the 2008 financial crisis. The
events of 2008 saw a betrayal of the public trust and an unpopular, divisive
bailout. Public opinion of executives in the banking sector is low and phony
populism is an effective mimetic delivery mechanism for extreme political views
that wrap themselves around a legitimate public grievance.[12] Much of the same
financial populism seen in the cryptocurrency ideology is also found in groups
such as Occupy Wall Street, albeit from a different political bent.

10.2 TRUE BELIEVERS

As in most high control groups, there is a set of thought-terminating clichés,
which are phrases or sayings that discourage critical thought and meaningful
discussion about a given topic[9] such as "The Lord works in mysterious ways," or
"Everything happens for a reason" Asking any critical questions about cryptocurrencies will most often result in a backlash in the form of one of the following
thought-terminating clichés:

1. "have fun staying poor" / "hfsp"
2. "If you don't believe it or don't get it, I don't have the time to try to
   convince you"
3. "we're all going to make it" / "wagmi"
4. "we're so early"

5. "hold on for dear life" / "hodl"
6. "the dollar is a Ponzi scheme" / "everything is a Ponzi scheme"
7. "now do the dollar"
8. "FUD"
9. "few understand"
10. "bullish"
11. "to the moon"
12. "diamond hands"

Other critical questions on most of the core issues result in whataboutism concerning state-backed currencies (often the US dollar) and the events of the global financial crisis. The dichotomy and perceived conflict between the traditional financial system and the so-called "crypto financial system" are also central to the ideology and incontrovertibly and unquestionably true for its believers. The central ideas of the ideology feed on this false dichotomy in which the frauds of the financial crisis and scams of cryptocurrency are an either-or choice in which one must choose the lesser of two evils. It rejects the logically consistent position to withstand the excesses of both.[7,16,6]

The demographics of socially active cryptocurrency users are difficult to state precisely. However, many articles have noted that cryptocurrency is a primarily male-dominated space[10]. One crypto fund's 2019 survey of recent blockchain startups found that 85% of employees and 93% of executives were men. A 2018 North American bitcoin conference had 86 male speakers and one woman, which is not surprising considering the party for the conference was held in a Miami strip club. The pejorative term *crypto bro* expresses the prevalence of a reactionary and unenlightened hypermasculine culture that overwhelmingly dominates cryptocurrency spaces.

The communities and ideologies for the cryptocurrency subculture are fostered through mediums such as Twitter, Telegram groups, 4chan message boards, Reddit, and Facebook groups. In cryptocurrency culture, promoting a specific investment is *shilling*[4] for the coin. The term shilling comes from casino gambling, where shills are casino employees who play with house money to create the illusion of gambling activity in the casino and encourage other suckers to start or continue gambling with their own money. For many involved with the cryptocurrency scene, shilling as well as pump and dump schemes are their primary source of employment. Their income and livelihood are locked up in the value of a specific portfolio, and the promotion of this token is their full-time job. A growing set of YouTube and Twitch streaming personalities derive income proselytizing for the movement and promoting specific investments without disclosing their financial interests.[11] Many crypto advocates are prone to using quasi-religious metaphors to describe cryptocurrencies, the best example of which is Michael Saylor, CEO of MicroStrategy whose unhinged tweets are somewhat legendary amongst bitcoin acolytes:

> Bitcoin is a swarm of cyber hornets serving the goddess of wisdom, feeding on the fire of truth, exponentially growing ever smarter, faster, and stronger behind a wall of encrypted energy

The softer form of these quasi-religious narratives that present bitcoin as a source of meaning in life are ever present throughout crypto discourse, as they often tweet out statements like:

> The best part of Bitcoin is the purpose it demands of us
> Through seeking the answer to the questions that bitcoin impels, a new world is opened—one where truth is elevated to its indelible position as the crown jewel of all ordering, renewing itself as the most important concept

For many millennials and young adults, organized religion and the nation-state are declining as a primary form of identity. The rise of a global communication network, free trade, and decades of relative peace has given rise to an internet culture that increasingly dominates our lives and shapes our primary identities. At the same time, traditional institutions such as family, unions, and religion are declining in the influence and ability to organize communities and provide meaning and purpose. Internet groups are where they spend their time, find friends and seek validation. For many in this mode of thinking, it is a seemingly natural proposition that the internet itself should be the issuer of money, employment, and identity independent of national boundaries.

The cryptocurrency ideology provides a psychological, philosophical, and myth-making framework[3] that, for many believers, provides sense-making in a world that seems hostile, rigged against them, and out of their control[1]. The crypto movement fits all the textbook criteria of a high control group; it provides a mechanism for determining an in-crowd and an out-crowd (nocoiners vs. coiners). It gives a framework for assessing the virtue of other followers based on their faith (HODLing) in the cause. It offers uncomplicated and pithy answers to complex economics and monetary policy issues. It gives a linguistic framework of thought-terminating clichés and acronyms to quell dissent. It provides a mechanism of social control in which one can acquire influence and status in exchange for proselytizing and onboarding more followers to buy tokens. And finally, the ideology presents an eschatological narrative of retributive justice about the end times of the global financial system, in which the true believers will be reborn with a new life in an anarcho-capitalist utopia.

> **The crypto ideology makes miraculous promises of wealth, not derived from labor or economic activity but purely from faith.**

The mission of proselytizing the currency takes on religious tones and requires constant displays of faith in the cause[7]. These communities are culturally isolated groups where dissent is met with hostility, ostracization, death threats, doxing, and harassment.

An unexpected result of the internet era is that negative sentiment and crackpottery spread more virulently than they did ten years ago. With the development of platforms like Facebook, movements that would have been relegated to the fringes of society have now found their path to the mainstream. It is unclear what to call phenomena such as QAnon and cryptocurrency. Some media outlets have identified the phenomenon as a *collective delusion* or *conspiracy cult*. These groups defy traditional definitions of religious movements by virtue of not being centrally organized or having single ordained messages. The inescapable truth remains that these phenomena are speaking to a sense of belonging and community people are not otherwise finding in their lives. In the future, increasingly elaborate and bizarre conspiracy movements based on economically-incentivized motivated reason will come in to fill this void in people's lives and will likely evolve into many new forms. The conspiracy movements of QAnon and cryptocurrency are the vanguard of emerging phenomena that society will be dealing with in the next century.

Casino Capitalism

"When the capital development of a country becomes a by-product
of the activities of a casino, the job is likely to be ill-done."

– John Maynard Keynes

These days the economy is growing both in complexity and in pace. The rise
of the complexity of financialization has led many in the public to question the
distinction between markets and a casino. From a particular perspective, the
behavior of stock speculators and casino gamblers may, in many cases, not be
that far apart. The historian Edward Chancellor wrote in his history of financial
speculation *Devil Take the Hindmost*[1]:

> The psychologies of speculation and gambling are almost indistin-
> guishable: both are dangerously addictive habits which involve an
> appeal to fortune, are often accompanied by delusional behaviour
> and are dependent for success on the control of emotions.

The distinction between gambling, speculation, and investing takes us to the
philosophical core of capitalism. In all its forms, capitalism is the strategic use
of competition amongst private parties to encourage economic production and
price discovery of goods and services. It is an assertion that markets are the best
solution to the *economic problem* of allocating scarce resources by balancing supply and demand to find an equilibrium that facilitates socially optimal exchange.
In capitalism, buyers compete with other buyers while sellers compete with other
sellers. This decentralized system will eventually converge on a Pareto optimal
economic state where fair and transparent markets allocate resources efficiently.

11.1 THE NATURE OF CAPITALISM

The use of competition to incentivize the creation of goods or services that the market demands are at the heart of the idea of capital formation[7,6]. By extension, public markets exist to allow the public to invest in the future values of collective enterprises in terms of the goods and services they will produce in the future. Inherently, predicting future events related to a joint enterprise is fraught with inherent risk; a company can succeed in the future only if it can deliver its future products. Yet, even a simple company selling hamburgers can be influenced by all manner of exogenous events; crop yields could fail due to poor weather, pandemics can disrupt supply chains, or consumer appetites could change. The market is a metaphorical "weighing machine" that takes all of these thousands of factors and data points and outputs an aggregate price with potential risks and possible returns priced into the present value of the company's stock. Asset prices reflect all available information, and on a risk-adjusted basis, it is almost impossible to "beat the market" since market prices should only react to new information.

However, this thesis does not exclude the possibility of manias, panics, crashes, and bizarre market behavior. At the height of the coronavirus pandemic, there was increased market interest in the video conferencing company Zoom. Investors rushed off to buy the stock with the ticker ZOOM. The only problem was that this stock belonged to Zoom Technologies Inc., a Chinese-based electronics manufacturer, and not the widely known American company Zoom Video Communication Inc, listed under the ticker ZM. Investors piled into the ZOOM stock, driving it up 1800% before the SEC had to step in to halt trading. These types of aberrant fat-finger events and irrational behavior occur and are an ever-present source of noise; however, these events are outliers.

The distinction between gambling and investing is subtle: **investing** in efficient public markets is inherently the activity of taking on the risks that arise naturally out of legitimate economic activity, and in fair markets, the risk and proportionally the possibility for returns are distributed to those who have the most accurate information and who can best understand the risks. In other words, investing incentivizes both information gathering and the building of predictive models, allowing more efficient allocation of capital and further economic growth and prosperity.

Proper investing is in stark contrast to **gambling**. Gambling involves creating risk untethered to any pretense of economic activity. Going to Las Vegas and repeatedly wagering money on Red-17 on the roulette wheel involves risk and the possibility of a return. However no economic activity is performed, no products or services are produced, and no new information is generated from statistically independent spins of the wheel. The casino creates artificial risk explicitly for its entertainment value, which appeals to a certain perverse desire for excitement and thrill associated with wagering on the outcome of random events.

Gambling involves wagering on artificial risk created for the purposes of wagering, while investing involves taking on calculated risks whose returns are based on actual economic activity[3]. Gambling is wagering money on an event that has an entirely unknowable outcome, whereas investing involves taking a calculated risk with an uncertain but predictable set of outcomes. This is where the primary difference between gambling and investing lies, and in an efficient market returns should be commensurate with risk.

However, many self-described "investors" are indistinguishable from gamblers. They may be driven by the same thrill-seeking and irrational behavior in picking stocks, just like they would pick numbers on a roulette wheel. One type of this investing is known as **speculation** which is investing in an asset for the sole reason that one believes that someone else will buy it for a higher price, regardless of the fundamentals.

However, overwhelming the market will correct the behavior of such individuals as picking investments independent of information gathering or fundamentals is a losing proposition that simply allows other market participants to outwit these low-information actors with better information. Activities such as day-trading, where individuals attempt to predict the short-term price movements of individual stocks on an intra-day basis, are a popular form of speculation that blurs the line between investing and gambling. On a risk-adjusted basis, day trading is highly economically irrational as it almost invariably has a negative expected return when taxes and transaction costs are factored into the equation. Retail traders who frequently trade vastly underperform retail traders who hold long-term investments. Warren Buffett once famously said the following of forecasting the market:

> The only value of stock forecasters is to make fortune-tellers look good. The short-term direction of stock prices is close to random. But why? It all comes down to human psychology and the relationship between markets and volatility. Time in the market beats market timing every time.

However, many new retail brokerages like Robinhood have been slowly training a new generation of young investors to do quite the opposite. By sending push notifications to trade more frequently and gamifying the experience of buying individual stocks, this new generation is learning to invest in a far riskier manner, which is, in many cases, indistinguishable from gambling.

11.2 LIBOR-cube Swaps

The pejorative term *casino capitalism* refers to an environment in which private businesses, especially banks, risk large amounts of money on high-risk investments based on a desire to make money quickly on short-term speculation. While not an accurate description of all capitalism and markets, there are indeed both markets and specific financial products that blur the line between gambling and investing.

Typically when sophisticated investors construct a portfolio, they aim to ensure their individual positions are *hedged*. A hedge is a supplemental investment made to reduce the downside price risk of an asset. Usually, a hedge consists of taking an offsetting or opposite position such that if one component of a portfolio goes down, another component of a portfolio will go up. There are a wide variety of tools and instruments for investors to hedge their positions. For instance, portfolios heavily dependent on agricultural yields might see a downturn in years with severe droughts or insufficient rainfall. To smooth out earnings, a portfolio manager could invest in a specific type of financial product known as a *weather derivative* which pays out buyers if a certain number of days of rain is recorded in a region. In most cases, this type of contract acts much like an insurance policy against the randomness of detrimental weather impacting profits. However, unlike an insurance policy, there is no requirement for insurable interest or proof of loss to receive a payout.

Buying weather derivatives in this fashion clearly has utility for portfolio managers to manage risk. However, the issuer of these derivatives will sell these types of products indiscriminately to anyone who desires to purchase one. It is therefore entirely possible to buy these products not as part of a hedging strategy but merely to gamble on the weather, much like one might do at a high street betting shop. There are some hedge funds that have been known to engage precisely in this type of behavior. Weather derivatives are an example of a product that is a sensible investment for one set of buyers, while for others, it is pure speculation depending on their larger portfolio composition.

Although derivatives have a negative connotation in the public consciousness following the events of the 2008 financial crisis, derivatives are an extraordinarily important and integral part of financial markets. Nevertheless, market makers have also been known to deliberately create complex derivatives and engage in the misselling of said derivatives to institutions unable to price the risk of these products accurately. In fact, for many American banks, we could effectively argue that this is their primary source of business; to sell the most sophisticated financial products to the least sophisticated investors possible.

A now-famous example is that of *interest rate swaps*. A swap contract is a hedging tool that involves two counterparties exchanging an initial amount of currency, then sending back small amounts as interest, and, eventually, swapping back the initial amount. Interest rate swaps are a specific type of swap contract where one stream of future interest payments is exchanged for another based on a specified principal amount. Interest rate swaps allow buyers to exchange fixed or floating rates to reduce or increase exposure to fluctuations in interest rates, thus hedging against changes in the underlying interest rate.

A commonly used interest rate is the London Inter-Bank Offered Rate (LIBOR), an interest-rate average that London banks compute daily to determine how much they would be charged to borrow from other international banks. The LIBOR rate underpins vast amounts of fixed income products and is used as the reference rate for many financial products.

In 1992, the American banking institution Bankers Trust Company was found to be selling interest rate swaps that did not use the base LIBOR rate, with the contract instead specifying the swap to be derived from the square or cube of the LIBOR rate—effectively the LIBOR rate multiplied by itself two or three times. This interest rate swap would help the fixed-rate payer wager on declining rates in a low-interest-rate environment. However, if interest rates increase, the losses from a LIBOR-cubed contract would grow exponentially.

Bankers Trust Company offered these power swap contracts to its clients, including one greeting card company named Gibson Greetings Inc, which reportedly lost $23 million on this type of transaction and was later sued for mis-selling[5]. This type of interest rate swap is an entirely absurd financial product as no portfolio has ever had a conceivable risk exposure as a function of the cube of LIBOR. While perhaps technically legal to sell, it is a product whose purpose is purely to place highly-leveraged and high-risk wagers on absurd outcomes indistinguishable from gambling.

Despite pathological examples of casino capitalism in the world, these types of behavior and products are overwhelming the exception and not the rule. When companies have positive quarterly earning statements, their stock price rises, and in contrast their stock price falls when they have negative earning statements. There are some exceptions to this, but in transparent developed equity markets, we do not see many extremely aberrant or mis-priced stocks completely untethered from their fundamentals. In other words, while it may be possible to play the stock market as a gambling game, it is not a winning proposition.

Cryptocurrencies are, on the other hand, the exact opposite. There is no mode of "investing" in crypto assets that is not gambling. The underlying assets themselves have no intrinsic value or fundamentals and are a pure manifestation of the greater fool theory; the value of a crypto token is only a gamble on what the next fool will pay for it. Crypto assets only add negative diversification to a portfolio, coupled with idiosyncratic and unquantifiable risk. From a rational portfolio construction perspective, cryptocurrencies are toxic.

The political philosopher Mark Fisher famously stated[4], "it is easier to imagine an end to the world than an end to capitalism," Indeed, capitalism is not going anywhere anytime soon and whether we like it or not, we are all forced to participate in markets. In democracies, however, we must insist on fair, orderly, and efficient markets that facilitate capital formation rather than reckless gambling. The purpose of markets is to perform price discovery on goods and services. If we remove the exchange of goods and services from the equation[2], we have nothing more than a gambling parlor just as the one we see in crypto markets.

Crypto Exchanges

"The beauty of doing business with a crook is that he always forgives you for catching him, so long as you don't stop doing business with him."

– Edwin Lefèvre

The vast majority of investors in the crypto market go through a centralized business known as a cryptocurrency exchange. These businesses, similar to regular exchanges, take traditional currencies such as dollars and euros at an exchange rate for a given amount of a digital cryptocurrency. The exchange rate between these two assets is called a *trade pair*. An example trade pair is USD/BTC, US dollars for bitcoin.

12.1 Neo-Bucket Shops

On one hand, these crypto exchanges act similar to standard stock brokerage accounts. Customers deposit funds which can be traded on the company's platform. The balances of their accounts are denominated in the currencies held and can be exchanged for other assets the exchange trades. For cryptocurrencies, the exchange acts as a temporary custodian for the funds. For national currencies, the exchange sometimes enables the withdrawal of funds into regular bank accounts[28]

Customers deposit funds with the exchange either through credit card payments, ACH, or international wire transfers to the exchange's correspondent banking partners. Ostensibly crypto exchanges make money by charging transaction fees, offering margin trading accounts, and taking a percentage of withdrawals from their accounts. However, in practice, these exchanges engage in all manner of predatory behavior and market manipulation activities[21]—a far more lucrative business.

Cryptocurrency exchanges are extraordinarily profitable, as they serve as the primary gateway for most retail users to interact with the market. However, these companies have a hidden risk that is transparent to many users. In the United States, exchange activities are only lightly regulated[5,14] at the state level under state-level money transmitter businesses, a framework that offers no consumer protection. In the events of fraud and market manipulation, customers have little to no recourse compared to what traditional brokers and equity market makers are required to comply with under securities laws.

The largest exchanges by volume have been set up outside of jurisdictions where the bulk of their customers' cash flow originates. There are a small number of regulated exchanges. Still, the major exchanges as a percentage of self-reported volume are unregulated and located in the Caribbean Islands and Southeast Asia. These businesses are commonly set up in jurisdictions with loose or corrupt financial regulatory regimes[13,1] which include, but are not limited to:

1. Antigua and Barbuda
2. Seychelles
3. Malta
4. Jersey
5. Gibraltar
6. Isle of Man
7. The Bahamas
8. Cayman Islands
9. Singapore

The largest cryptocurrency exchange globally is Binance, which was formed in China, moved to South Korea, thereafter to Malta[3], and while it is currently unknown where the company office is headquartered it is is allgedly based in the opaque tax haven of the Cayman Islands[2]. Binance has had consistent issues maintaining its banking relationships in United States, Europe and the United

Kingdom, which according to regulators, is because of the opaque nature of the corporate entities[9].

Many of the CEOs and founders of these exchanges are regularly seen in jurisdictions on the Financial Action Task Force (FATF) blocklist, interacting with sanctioned persons. Most personally avoid traveling to both the European Union and the United States for fear of prosecution.

The corporate structure of offshore crypto exchanges is purposely set up to avoid regulation, auditing, and any reporting requirements since these exchanges regularly engage in forbidden activities in traditional markets such as wash trading, order tampering, price manipulation, pump and dump schemes, front-running, painting the tape, and trading against their own clients.[9]

12.2 FLAVORS OF MARKET MANIPULATION

Pump-and-dump schemes are rampant in these markets[24,11,10,29,17,18,15], and there is no protection against the exchange directly participating in this activity. The hazards of pump-and-dump schemes result in wealth transfers from less sophisticated participants to market manipulators. According to Dhawan and Putniņš's 2020 study[6] of cryptocurrency market distortions:

> Unlike stock market manipulators, cryptocurrency manipulators openly declare their intentions to pump specific coins, rather than trying to deceive investors. Puzzlingly, people join in despite negative expected returns. [..] Analyzing a sample of 355 cases in six months, we find strong empirical support for both mechanisms. Pumps generate extreme price distortions of 65% on average, abnormal trading volumes in the millions of dollars, and large wealth transfers between participants.

..

> There is at least one pump on 133 days out of the 175 days in our sample, indicating that there is almost one pump per day on average. Such a high rate of manipulation is unprecedented in financial

markets

Usually, the construction of an order book is a regulated activity that informs how price formation on traded assets can occur. The SEC enforces a policy known as the National Best Bid and Offer (NBBO) in the United States, which requires brokers to execute customer trades at the best available prices across multiple exchanges. No such rule exists for unregulated cryptocurrencies, and a commonly seen pattern in this kind of market is the abuse of *order spoofing* or phantom bids. The exchange places a buy order and then cancels it seconds later after a trader wants to fill the order to sell. As soon as the order is placed, the price of the asset jumps and deceptively signals fake demand.[4]

The order of execution for trades is also an area where the exchange has privileged information that it can use to its advantage. Many exchanges operate their own for-profit proprietary trading desk, effectively acting as an in-house hedge fund that can trade using non-public information of its clients against its own clients.

There is no regulation preventing any exchange employees from trading on non-public information or prioritizing their personal trades, manipulating the construction of the exchanges' order book, or interfering with clients' orders. Indeed, the ability to insider trade is seen by employees as one of the perks of working for a crypto exchange.

Many exchanges are subject to sudden and arbitrary "system overload" events and market halts, which the exchange can use to intentionally block trades across the entire market when it advantages their corporate positions.[20,19]

Moreover, exchanges often interact with customers through mobile apps, which allow customers to place orders directly from a mobile phone. This family of apps uses the same dark patterns as Silicon Valley social media companies, such as behavioral nudges and push notifications, to push consumers into buying risky products and create "fear of missing out"[16], to encourage customers to gamble more.

On the opposite side of direct manipulation, exchanges will offer extremely risky leverage. In regular markets, *leverage* is when a trader who holds a positive marked to market position in a stock can use their holdings in that stock as collateral to borrow more money to trade an even larger position. However, suppose the price of the underlying stock decreases below a threshold where the value of the collateral no longer reflects the risk on the loan. In that case, the broker who offered the loan can ask the trader for additional capital in an event called a *margin call*. If the trader cannot post more capital to maintain their position, the broker can reclaim the stock from the trader in a process called *liquidation*. Leverage, usually in the range of 2-4x, is a normal part of traditional markets, although it is inherently a mechanism that increases trading risk.

However, many crypto exchanges over margin accounts allow up to 100 or 125 times, figures that are deeply predatory, and unseen in traditional markets. The extreme volatility of cryptocurrency makes these accounts unimaginably risky and highly vulnerable to even small amounts of market manipulation. Market manipulators need only shift asset prices a 1% at this level of leverage to liquidate high leverage positions. Many exchanges profit from liquidating some accounts as well as taking transaction fees on top of these insanely risky positions. Several class-action lawsuits filed in the United States allege exchange involvement. In a class-action lawsuit brought against several exchanges in the US, the plaintiffs allege:

> [The defendant] acts like a casino with loaded dice, manipulating both its systems and the market its customers use for its own sub-
> stantial financial gain.

It is challenging to secure reliable information about these exchanges and their transaction volumes. Most of the volume between exchanges themselves may be a complete fabrication as it is in the interest of exchanges to simulate liquidity on their markets by a process known as *wash trading*. Wash trading is when market participants repeatedly buy and sells products to themselves in order to to simulate market action to accounts they control. Wash trading is illegal in all other regulated markets except the crypto market, because it creates false price signals which do not correspond to any actual economic activity.

Similar to wash trading is *painting the tape*, a form of market manipulation whereby an *economic cartel* of insiders coordinate to influence the price of an asset by buying and selling it amongst themselves purely to create the illusion of demand. Cartels are undesirable in markets because they give rise to information asymmetry and warp price formation of assets in ways that degrade public trust in the market and inhibit legitimate commerce.

How many transactions on the bitcoin network are real exchanges between independent individuals, or how many non-economic transactions are being created to simulate volume remains largely unknown. The closest insider information on this data is the Bitwise ETF proposal to the US Securities and Exchange Commission, which posits that 95% of cryptocurrency exchange volume appears to be fake or non-economic wash trading.[27,12]

Exchanges that operate in the United States must collect KYC identity information on those opening up accounts. However, regulations around customers can often be less stringent outside the United States. An unspoken feature of many offshore exchanges is neither having anti-money laundering (AML) enforcement nor know your customer (KYC) obligations. This allows customers to transact outside the law unbounded by any domestic regulation.[23]

Executives at exchanges note that a cat and mouse game is being played, interfacing this wild west environment with the existing banking infrastructure. Exchanges that allow dollar withdrawals must go through a constant cycle of shifting shell entities and opening new corporate bank accounts whenever their previous accounts gather scrutiny or become frozen by officials. This network of banks and correspondent banks forms the network by which these exchanges can interface with existing domestic and international transfer systems in the United States and Europe by routing through proxy institutions which mask the suspicious origin of funds to and from the exchange.

Cryptocurrency exchanges are also notorious for platform risk. The highest volume exchanges are almost exclusively the main entry point for new retail investors and are overwhelmingly unregulated and unsupervised, with little recourse in the courts when fraud occurs. Exchanges in Asian markets have a mixed variety of legal reputations, and in Japan, there have been significant issues with the exchanges acting as gateways for money laundering. In 2018, Japanese regulators issued orders to six major exchanges: Bitflyer, Tech Bureau, Bitpoint Japan, Btcbox, Bitbank, and Quoine, for additional scrutiny on transactions. Many of these exchanges had some form of involvement with the Japanese organized crime group, the Yakuza.

In September 2020, the United States Justice Department issued a civil forfeiture complaint against 280 cryptocurrency accounts linked to 11 exchanges in the Korean region. These accounts were tied to laundering efforts by the government of North Korea to evade NATO sanctions on the country.

Since exchanges hold customer funds, they are enormous targets for hackers[26]. Cybersecurity problems have been a constant problem for exchanges, and the sector's history is full of high-profile hacks that have wiped all of the deposits of many customers. To enumerate the list of hacks could be the subject of an entire book unto itself, as they are so commonplace. Recently the largest hack was the Japanese exchange Coincheck, where hackers stole $530 million worth of cryptocurrency. As of September 2020, an average of approximately $2.5M is stolen every day in cryptocurrency exchange hacks.

In addition to cybersecurity risk, exchanges are often highly vulnerable to control fraud by their directors. The Canadian exchange QuadrigaCX lost $140 million in customer deposits after its director died under strange and dubious circumstances and had not shared the keys to accounts with any other employees in the company. After the executive's alleged death, the exchange's cold storage cryptocurrency wallets were mysteriously drained.

The nature of trading cryptocurrency requires investors to simultaneously manage platform risk, counterparty risk, market risk, and asset-level risk[25] and far above the due diligence requirements of traditional markets and vastly beyond the skills of most retail investors.[22]

Crypto exchanges, just like casinos[7], entice customers with false promises of financial windfalls and get-rich-quick schemes. And they often omit the unspoken truth that the intermediary company sitting between investors and sellers is often a dodgy network of shell entities with predatory intentions and which could disappear with a moment's notice[8]—leaving customers with no legal recourse.

Digital Gold

"In truth, the gold standard is already a barbarous relic."

– John Maynard Keynes

In the absence of cryptocurrency's efficacy as a peer-to-peer electronic payment system, the narrative around the technology has shifted away from the use case outlined in the original paper and onto a new proposition: cryptocurrency is "digital gold" or a "store of value."

The overarching issue with this narrative is that, unlike gold, cryptocurrencies have not proven themselves as a consistent store of value on any significant time period and lack the essential properties of a store of value investment[7]. Traditional stores of value such as gold have persisted and retained value through long stretches of human history, famines, wars, recessions, and the rise and fall of empires, while almost all cryptocurrency tokens have imploded on short time scales[2]

13.1 Fools Gold

The argument of crypto promoters is that cryptocurrency can be a store of value suitable for the world at large and form an economic basis for global economies on a long time scale. The "digital gold" terminology implies that cryptocurrency could replace precious metals, such as gold and platinum, as a store of value. The argument seems plausible at face value but has several flaws which stem from the economic criterion required for such a system and several existential problems that prevent cryptocurrency from being suitable or long-lived enough.

> **Cryptocurrencies are not stable over time, and are thus not a reliable store of value.**

First, a store of value is an asset that maintains its value without depreciating. It is a physical item or asset that can be retrieved and predictably exchanged at any point when needed by the holder. While the asset price may fluctuate gradually, they are unlikely to lose all value. Historically physical items like precious metals and gemstones have served this role.

A store of value must have a low variance in price movements; thus, a store of value investment cannot "go to the moon" or vastly appreciate in value. Purely speculative investments, such as bitcoin, with the expectation of price appreciation, are therefore the exact opposite of stores of value. Instruments such as stocks do not form a stable store of value as they are exposed to factors that fluctuate with the economy and, over long periods, tend to dissipate as companies dissolve and are replaced as civilization evolves. Cryptocurrencies are the purest exemplar of speculative investment and are one of the most volatile assets ever conceived. Cryptocurrencies have seen ludicrous price movements in response to global events such as the 2019 coronavirus outbreak, regulatory clampdowns, and exchange hacks. Drawdowns of 40-50% of value regularly occur with seemingly no underlying reason for the movements. Since the asset has only been created in the last decade, it is easy to cherry-pick regions of growth and falsely claim that this is an indicator of a general trend. However, as a store of value, cryptocurrencies simply have to this day not predict held their value and have been subject to shocks that would be unprecedented in any other asset classes.

> **Gold and other precious metals are maintenance-free commodities and do not require investment to sustain their physical properties. Cryptocurrencies need a constant influx of money in mining energy to maintain their existence.**

The second argument against cryptocurrencies stems from the continuity of the asset. Most cryptocurrencies that have been launched have died; the value that investors held in them simply vanished when they ceased trading. The median risk-adjusted return of cryptocurrency investment is zero. A few currencies such as bitcoin and ethereum have stood a short test of time; however, their future is fraught with uncertainty. If it is being proposed that assets are long intergenerational stores of values, it is worth asking the fundamental question of what it would take for one of the top ten tokens to collapse and how long these pure digitally ledger structures could even theoretically persist.

To all but the most faithful, the question "Do you see your grandchildren storing their savings in bitcoin?" is difficult to answer. A sensible answer would be probably not. To those who believe in the continuation of rapid technical progress, it is difficult to predict technology trends two to three years in advance, much less decades. As a thought experiment, if we believe in the bitcoin-maximalist (or any maximalist vision) rhetoric that "there can be only one global token," that first-mover advantage dominates all other factors, this precludes any competitors from ever existing. In this model, the bitcoin ledger is the final authoritative store of value whose continuity is eternal.

Thus all subsequent technologies will either build on top of bitcoin sidechains or are fundamentally heretical in their vision. This vision can ultimately be reduced down to an argument that bitcoin is the end of history, and even if a technically superior cryptocurrency were to launch, it would be irrelevant by virtue of it simply not being bitcoin. To the bitcoin devotees, the token's value is derived from its immaculate conception: it emerged in perfect and final form as a manifestation of the divine.

Taken to its logical conclusion, bitcoin maximalist arguments are absurd, and if one genuinely believes in the technical merits of the technology itself and recognizes the historical trend of technological progress. The argument for a flawless and imperfectible technology is a clear appeal to absurdities.

The non-maximalist view argues against any single cryptocurrency universality. If we play devil's advocate and assume cryptocurrency technology is not a technical dead end, then cryptocurrency markets can be seen as an economy of ideas in which the best and most technically efficient solutions attract the most investment. Rational investors will choose to store the most value in proportion to their merits. However, in this model, anyone's current token can and will be replaced by a better one at some point, and this must repeat ad infinitum. Unless there is a continuity of account states between evolutions of the technologies, then the value held in deprecated chains will eventually be subject to flight to safer and more advanced chains. Under this set of assumptions, we again conclude that any one cryptocurrency cannot be a store of value. Their structure is identical to stock in companies that rise and fall tethered to human activity and is inconsistent with the store of value model.

On the separate question of continuity, we have to ask if there are any existential threats to the cryptocurrency model. Are there events that could break the trust model and destroy stored value? The most likely possibility is a catastrophic bug in the software, either introduced accidentally or intentionally. If not handled properly, such an event could result in the complete destruction of anyone's network. While many of the widely used protocols are peer-reviewed and many reviewers oversee the code changes, this has not stopped similarly high profile software projects from suffering similar failures. Many public vulnerabilities have been discovered in widely used server software and under the names of Heartbleed, Spectre, and Shellshock. For most commonly used public software, it is not a question of if there will be a vulnerability but only when.

Cryptocurrencies are not a risk-off asset.

The second existential threat is an attack on cryptographic algorithms to secure any protocol. Several primitives used in protocols such as bitcoin are theoretically sound, but their models do not preclude the existence of mathematical attacks and the use of future technologies to undermine their integrity. There is no proof that core hash functions (SHA-256 and RIPEMD) used in bitcoin are not easily reversible, even though no method is currently known. Attacks on the cryptographic operations used in cryptocurrencies could allow users to breach other users' wallets, spend their tokens, or corrupt data on the blockchain itself. An advance in the mathematics of elliptic curves could theoretically yield a more efficient factoring technique that would render the specific choice of primitives used in historical wallets vulnerable to attack. While there is currently no known attack on the particular curve used in bitcoin, but however alternative technologies like IOTA have chosen combinations of specific, unverified primitives that have been proven unsound.

The third existential threat is the theoretical application of *quantum computers* to breaking cryptographic primitives used to secure cryptocurrency networks.

Quantum computers are theoretical computing devices that use the quantum mechanical properties of superposition and entanglement to perform computations faster than traditional computers. These devices have yet to be practically realized. In principle, however there are classes of problems in which these devices could perform orders of magnitude faster than classical computers. These problems overlap with cryptography and potentially introduce workarounds by which actors who possess a quantum computer could undermine several standard cryptosystems. The presence of an actor who possesses a quantum computer could theoretically be used to undermine and destroy cryptocurrency networks. However, it is still an open question in physics whether quantum computers are even physically realizable.

A standalone against cryptocurrency as a store of value is purely statistically. The exchange value of most cryptocurrency markets is highly correlated. As bitcoin moves, so does the whole crypto market. Both ethereum and bitcoin have a correlation coefficient of 0.9. Buying into any cryptocurrency besides bitcoin means one's investment is overwhelmingly exposed to bitcoin's extraordinarily volatile price movements[3]. Given bitcoin's dominance and its distinction in driving the price of all other tokens, there is little reason to invest in anything but bitcoin.[5] In addition to the correlations between cryptocurrencies, the overall crypto market is increasingly becoming correlated with NASDAQ tech equities, and thus offers no diversification over simply investing directly in the tech sector. In times of market volatility bitcoin crashes along with the rest of the sector.

> Cryptocurrencies are not a hedge against inflation and do not have a consistent relationship with macroeconomic factors that explain their volatility. Historically they have proven not to be a safe haven in times of market volatility and recently are overwhelming correlated with the market.

The consensus mechanism behind most cryptocurrencies also gives rise to several situations which could threaten them as a store of value. A so-called 51% attack on a network is an event where a miner or group of miners controls over half of the hash rate used to confirm new blocks. The miner rebellion could then interrupt the recording of new blocks and prevent others from completing blocks. This event would allow the attackers to double-spend their own tokens.

	Entities in control of >50% of voting/mining power
Bitcoin	4
Ethereum	3
Dogecoin	4
Ripple	1
Cardano	1
ZCash	2
Litecoin	3
Nano	3
IOTA	1

Blockchains such as the ETC chain have recorded these events, and we have seen successful attacks frequently occur in the wild. This kind of attack would be expensive and energy-intensive. However, given the mining centralization, it is already the case that four companies on the Chinese mainland control over 60% of the bitcoin hash power. This context represents a situation where four Chinese executives potentially are a social attack vector. The continuity of their interests is inexorably linked to bitcoin's proposition as a store of value.

Many cryptocurrency mining networks are in fact almost entirely centralized in the hands of a very small group of interests:

Additionally, blockchains governed by standard consensus algorithms have regularly seen the emergence of so-called *forks*. A fork is when a subset of miners and participants diverge on their use of a single chain of blocks, resulting in two historical ledgers with different spending activities. Most major cryptocurrencies have seen forks, including bitcoin, which has *bitcoin cash*, *bitcoin SV*, *bitcoin gold*, while ethereum has *ethereum classic*. Economically this is an extraordinary event since the holders of wallets have active accounts on both chains, and their tokens now have two historical accounts of their provenance.

Physical commodities cannot "split" and have multiple versions of themselves that pop into existence from nowhere. A cow in a field will never suddenly spawn into two cows, and gold bricks do not suddenly manifest duplicates of themselves. However, crypto tokens can split and fracture indefinitely, and in this scenario, the asset holds the same past but a divergent future. The usual outcome of this abnormality is that one chain will take precedence, and the other will die off or divide market activity between them and continue. Forking is a legitimacy problem for the store of value since choosing the wrong fork to transact on will nullify transactions or potentially destroy holdings.

13.2 Not an Inflation Hedge

Another existential threat to cryptocurrency is an outage, restriction, or attack on the internet. Mining centralization has given China an outsized influence on the bitcoin ecosystem and exercises enormous controls over its domestic internet through the Great Firewall. In their research, Kaiser et al.[4] identified 19 different attacks the Chinese government could perform which could cripple the network or fundamentally alter its economics. The centralization of mining efforts has also led to dedicated networks such as FIBRE (Fast Internet Bitcoin Relay Engine), a private network of miners set up with nodes in China, Europe, the United States, Russia, and Southeast Asia. State-level actors who thought bitcoin was a threat to sovereignty would be capable of causing mass disruptions or even destroying the network. If not fatal, such an attack would likely cause a massive movement in price that could effectively annihilate global liquidity. The most likely actor to engage in this kind of attack in terms of capacity and incentive is the People's Republic of China.

A political attack on bitcoin itself is also within the realm of possibility. During the lifetime of bitcoin, sitting United States presidents from both political parties have stated that the political program of bitcoin was not in the geopolitical interests of the United States. President Barack Obama discussed bitcoin at the technology conference SXSW and expressed his opinions on widespread cryptocurrency use: "It would be as if everybody has a Swiss bank account in their pocket."

While the US has only increased its prosecution of domestic criminal activity related to cryptocurrency, it has not generally extended its reach abroad or shut down domestic exchanges. This wait-and-see attitude has been the dominant philosophy among most politicians who have either been indifferent or too concerned with other matters to pursue additional activity against the network.

If the United States would wish to bring bitcoin to heel, it has the political tools and international alliances to restrict the asset's trade severely.

The US dollar's role as the international reserve currency and influence over domestic companies such as Visa and Mastercard, in addition to oversight over the SWIFT interbank network, means that the United States could effectively halt transfers to and from international cryptocurrency exchanges. With most users of the exchanges not able to withdraw their deposits, there would be a liquidity freeze and likely global shock in exchange price, as most users would attempt to flee to safe havens away from US sanctions. This endgame scenario may not completely destroy the network but could effectively destroy its value and ability to trade in many western allied countries. The United States federal government and the Treasury absolutely have the capacity and means to perform this level of action if there would be such political will.

> **Bitcoin is not a safe-haven from tyrannical regimes or a mechanism to hide assets from governments.**

The question of bitcoin as a store of value in these catastrophic events is three-fold: whether they are possible on short time scales, whether they are possible on long time scales, and on what time scales is the destruction of value possible. The externalities of nation-states failing or quantum computers are irrelevant to the continuity of physical commodities' value. No process could cause all land, precious metals, or stones in all of the world to devalue simultaneously.

Gold's historical claim as a store of value are a complex mix of factors: its industrial uses, decorative uses, long history of price stability, non-perishability, maintenance-free storage, and its millennia spanning narrative and collective fiction. Crypto advocates want to declare bitcoin as their new "digital gold" and yet all they bring is a weak fiction detached from the other necessary properties of a store of value.

Cryptocurrencies can never function as a store of value or digital gold. Instead, they are purely speculative volatile assets whose intrinsic value is built on nothing but faith in an expanding pool of greater fools that must expand infinitely and forever[1,6].

Smart Contracts

"Recasting all complex social situations either as neatly defined problems with definite, computable solutions or as transparent and self-evident processes that can be easily optimized—if only the right algorithms are in place!—this quest is likely to have unexpected consequences that could eventually cause more damage than the problems they seek to address."

– Evgeny Morozov, *To Save Everything, Click Here*

Smart contracts are a curiously named term that has sparked a great deal of interest due to the confusion of its namesake. Like many blockchain terms, a smart contract is a semantically meaningless term in the larger corpus of discussion, and its usage has been defined to mean a great many different things to a great many people.

Put simply, a smart contract is an app, much like the ones that run on your phone: a piece of computer software that runs code that controls a pool of crypto casino tokens. The aspect that separates this type of software from normal software is that this application is forced to respond to any request by the design of the blockchain platform it runs on. Internal to this software, there are a set of rules written by another human being that describe a process by which users can interact with the casino tokens locked inside it.

The dumbest smart contract would be a metaphorical box in which users can deposit tokens. When they deposit a fixed amount of tokens, N, they get a receipt that remembers how much they put into the box, and when they return with the receipt, they can withdraw N tokens. This example is a simple process to state in English, and an equivalent transcription of this idea can be encoded in a computer program and run in a smart contract.

A contract in Common Law jurisdictions is an interaction between two parties recognized by the law where an offer and an acceptance are established around a shared set of terms. Both the offer and acceptance can take many forms, including actions such as signatures, the production of shared documents, or digital interaction. The contract terms are interpreted in a given governing law, which defines the environment in which the contract's terms are valid and gives a mechanism to settle disputes. The basis of this system is the interpretation of legal terms in the minds of judges and magistrates, which interpret the law in a historical and situational context.

> **Smart contracts have absolutely nothing to do with legal contracts.**

If there is one takeaway before we delve into the technical details, it is a simple observation that the term is deeply flawed. However, the technology has benefited from convenience in confusion around the name; indeed, smart contracts are a contradiction in terms as they are neither smart nor contracts.

14.1 Smart Contracts are not Contracts

To unpack this term, we will refer to two different types of programs colloquially called smart contracts: bitcoin scripts and solidity scripts. Bitcoin scripts are a very simple mechanism for including small units of logic alongside bitcoin transactions. These can be used to orchestrate the flow of transactions according to a minimal set of logical operations. The script itself is interpreted in a simple "computer" called a stack evaluator, a set of simple instructions evaluated left-to-right that can view and manipulate a mutable list of values. Many programming languages such as Python and Ruby are based on stack virtual machines. Bitcoin scripts on the other hand are intentionally minimal for performance reasons and to not overcomplicate the protocol. For instance you can express a simple program that locks a set of bitcoin values until a given time in the future, but you cannot write a calculator or chess engine inside of a bitcoin script. In computer science terms, the bitcoin script is not Turing-complete since it is a language that is not capable of expressing general computation and has no looping operation or means to evaluate terms recursively. Not being Turing-complete drastically restricts the set of possible programs that can be expressed in the language. In practice, bitcoin scripts are not widely used, and there is a class of about five commonly used tasks for which the logic is simple enough. An example bitcoin script for a Pay-to-Public-Key-Hash (P2PKH) transaction looks like the following:

```
OP_DUP
OP_HASH160
62e907b15cbf27d5425399ebf6f0fb50ebb88f18
OP_EQUALVERIFY
OP_CHECKSIG
```

The Ethereum network has taken a different approach to its protocol and embedded an entire virtual machine (called the EVM) inside the evaluation of Ether transactions. This method for achieving this executable blockchain logic was outlined in the 2014 ethereum whitepaper. The EVM is a virtual machine that is also stack-based but provides more primitives and operations to manipulate stack data. The ethereum virtual machine serves as a target for higher-level languages (Solidity, Viper, etc.), which take human-readable source code and translate it into a set of machine-readable EVM instructions. These instructions are encoded as numerical codes inside ethereum transactions sent to the public network. The primary language that ethereum contracts are written in is Solidity, a blockchain-specific scripting language most comparable to the standard web scripting language Javascript.

Solidity logic can mediate the exchange of ethereum tokens according to arbitrarily complex logic, including arithmetic, mathematical operations, logical control flow, and manipulation of simple data structures such as associative maps and lists. In a suppositional sense, Solidity is Turing-complete. In practice, however, it has a restriction on its runtime imposed by its runtime. This restriction is known as bounded evaluation, which assigns a specific cost to each operation which incurs an economic cost to the issuer of the transaction known as gas. This gas is capped per transaction and effectively prevents infinite-looping events while evaluating a block of transactions. This restriction prevents the network from being globally stalled while evaluating a transaction's potentially arbitrarily complex program logic.

```solidity
pragma solidity >=0.4.22 <0.8.0;


contract OwnedToken {
    TokenCreator creator;
    address owner;
    bytes32 name;

    constructor(bytes32 _name) {
        owner = msg.sender;
        creator = TokenCreator(msg.sender);
        name = _name;
    }

    function changeName(bytes32 newName) public {
        if (msg.sender == address(creator))
            name = newName;
    }

    function transfer(address newOwner) public {
        if (creator.isTokenTransferOK(owner, newOwner))
            owner = newOwner;
    }
}
```

Solidity falls out of a previous tradition of open-source programming tools that have taken a *move fast and break things* approach to development philosophy, prioritizing time to develop over theoretical concerns of semantics, correctness, or best practices of language design. Solidity was meant to appeal to the entry-level Javascript developer base, which uses coding practices such as copying and pasting from code aggregator sites like Stack Overflow. As a result, Solidity code generally has a very high defect count and has resulted in a constant stream of high-profile security incidents directly related to coding errors. Some studies have put the defect count at 100 per 1000 lines.

A cottage industry has arisen around trying to prevent security flaws related to the coding errors in smart contracts. These companies have taken two approaches: a technical one in the form of a process known as software verification and a heuristic one in which third-party independent contractors audit code to attest to the integrity of the contract's logic before it goes live. The formal verification approach builds on a branch of computer science known as formal methods which attempts to model the behavior of programs by reducing them down to a mathematical description of the values computed by individual components.

The primary issue arises when the transcription of ideas into a computer program becomes more complicated. It then becomes challenging to confirm whether the programmer's code matches the intent. A specialized branch of software engineering is concerned with just this problem, known as software verification. Unfortunately, most of the general solutions required to do this process, in the general case, are open problems or reduce down to equivalent open problems in mathematics and theoretical computer science.

Moreover, smart contracts introduce a whole other dimension of complexity to the problem by forcing developers not only to verify the internal consistency and coherence of their software logic but also to model any and all exogenous financial events and market dynamics surrounding the price of the casino tokens used in the software. This hostile execution environment turns a pure computer science question into a composite question of both finance and software and expands the surface area of the problem drastically. At some point in the future, our theoretical models may be able to tackle such problems, but likely not for long time as these problems are of a truly staggering complexity.

The degree of engineering required to prove the correctness properties of these contracts' logic is expensive, and the return on investment for that level of engineering would do little to mitigate the risks when the underlying platform itself is unable to be changed. However, it is much easier in practice to deceptively market a project as "having formal verification" or "having a code audit," as there is very little due diligence done on these projects in the first place. In practice, both audits and formal verification approach has thus mainly been performative and yielded little success in preventing catastrophes in live contracts.

Meanwhile, the reality is that today smart contracts are an unimaginably horrible idea and it is a genuinely horrifying proposition to base a financial system on these structures. Smart contracts synthesize brittle, unverifiable, and corruptible software with irreversible transactions to achieve a result that fails in the most violent way possible when the wind blows even slightly the wrong way. They further lack a key component that most software engineering deployed in the wild requires, a *human-in-the-loop* to correct errors in the case of extreme unforeseen events such as fraud and software failure.

Thus the very design of smart contracts and blockchain-based assets is entirely antithetical to good engineering practices. The idea of smart contracts is rooted in libertarian paranoia concerning censorship resisters and ignoring externalities instead of a concern for mitigating public harm.

The most catastrophic smart contract was undoubtedly the DAO hack. The DAO was an experimental, decentralized autonomous organization that loosely resembled a venture fund. Exampled simply, it is a program that would allow users to invest and vote on proposals for projects to which the autonomous logic of the contract would issue funds as a hypothetical "investment." It was a loose attempt at building what would amount to an investment fund on the blockchain. The underlying contract itself was deployed and went live, consuming around $50 million at the then exchange rate with Ether cryptocurrency. The contract contained a fundamental software bug that allowed an individual hacker to drain DAO accounts into their accounts and acquire the entirety of the community's marked investment. This hack represented a non-trivial amount of the total Ether in circulation across the network and was a major public relations disaster for the network. The community controversially decided to drastically roll back the entire network to a previous state to revert the hacker's withdrawal of funds and restore the contract to regular operation.[7]

Among the programming language ecosystem, there is a niche subset of languages known as functional languages, which are notable for their applications in high-assurance software applications, ones where the correctness of code can be proven in more cases. A sizable number of practitioners in the functional programming ecosystem have spent efforts looking at the problem of smart contract languages. Many proposals and prototypes have been made that would make theoretical guarantees of correctness beyond the current state of affairs. However, none of these projects have gained any traction or born fruit, as the fundamental problem of retrofitting these tools onto existing runtimes and training existing practitioners in unfamiliar tools within their profession. Hard computer science problems just get in the way of easy money.

The grandiose promise of smart contracts was for applications that build decentralized internet applications called dApps. These dApps would behave like existing web and mobile applications but counter interface with the blockchain for persistence and consume or transmit cryptocurrency as part of their operations. There are endless proposals for ideas like decentralized clones of existing services such as Airbnb, Uber, LinkedIn, and nearly every other commercially successful web application. The implicit assumption of these proposals is that a decentralized application would allow the applications to be superior due to being run "by the people," independent of corporate governance, and free of privacy and data collection problems. Much of the smart contract narrative is built around phony populism and the ill-defined idea that there is an upcoming third iteration of the internet (a Web 3.0) that will interact with smart contracts to provide a new generation of applications. In practice, none of that has manifested in any usable form, and the fundamental data throughput limitations of blockchain data read and write actions make that vision impossible.

Most live smart contracts instead fall into a limited set of categories: gambling, tumblers, NFTs, decentralized exchanges, and crowd sales. The vast majority of code running on the public ethereum network falls into one of these categories, with a standard set of open-source scripts driving the bulk of the contract logic that is evaluated on the network. However, there is a wide variety of bespoke scripts associated with different ICO companies and high-risk gambling products that are bespoke logic and act independently of existing community standards and practices.

The most common script is an *ERC20 token*, a contract that allows users to issue custom token crowd sales on top of the ethereum blockchain. These tokens were a custom registry that mapped holdings of addresses to their balances of the custom token. By transacting with the contract (i.e., offering party), users could exchange their ethereum tokens to "buy into" the custom tokens offered at a specific value. The total supply of these tokens in any one of these contracts was a custom fixed amount, and by interacting with the ERC20 contract, the buyers' tokens were instantly liquid and could be exchanged with other users according to the rules of the contract. This is the standard mechanism that drove the ICO bubble and related speculation, and this token sale contract is overwhelmingly the most common use case for smart contracts. Quite commonly, these ERC20 tokens were tied to a *SAFT* (Simple Agreement for Tokens), a legal contract in US law that mapped owners in the token registry to the purchasers of those securities inside the US legal system. This SAFT agreement was structurally similar to a SAFE (Simple Agreement for Equity), which companies in the US typically use for early startup fundraising to offer equity to venture capitalists and early investors.

Tumblers–such as tornado.cash–are another application of smart contracts which allow users who have engaged in darknet transactions to clean their money by exchanging their dirty tokens with clean tokens through a set of random swaps which preserve the value but obscure the provenance. These tumblers use several evasion techniques such as random transactions, time-delayed transactions, and swaps with other chains with private transactions to return the clean money back to the client. In traditional financial services, this would be called a criminal activity known as money laundering. Traditional money custodians and money transmitters are typically required to maintain audit logs and prevent this form of activity as part of their licenses and regulatory oversight.

Another class of projects is the digital collectibles and digital pets genre. One of the most popular is *CryptoKitties*: a game in which users can buy, sell, and breed cartoon kittens. The sale of digital cats was responsible for 6.2% of all ethereum traffic in 2018. The number of transactions on this one application represented a significant fraction of all contract logic and drastically congested the global network when many individuals began trading digital cats.

Gambling products overwhelmingly dominate the remaining set of contracts. Aside from illegal securities offerings, gambling is the primary domain for blockchain apps. This script allows participants to gamble their tokens in games of chance against other blockchain users. There are a variety of so-called dApps (distributed applications) which offer lotteries and games in which users stake ethereum tokens, and the game makers offer opportunities to play in exchange for transaction fees. Some of these games are classical Ponzi schemes in which players pay into a pool of tokens, and early investors are paid out from the increasing pool of subsequent investors[6,3].

The ICO bubble marked a significant increase in the interest in smart contracts arising from outlandish claims of how cryptocurrency ventures would disintermediate and decentralize everything from the legal profession and electricity grid to food supply chains. In reality, we have seen none of these visions manifest, and the technology is primitive, architecturally dubious, and lacking in any clear applications of benefit to the economy at large. The ecosystem of dApps is a veritable wasteland of dead projects, with none having more than a few hundred active users at best.

14.2 SMART CONTRACTS ARE NOT SMART

The very design of a smart contract is to run on an unregulated network which prevents it from interfacing with external systems in any meaningful fashion. This confusion around the namesake of smart contracts has been exploited by many parties to sell products and services.

The fundamental limitation of smart contracts is best exemplified by a technical limitation referred to as the *oracle problem*. In blockchain systems, there is a data boundary between data stored on-chain, referring to data stored natively on the blockchain database such as transactions, wallet address, and smart contract state. Data that is off-chain colloquially means anything not within the blockchain database, such as the public internet, data stored in traditional databases, and data feeds for news events or financial markets. The efficacy of many applications of smart contracts was predicated upon the ability to query events that would occur outside the blockchain network, which would be either self-reported or attested to by an authoritative source.

> Smart contracts claim to not trust external central authorities, but they cannot function without them. Thus the idea is doomed by its own phi-

losophy.

This problem poses a fundamental contradiction in the theoretical value proposition of decentralized dApps; if their operation was run on a decentralized platform, but the core mechanism for operation depended on a central authority, this resulted in a system that is functionally equivalent to an existing centrally operated application. Stated another way, if a blockchain financial product depends on the weather or value of the S&P 500, the smart contract would have to extend its trust boundary to the included National Weather Service or a Bloomberg for its operation to function. At this point the entire setup provides a service that is no better or different than running the same program on a centralized server. This is not only a problem, but an inherent contradiction. The oracle problem for smart contracts is metaphorically like creating a safebox with six sides, but while five walls are made out of steel and the sixth is made out of tissue paper. The vulnerability undermines the entire principle of the construction.[2]

Within the domain of permissioned blockchains, the terminology has been co-opted to refer to an existing set of tools that would traditionally be called *process automation*. In 2018 so-called enterprise "smart contracts" were the buzzword du jour for consultants to sell enterprise projects. These so-called enterprise smart contracts had very little to do with their counterparts in public blockchains and were existing programming tools such as Javascript, Java, and Python rebranded or packaged in a way that would supposedly impart the "value of the blockchain" through undefined and indeterminate means. Indeed one of the popular enterprise blockchain platforms, IBM Hyperledger, provides a rather expansive definition of smart contracts[4]:

> A smart contract can describe an almost infinite array of business use cases relating to immutability of data in multi-organizational decision making. The job of a smart contract developer is to take an existing business process that might govern financial prices or delivery conditions, and express it as a smart contract in a programming language such as JavaScript, Go, or Java. The legal and technical skills required to convert centuries of legal language into programming language is increasingly practiced by smart contract

auditors.

While the public blockchain company Dfinity[5] claims to creating a technological singularity of infinite possibilities:

> We aim to create a "blockchain singularity" in which every system and service is rebuilt and reimagined using smart contracts and runs entirely from infinite public blockchain without need for traditional IT.

Both these meaningless paragraphs are the embodiment of the blockchain meme. It is an extension of the terminology to include "infinite use cases" through a meaningless slurry of buzzwords. Smart contracts simply are not useful for any real-world applications. To the extent that they are used on blockchain networks, smart contracts strictly inferior services or are part of gambling or money laundering operations that are forced to use this flawed system because it is the only platform that allows for illicit financing, arbitrage securities regulation, or avoids law enforcement.

The insane software assumptions of smart contracts can only give rise to a digital wild west that effectively turns all possible decentralized applications into an all-ports-open honeypot for hackers to exploit and manifests the terrible idea that smart contracts are just a form of self-service bug bounty. These assumptions give rise to an absurd level of platform risk that could never provide financial services to the general public given the level of fraud and risk management required to interact with it.

Transaction reversal and fraud mitigation through due process and the courts[8] are essential for all financial services. Nevertheless, adding this capacity to a permissionless system would undermine the very decentralized premise on which it was built, and therein lies an irreconcilable contradiction.

Append-only public data structures, permissionless consensus algorithms, and smart contracts are all technically exciting ideas; however, combining all three is a nightmare[1] that could never be a foundation for a financial system or for handling personal user data. The technology is not fit for purpose and cannot be fixed. To put it simply, smart contracts are a profoundly dumb idea.

Blockchainism

"You can't convince a believer of anything; for their belief is not based on evidence, it's based on a deep seated need to believe"

— Carl Sagan

In the middle ages, a widely practiced proto-scientific tradition called *alchemy*, was concerned with finding ways to turn worthless metals into gold. For centuries the most brilliant medieval scholars strived in their laboratories to find a chemical process that would transmute so-called "base metals" into "noble metals," under an assumption that it was physically possible and that it was inevitable they would discover it. Alchemy is one of the first examples of the synthesis of economically motivating reasoning bleeding over into scholarship and warping the epistemological foundations of its practitioners.

Today *blockchainism* is the new alchemy of the internet age; a pseudoscience that metaphorically aims to transmute technology into trust, and trust into digital gold. The ideology of blockchainism arises out of the proposition that blockchain technology is a vehicle to enact change on social issues. It is primarily bracketed to the entrepreneurship and business development contexts in which blockchain is the catalyst for new ventures and corporate transformation projects. It is perpetuated by the over-exuberance of blockchain articles in trade journalism and a reasonably continuous conference cycle centered around blockchainism[9].

15.1 THE PSEUDOSCIENCE OF TRUST ALCHEMY

The alchemy of blockchainism is a concept rooted in the mystique and mis-understanding of the nature of bitcoin's original approach to establishing trust between otherwise unrelated parties over an untrusted network. Bitcoin has a partial answer to this problem for a specific data structure of a particular applica-tion. The core fallacy of blockchainism is extrapolating that cryptocurrency has solved trust[8] in generality rather than specificity. What "solving trust"[3] means will depend on context, but this thesis is central to many books, including *Real Business of Blockchain*, *Blockchain Revolution*, *The Trust Machine*, *The Infinite Machine* and dozens more books.[7]

Technology has always had a loose affiliation with futurism and science fic-tion. Speculative fiction is the stories our civilization tells itself about where we might end up and, ultimately, the ethical and philosophical problems we will encounter on that journey. Science fiction, for many programmers, is an outlet for philosophical discussion and a cultural touchstone that influences our work. The history of science fiction literature has anticipated or inspired many of the everyday technologies we use in our lives.

However, since the 1980s, science fiction's tone has shifted toward a darker and more bleak view of the future. The cyberpunk genre of the 1980s often envisioned dystopian futures in which institutions had broken down, leaving lawless plutocracies. The combination of "low life" and "high tech" is the defin-ing attribute of this fiction. Often these genres concern the clashes between authoritarian governments, powerful corporations, and hackers. The themes of surveillance states, privacy, and internet politics are familiar storylines, and in hindsight, much of the writing is quite prescient concerning the current state of affairs. Many brilliant authors and speakers fall into this category, and a diversity of perspectives and visions overwhelmingly enriches the field. However, many of these visions are extraordinarily speculative, and the line between speculation and reality is often one that becomes confused.

The software industry is in a constant state of technical booms and busts. Professor at Stanford Roy Amara once said of the software field that "we overes-timate the impact of technology in the short-term and underestimate the effect in the long run." In the past decade alone, we have seen trends rise and fall of many buzzwords such as artificial intelligence, big data, internet of things, cloud computing, edge computing, and most recently, blockchain. In most technologies, there is at least some kernel of a novel idea that has the potential to alter the technology landscape and create new lines of business. However, technology journalism tends to drastically overstate the impact that any one of these ideas will have. Indeed most entrepreneurs are strongly incentivized to enormously exaggerate the impact of their ventures both for investors and for the general public.[17]

The rise of social media has also meant that many non-technical users have stumbled on the surprising truth that they can significantly boost their professional careers by becoming technical thought leaders with very little understanding of technology or software. The rise of venture capital microfunds (funds with less than $50 million assets in management) has given rise to a particularly vocal set of associates in these funds whose job is ostensibly to scream extremely loud, contrarian, and bombastic opinions about technology trends. A large part of technology culture is a dialogue about mundane ideas expressed through hyperbole and over-extrapolation.[2,13]

This model presumes that the advent of cryptocurrency has given rise to breakthrough technology and a global network in which arbitrary data can be globally written, verified of integrity, and shared with relevant parties without intermediaries. In this "game-changing" paradigm shift, any existing process that requires a single authoritative source of truth has now found the ultimate vehicle for storing that single source of truth without the authority component. The blockchain (often referred to in singular form) will decentralize power and disintermediate the global economy unlocking new opportunities and building international reciprocity and trust. The seductive marketing around this cliché is that without cryptocurrency, the blockchain itself could convey the same disruptive power as bitcoin for any domain.[12]

The model is simultaneously a massive oversimplification and over-extrapolation that stems from a fundamental misreading of the technology. At face value, it has an illusory coherence and loose affiliation with the original intent and ideology behind cryptocurrencies however public blockchains are generally an awful form of database for most applications. The assumptions baked into their design are entirely at odds with almost all business and government applications. For many involved with blockchainism, the idea of a project is as far as their knowledge and expertise will ever carry them. The feasibility details are simply an implementation detail to be resolved by others. These details are often addressed with a cliché "blockchain not bitcoin" or hand-wavy that the "the underlying blockchain technology is here to stay."[16,13,15]

This mentality is a partial path back to sensibility for most but confusingly carries this blockchain semantic baggage. The problem most of the ventures will quickly discover is that generally, most human processes that one would attempt to digitize require an implicit degree of control, governance, and privacy. For example, companies operating in Europe are under the General Data Protection Regulation (GDPR)[10,6] required to allow users to erase personally identifiable information upon request. Blockchain is semantically ambiguous, but the general ideas are multiparty networks that are decentralized, trustless, and immutable. Suppose, hypothetically, an organization sets up a new blockchain project where the servers are centrally controlled. In that case, access is granted by a central authority, and data is revocable; then, one has created the exact opposite technology and confusingly labeled it the same as its polar opposite. This contradiction is the bizarre marketing-driving logic of blockchain solutions looking for problems[1,5,14].

15.2 THE BLOCKCHAIN MEME

The form of technology that many of these ventures may build is not novel at all; cryptographic ledgers and databases that maintain audit logs have been used since the early 1980s. In practice, the term blockchain is often used to refer to regular databases is a widely noted phenomenon. Rauchs et al. refer to this phenomenon as the *blockchain meme*, explaining it in a 2019 whitepaper as follows:[11]

> Unclear terminology and marketing hype have contributed to the "blockchain meme": 77% of live enterprise blockchain networks have little in common with multi-party consensus systems apart

from incorporating some of the same technology components (e.g. cryptography, peer-to-peer networking) and using similar nomenclature. The "blockchain meme" nevertheless acts as a powerful catalyst to overcome corporate inertia and spur wide-reaching organisational change, both within and across organisational boundaries.

The blockchain meme has been associated with all manner of outlandish endeavors. In the United Kingdom, the government finance minister has publicly suggested that blockchain may be a solution to Britain's Brexit problems regarding trade along the Northern Ireland border. One of the most egregious examples of blockchain opportunism is the introduction of California A.B. 2004. This bill would create a pilot program for using "verifiable health credentials" to report COVID-19 test results publicly. The bill was opposed by both the ACLU and EFF for several core issues regarding privacy rights.

Considering trade journalism and press releases from 2018, we see blockchain proposed by many seemingly sensible people as the solution to everything from human trafficking, refugee crises, blood diamonds, and famines to global climate change. This despite most technologists having minimal experience working with vulnerable groups or understanding the political complexities. This kind of thinking that blockchain somehow has the answers to our problems has infected consultants, executives, and now even politicians. The one group of people who are not asked about the efficacy of blockchain is programmers themselves, for whom the answer is simple: just use a normal database[4].

Jack Dorsey, the creator of Twitter, even goes so far as to claim that bitcoin will bring about world peace. The very embodiment of blockchainist delusion.

#Bitcoin will unite a deeply divided country. (and eventually: world)
https://twitter.com/jack/status/1424854924194729984

And therein lies the problem, blockchainism is a siren song of aimless utopianism whose whispers are so soft that every person will precisely hear what they dream of: a Rorschach test in which everyone will see something different. The charitable interpretation of this phenomenon is that this is simply an inefficiency in human language that results from civilization collectively defining new terminology and expanding its understanding of technology. However, the terminology itself lends credibility to a domain that primarily consists of gambling, illicit financing, and financial frauds. Blockchain consultants have become strange bedfellows with international charities and non-government organizations advancing humanitarian causes.

The reach of this philosophy is vast, and advocates of blockchainism are invited to speak at the United Nations and the World Bank and attend meetings at the World Economic Forum in Davos. On the back of this access, humanitarian groups and NGOs have pumped millions of dollars into this sector for technologists to look into the problem of applying "The Blockchain" to all manner of problems. Humanitarian work is often thankless, and the ability to add "innovative solutions" such as a blockchain may generate publicity but ultimately comes at the opportunity cost of doing high-impact but much less glamorous projects that could actually improve the world.

Frauds & Scams

"The next man who has as large a capacity and as genuine a taste for swindling, will succeed as well. Pardon me, but I think you really have no idea how the human bees will swarm to the beating of any old tin kettle; in that fact lies the complete manual of governing them. When they can be got to believe that the kettle is made of the precious metals, in that fact lies the whole power of men like our late lamented."

— Charles Dickens, *Little Dorrit*

Cryptocurrency markets are undeniably rife with fraud, scams, and abuse. Nevertheless, to understand the reasons for the proliferation of scams, we need to understand how and why fraud occurs in the modern business environment.

Trust is an essential part of any business relationship, and the foundations of trust in any business relationship have three components: judgment, expertise, and consistency. Positive business relationships are gained from interactions between counterparties that reinforce the positive experiences that both parties go through. Judgment and expertise are achieved when a party proves that they can make successful decisions based on specialized knowledge and expertise. Consistency is the repeated successful reinforcement of expectations.

Transitive trust is a phenomenon in which the trust of one party is extended to another party based on their trusted parties:

A trusts B,
B trusts C,
therefore A trusts C.

The primary attack vector in many frauds is exploiting some notion of *transitive trust* to use the fact that due diligence is often not performed under the assumptions that others have already performed all the necessary checks.

In advanced economies, fraud is always a possibility, but it is usually a tail risk that occurs with a low probability compared to the bulk of routine transactions. Fraud controls and rigorous due diligence are expensive relative to the likelihood of the fraud and, unless otherwise required by law, are many times discarded for the sake of saving cost.

In high-trust sectors such as tech, a company is often trusted by its employees simply by virtue of its existing as an incorporated entity. Starting a company typically involves going through a process involving government and banking approval since a company requires legal and financial legitimacy for its existence. Transitive trust naturally exists in firms because it is assumed that the government and banking institutions have done their due diligence to allow it to exist at some minimum level. This transitive trust is a behavioral heuristic that scammers and con men often exploit[1].

Inside the enterprise itself, lawyers and accountants act as a line of defense against fraud. However, these professionals are not immune from corporations or influence. It is easy for well-funded actors to penetrate this line of defense, and once it is penetrated, the fraud can often run unchecked. Insiders to organizations do not often check up on activities "signed off" activities. The facade that an activity, however dubious, has been "signed off on by the lawyers" or "approved by the compliance department" is often the primary method for initiating a fraud inside of an existing enterprise. Once the fraud is within the perimeter, the fraud can easily expand by layering on this trust.

16.1 FRAUD TRIANGLE

The Fraud Triangle is a framework for identifying environments and incentive structures that may be vulnerable to fraud by their observed prevalence at the intersection of three factors. The framework was first described by American criminologists Donald R. Cressey and Edwin Sutherland and has become a cornerstone of modern risk management[4].

- **Motive** - The perpetrator personally requires resources beyond what they can acquire by honest means, which can be:

  1. Debt
  2. Greed
  3. Lifestyle needs
  4. Vices (gambling, drugs)

- **Opportunity** - The perpetrator has the means to bypass checks and controls that would otherwise prevent the fraud, such as:

  1. Checks are not enforced
  2. Checks are not monitored
  3. No segregation of duties
  4. Single controller

- **Rationalization** - The perpetrator requires logical or emotional reasons for why the fraud is not causing harm or is just temporary, including:

  1. "I'm not paid what I'm worth"
  2. "I intend to pay it back"
  3. "Everything is a scam anyways"
  4. "Nobody will miss the money"
  5. "Everyone else is doing it, so why shouldn't I"
  6. "The banks are doing it as well"

onsidering cryptocurrency fraud, the rationalization and opportunity aspects are particularly pathological. With any consumer business (or fraudulent investment scheme), a network effect dominates the venture's success. Often, a critical mass of users is required to reach maturity or sustainability for the business model. The path to sustainability can often be complex. It can create a perverse incentive for the orchestrator to get there "by growth at any cost" and justify any fraud that occurs to get there by the ability to offset its harm at a future date when resources are more abundant. This phenomenon is best exemplified by the series of tech ventures in the late 2010s, such as WeWork, Theranos[9], and Uber, all mired in scandals related to rapid growth models that ultimately masked rampant corporate wrong-doing, and in some cases, outright fraud.

In the growth rationalization model, if one is launching a new currency, then whatever it takes to bootstrap a market around it is simply the cost of doing business; and investors can be made whole later. Moreover, if this means faking invoices, simulating market activity, or lying to investors, this is all justified by the returns these people will eventually see at some future date. This fallacy central to some entrepreneurial fraud is rooted in underestimating the probability of failure. Their enterprise is, in effect, over-leveraged on delivering the impossible, which becomes a deeper and deeper hole to dig oneself out of, leading to increased desperation. Enterprises such as Fyre Festival and Theranos are textbook examples of this phenomenon.

Libertarian conspiracy theories and the cult-like culture of cryptocurrency present a convenient rationalization narrative that "all money is a Ponzi scheme" or that all financial business models are based on fraud. This line of thinking is the most internally consistent rationalization for engaging in cryptocurrency fraud and is perpetuated by its culture. In this narrative, any fraud can be justified by rationalizing their crimes against allegedly more significant crimes perpetrated by banks or politicians.

The opportunity for cryptocurrency fraud is pervasive simply because the lack of regulatory checks and controls on these ventures is relatively lax or nonexistent. In an environment where a single user can abscond[4] or run away with large amounts of investor money, seemingly with little risk to themselves, it will create an environment that will attract less scrupulous individuals. Cryptocurrency businesses are the perfect storm in the fraud triangle, and crypto fraud is today's most straightforward and widespread form of securities fraud.

16.2 PONZI SCHEMES

The term Ponzi scheme comes from Charles Ponzi, a swidler in the 1920s who convinced investors of a 50% payoff in 45 days or 100% in 90 days. Supposedly, the investment was in overseas discounted postal reply coupons. In actuality, it was a massive scam that resulted in a $20 million loss within a year and destroyed six banks in Boston.

The mechanism by which a Ponzi scheme function is the following: new investors' money is used to pay off existing investors, effectively "robbing Peter to pay Paul." So as long as the incoming capital flows are greater than the outgoing capital, the scam goes on and gets larger. Incentivized recruiting of new investors leads to a pyramid scheme structure. The most notorious version of a Ponzi scheme in recent history is the story of Bernie Madoff's Ponzi scheme, which lasted decades[13] with nearly 5,000 investors and resulted in $64.5 billion of losses. In the world of cryptocurrency, several similar scams have been uncovered[18].

> The key to sustaining a Ponzi scheme is controlling redemptions to create the illusion of solvency.

The BBC reported on the most famous cryptocurrency pyramid scheme in a series of podcasts *The Missing Cryptoqueen*. Ruzha Ignatova was an Oxford-educated charismatic fraudster who convinced people that OneCoin would become the largest cryptocurrency in the world. The company was a pyramid scheme with no technology or network and encouraged people to buy packages of digital tokens that investors could hypothetically later redeem. By 2017, the United Kingdom, Austria, Thailand, Italy, and Germany had warned and blocked accounts within their territories. Authorities have arrested collaborators such as her brother and lawyer, but Ruzha's whereabouts remain unknown. OneCoin lasted from 2014 to 2017 and resulted in $5 billion in damages to its victims. Most of the investors hurt most were low-income individuals and retail investors who had been sold on narratives of financial windfalls and financial prosperity on the back of Ruzha's marketing.

Another example that we have already covered is BitConnect, which was active from 2016 to 2018 and run by an individual named Satish Kumbhani. The scheme promised 40% profit per month, with $1000 initial investment making $50 million in 3 years. The platform was created as a trading bot, yet the platform was set up to lock investors' funds and give new investors money from old investors. By January 16, 2018, regulators from Texas and North Carolina issued a cease and desist to BitConnect's lending and exchange operations, pointing to unrealistic investment payout expectations and a multi-level marketing structure of a Ponzi scheme.

16.3 PUMP AND DUMPS

Pump and dump schemes have been a common form of market manipulation ever since the first stock markets. They are a form of ostensibly victimless crime in which a set of insiders manipulate market information to distort price formation to their advantage. Pump and dump schemes were rampant leading up to the Great Depression and became illegal in the United States in the 1930s after the passing of the Securities Act.

The 2013 movie *Wolf of Wall Street* fictionally depicts the misadventures of the notorious charlatan Jordan Belfort and his firm Stratton Oakmont, which defrauded investors through boiler room tactics that resulted in a $200 million loss to investors. Pump and dump schemes involve a group of individuals communicating with potential investors to "pump up" and drive up the price of a security with inflated artificial demand by investors that were pressured and that at a specific high price point, "dump" and sell the security. This event crashes the value of the underlying security and causes a significant capital loss to the investors who were convinced to join.

Since cryptocurrencies are generally an unregulated market, pump and dump schemes run rampant. Unlike the days of the phone call-based boiler rooms of the past, modern crypto boiler rooms use Telegram, Discord, and other social media platforms to create investment groups requiring paid membership. The scammers then run the price up of a particular crypto coin and exit before the advertised high price, leaving many followers at a loss. In 2018, The Wall Street Journal ran an exposé that found $825 million in trading activity within six months across 125 pump and dump schemes. The largest one Big Pump Signal, has over 74,000 followers.[15]

A study of pump and dump schemes has found that 30% of all cryptocurrencies are used in 80% of pump and dump schemes. Once used on a particular crypto successfully, it is very likely that another pump and dump will be done on that same coin again. More importantly, studies show that pump and dump crypto schemes occur with low volume coins with significant wealth transfers from outsiders to insiders, and resulting in detrimental effects on market integrity and price formation.[16,6,12,11,8,7]

16.4 GIVEAWAY SCAMS

With the advent of social media, a new class of simple crypto scams has arisen that utilizes celebrities to claim victims. The premise is simple: a receiving party suggests one must first send a small amount of cryptocurrency to a given address with a claim to "double" the amount sent. The sender commits the transaction, and the receiver runs off with the funds. Since cryptocurrency payments are not reversible or subject to regulatory protections, the receiver will make off with the amount sent to their address. This scam is particularly prevalent because it has virtually no overhead, can reach a mass of victims quickly, and is unlikely to be traceable if the captured funds are laundered. It is common to impersonate the names and likeness of cryptocurrency celebrities like Elon Musk to push their scams.

16.5 DISTRIBUTED CONTROL FRAUDS

Frauds need not necessarily have a single origin or perpetrator, and in today's world, it is often increasingly difficult to identify the origin of some of the worst scandals of our time. In corporate fraud, a common situation is when directors of a company set up an organization with a criminogenic culture that encourages fraudulent activity but does not explicitly direct employees to perform the actions. A working environment that rewards the correct type of employees via a particular system of incentives and deterrents implicitly guides the employees to conduct the fraud themselves, leaving the company's directors with no criminal liability. Such a setup is known as a *distributed control fraud.*[5,3]

In the United Kingdom, one of the largest financial scandals of the last century was the Payment Protection Insurance (PPI) misselling scandal. Since the early 1990s, banks had begun offering a scheme in which customers could purchase insurance plans such that if their job was made redundant, they could claim the insurance policy which would cover their mortgage payments until they found a new position. High street banks offered these products alongside mortgage and credit offerings and turned into an enormously lucrative business for the banks. This business was so lucrative for the company that branch managers were strongly incentivized by their bonuses in terms of how many PPI products they sold to their customers. This situation would result in misselling activity in which products were sold to clients unsuited for the policy or silently bundled with mortgages in hopes that the client would not notice. This created an incentive for rank-and-file employees to ignore the clients' wishes and push the products on their customers simply because their internal performance was measured. The employees overwhelmingly did not profit from this action and, while technically to blame, were not themselves the beneficiaries of the fraud.

A similar situation occurred in the United States during the bank 2018 Wells Fargo account scandal. In the same kind of setup, the local branch managers were opening accounts for individuals in their communities without explicit authorization from these people. This resulted in Wells Fargo opening checking accounts, credit cards, and a variety of financial products to generate cash flows for the bank. Just as in the PPI scandal, the rank and file employees were directed to perform their regular duties but at a scale that was unsustainable. The employees were not directly told to open accounts; however, the bank's practices incentivized fraud indirectly by creating a criminogenic environment.

It is difficult to label any one party as guilty in this action; the directors are simply acting within the fiduciary interests of the organization they represent and whom themselves did not explicitly commit fraud. No one person is to blame, and the ethical problems[10] are spread across the entire organization such that no one person is likely to have the entire picture. This setup is a near-perfect corporate crime as the legal system rarely can handle the evidentiary standard needed to prove fraudulent intent for anyone but the unsophisticated rank and file employees.

The essence of distributed control fraud is to create bubbles of willful ignorance in which fear, software obfuscation, or financial incentives create an environment wherein those involved do not have complete knowledge of the crime.[2]

The rise of companies whose business is conducted exclusively using cryptocurrency networks presents a new form of distributed control fraud where one uses perverse incentives encoded into the software and network itself to induce criminal activity. Many cryptocurrency companies, especially during the ICO bubble, offered thinly-veiled securities that are marketed and sold to the public with a wink and a nod. Insiders to these companies can manipulate these assets and trade on non-public information because the company has no internal policy on these activities, and the products are unregulated by external parties. Software-based distributed control fraud is a vastly under-reported area of fraud associated with crypto assets and may be very difficult for law enforcement to detect or prosecute.

In many jurisdictions, directors of the company are explicitly banned from touting the expected returns of the investment. However, if one constructs an anonymous community in which others (outside the company) market the token's investment opportunity, this can be sufficient to drum up market interest in the security. A digital pyramid scheme structure can be encoded indirectly into the computer program that dictates the network's payouts, and this can create indirect kickbacks and incentives for early promoters. This decentralized and self-organizing fraud leaves the directors' hands completely clean as low-level employees and outside actors purely perform the actions.

These new forms of software-based distributed control frauds are a brave new world for regulation and the courts. If left to grow unchecked, these types of fraud will claim millions of victims while the courts are still left scratching their heads to understand the technology and mechanisms of the fraud.[14,17]

Web3

"Technological progress has merely provided us with more efficient means for going backwards."

– Aldous Huxley

In recent years, the cryptocurrency project experience something of a public relations problem; leading various actors to choose to refer to cryptocurrency under a different name, "web3". The narrative of web3 is somewhat intentionally amorphous and open to a wide variety of interpretations. Therein lies the rhetorical power of ambiguous buzzwords in that it acts like an aspirational Rorschach test where everyone will see something different, but everyone assumes it means something positive[14].

Many stories are told about what web3 means, but in broad strokes, it refers to the narrative that the internet of today is heading towards a new and improved form that is both "inevitable" and "better" in some way because it involves blockchain[15]. It is a narrative that resonates with a deep distrust[3] of existing American tech companies who have burned through much of their previous goodwill and are now mostly seen as malign actors by many in academia, the press, and politics. Thus, the premise is that there might be better ways of building platforms than companies with pathological business models[19] like Twitter and Facebook could provide. Like many other areas of crypto, it is difficult to discern where the line between true believers, grifters, opportunists, and delusional idealists; sometimes the boundary between these categories is quite blurry[23].

While web3 may not be well-defined, five technology categories loosely correspond to some new crypto products[19] that are being marketed under the web3 umbrella term: NFTs, DAOs, Play-To-Earn, DeFi, and the Metaverse.

17.1 NFTs

A significant part of the web3 ecosystem is creating digital assets known as NFTs. Unlike cryptocurrencies, which are fungible, any individual digital assets are interchangeable with other digital assets. NFTs are a specific type of smart contract which lives on one of the ethereum or other blockchains that allow programmable blockchain logic.

An NFT is a tradable cryptoasset that internally contains a URL, like those typed into a browser (e.g., https://www.google.com), which points to an external piece of data. This external piece of data could be a document, a file, or an image, but it is stored externally to the NFT itself. Since the image or data associated with an NFT is stored on a public server, any member of the public can "right-click" on the data to access the information independent of the blockchain.

Examples of NFTs include the opportunity to buy the abstract concept of "owning" Jack Dorsey's first tweet. Companies such as the Bored Ape Yacht Club have sprung up that offer collection of procedurally generated images of monkeys that are sold based on their sign value of conspicuous consumption as Veblen goods to Hollywood celebrities and cryptos nouveau riche. Many collections are intentionally absurd such as EtherRocks, which are literal clip art pictures of rocks. On top of these high-profile collections, hundreds of copycat collections simply copy an "artistic" style and attempt to profit from it.

Some NFTs are even purely conceptual and do not link to any data. In these situations, abstract notions and contextual narratives about the NFT are the product being sold to investors. This setup may be done as a piece of performance art or as a thinly veiled way of raising money on an unregistered security investment as a proxy for illegal equity raise in a common enterprise by disguising it as an "NFT project."[16]

Buying an NFT is conceptually similar to Name-A-Star registries in which a person pays another person to record their name in a registry, allegedly associating their name to an unnamed star in the sky. The registry conveys no rights, obligations, or rewards, but it is an artificially scarce commodity based on a collective belief in the supposed value of the registry. It is like a tradable receipt with no physical good or rights attached, which only signifies a proof of purchase based on some bizarre and logically self-inconsistent redefinition of ownership or to signal sign value or class status as a form of conspicuous consumption within the crypto community. Many people who sell NFTs are willing to make the conceptual leap that this registry with a smart contract somehow conveys some abstract digital notion of "ownership." However, this premise has several technical, legal, and philosophical problems.[6,7]

17.1.1 The Reproducibility Problem

Ownership is the act of possessing something by both having access to it and controlling its use[10]. Possessing an NFT does not grant exclusive access to the underlying data or art, nor does it allow an individual to control the data's use, as it remains public and infinitely both shareable and reproducible.

17.1.2 The Duplication Problem

NFTs have been criticized for having no way of guaranteeing the uniqueness of the datum or hyperlink. Since multiple NFTs can be created that reference the same artwork, there is no canonical guarantee of uniqueness that an NFT purchased is "authentic". It remains unclear what "authentic" would mean regarding infinitely reproducible hyperlinks.

17.1.3 The Plagiarism Problem

Given the duplication problem, many artists have also criticized NFT sales that involve plagiarized[11] versions of art whereby a pseudonymous party will "steal" or reference the work of another when deploying the smart contract allowing the third party to potentially profit off the work of another with no attribution or royalties paid to the original artist.

17.1.4 The Multiple Chain Problem

The NFT definition of "ownership" has been criticized as having no single source of truth since multiple blockchain networks can be created and operated in parallel, all of which can give rise to independent and potentially conflicting suppositions of ownership for the same piece of data. The same NFT can be minted on the Tezos blockchain and the Ethereum blockchain, with the same content but with two competing definitions of "ownership." Given this contradiction in the design, there is no canonical way to say a priori which blockchain network represents the base concept of ownership. This premise presents an intractable logical contradiction at the heart of the definition of NFT redefinition of "ownership". Having something multiply-owned in different contexts with different sources of truth introduces an irreconcilable multiplicity to the idea of ownership, which results in a philosophical contradiction.

17.1.5 The Link Rot Problem

NFTs have also been criticized because the hyperlinks to the data in the smart contract do not point to blockchain-hosted data but instead to content served on the open internet on private servers. These servers are themselves operated by third parties which may cease to exist or serve the content that the NFT points to on the internet. When the content goes down, the hyperlink is said to *link rot*, and the underlying data is no longer accessible by the alleged "owner" of the NFT, with the NFT effectively referencing nothing.

17.1.6 The Tinkerbell Effect

Another criticism of NFTs is that they only have value derived from the *Tinkerbell effect*. A phenomenon in psychology where the veracity of a belief or meme is only derived from the number of people who place their shared faith in the delusion. Not coincidentally, much of the NFT culture resembles either a pyramid scheme[13] or cult-like high-control group, which is coercive in maintaining a shared delusion amongst members of an ingroup who have a financial incentive to create a market bubble. Members of NFT communities often ceremoniously greet each other with coded language such as "gm," "frenz," and "wagmi," which are meant to signify devotion to the ingroup and its ideology ritualistically.

17.1.7 Market Manipulation

Finally, NFTs have been criticized for excessive amounts of market manipulation and, in particular, significant cases of wash trading that are now expected and normalized in the market. These phenomena make it challenging to ascertain what (if any) of the price formation is organic versus the work of a coordinated cartel attempting to create asymmetric information.

Melania Trump, the wife of the 45th President of the United States, held an NFT auction in which she offered digital images of some of her clothing worn in the White House. Bloomberg reported that Melania, or someone acting to facilitate the auction on her behalf, engaged in wash trading thus buying her NFTs from herself to create the illusion of the demand in her NFT collection.

17.2 PLAY TO EARN GAMES

Play-to-earn games are a form of video game that attempts to incorporate NFTs into the gameplay as either a game mechanism or to generate additional revenue from players. However, the video game community is another cultural group that NFTs have attempted to convince to jump on the crypto bandwagon—alebit with far less success. Video gamers often perceive NFTs negatively, and gaming literature usually refers to them in such colorful terms as "the death of video games" and "a soulless studio cash grab." NFTs are seen by many video gamers as simply a new potential way for game companies to attempt to get more money from their gamers, like *microtransactions*: not not an effort make a game more fun, but simply to make it more expensive.

Some video game company executives saw the popularity of play-to-earn game startups, and announced that they would be creating copycat games or incorporating NFTs into their titles. Major game publishers such as Ubisoft, EA, Square Enix, and others have expressed interest in including such NFT items in their games. The backlash has been tremendous, as serious gamers see it as a shameless unethical money grab. With graphic card pricing spiking due to crypto miners' demand, this only added fuel to the flames. The backlash from gamers has been swift with publicly announcing their contempt for NFT and NFT-based games, which led to many apologies and reversals from these gaming companies' executives.

A popular collectible game called Axie Infinity is the largest so-called play-to-earn game. It is a game where players buy NFTs of imaginary monsters who fight in virtual competitions for a form of the company's private game scrip called *Smooth Love Potions*. In November 2021, the game had 2.7 million players, including 35% of their active daily user base in the Philippines. The game contains a mechanic where wealthy users can use their monsters in a scheme, not unlike share-cropping, where the digital animals are rented out—in what is called a *scholarship*—to less-wealthy users who fight on the "landowners" behalf while keeping a fraction of the profits.

Some critics and journalists have described this system as "digital serfdom." There is a fundamental question about the productive economic value for the Philippines as a whole, having a non-trivial fraction of its population reselling virtual cartoon characters for a hyper volatile corporate scrip. The game has been criticized for synthesizing components of a pyramid scheme, of casino gambling, and of a multilevel-marketing scheme. In a brilliant article by the technologist and blogger Paul Butler[5], the play-to-earn schemes are described in terms of the concept of bullshit jobs[9] conceived by the late anthropologist David Graeber. Graeber defines bullshit jobs, like video game labor, as jobs that even the person doing the job cannot justify the existence of, but they have to pretend that there's some reason for it to exist.

> Ultimately, in-game labour is just a re-branding of gameplay designed to be dull enough that rich players will pay to outsource it to poor players. In spite of being presented as the future of work by some venture capitalists, the incentives just don't make sense. Floors don't have to be swept in the metaverse unless they're designed to need sweeping.

At present, the purpose of these games seems to be to create in-game incentive structures to utilize people in developing countries to grind on meaningless in-game tasks for no reason. The Greek economist Yanis Varoufakis described such games in his article *Crypto & the Left and Techno-Feudalism*[20]:

As long as we do not have these mechanical slaves catering for humanity as a whole (and not just producing commodities owned by the 1% of the 1%), the idea that people must now play like robots to earn a living so as to be human in their spare time is, indeed, the apotheosis of misanthropy.

While some users in developing economies have temporarily been able to use the game to generate a minimal income stream, it remains unclear how this non-economic process could ever be sustainable. In addition to the concerns about the business model, the BBC reported that the Axie Infinity treasury was recently hacked by the state hackers of the Democratic Republic of North Korea. In this hack, $620 million in crypto were stolen from players and, if successfully laundered by the regime, would likely be used to fund the country's concentration camps and nuclear programs.

17.3 DAOs

A DAO or decentralized autonomous organization is a form of smart contract which aims to reproduce the governance structure[17] of a corporation or coop associated with the cryptoasset[4] held by the smart contracts. DAOs are experiments in autonomous governance and voting structures (quadratic voting, continuous voting, etc.) that give voting rights proportionally to the "shareholders" based on their percentage of ownership of the governance token issued by the DAO[8].

DAOs are a form of regulatory avoidance which attempt to recreate the regulation of creating voting shares in corporations. DAOs place this practice outside the regulatory perimeter and have no recourse for shareholders in the case of embezzlement or fraud. They are best understood as shares in a common enterprise run by potentially anonymous entities and with no restrictions on the provenance of funds held by the "corporation." However, they may be attached to an enterprise attempting to solve a complicated public goods problem such as fixing climate change or providing universal basic income.

The notion that we should create unregistered corporate structures whose assets can be transferred to anonymous entities with no corporate reporting obligations is somewhat challenging from a fraud mitigation perspective[21], especially in a post-Enron world. It remains unclear what the killer use case is for anonymously controlled governance structures around slush funds, other than crime or projects that need avoid regulation.

17.4 DeFi

Defi is a broad category of smart contracts that loosely correspond to digital investment schemes running on a blockchain that allows users to create loans out of stablecoin and have side payouts in so-called *governance tokens*.

DeFi generally refers to a collection of services that offer lending products offered by non-banks and which exist outside the regulatory perimeter[2] as a form of regulatory arbitrage and to fund margin trading activities to speculate on cryptoassets.

DeFi projects use all manner of complicated financial jargon and insider lingo to describe their functioning, and it can be hard to parse what these investments actually are or do. On the Bloomberg podcast *Odd Lots*, one executive of a major crypto exchange described the process quite bluntly[18,1]:

> And now all of a sudden everyone's like, wow, people just decide to put $200 million in the box. This is a pretty cool box, right? Like this is a valuable box as demonstrated by all the money that people have apparently decided should be in the box. And who are we to say that they're wrong about that? Like, you know, this is, I mean boxes can be great. Look, I love boxes as much as the next guy. And so what happens now? All of a sudden people are kind of recalibrating like, well, $20 million, that's it? Like that market cap for this box? And it's been like 48 hours and it already is $200 million, including from like sophisticated players in it. They're like, come on, that's too low. And they look at these ratios, TVL, total value locked in the box, you know, as a ratio to market cap of the box's token.
>
> And they're like 10X that's insane. 1X is the norm. And so then, you know, X token price goes way up. And now it's $130 million

market cap token because of, you know, the bullishness of people's usage of the box. And now all of a sudden of course, the smart money's like, oh, wow, this thing's now yielding like 60% a year in X tokens. Of course I'll take my 60% yield, right? So they go and pour another $300 million in the box and you get a psych and then it goes to infinity. And then everyone makes money.

Despite all the fancy language and rhetoric around DeFi and some idealized appeal to "decentralizing finance," all these protocols do at a high level can be described quite simply.

1. Investors put money in a box

2. People believe really hard in the "utility" of said box.

3. The box "goes to infinity", and everyone gets more money out of the box than they put in.

If this sounds problematic and economically unsound, it is because it is. DeFi is essentially an technobabble obscurantist wrapper around Ponzi schemes.

17.5 THE METAVERSE

The metaverse is another intentionally ambiguous term for an alleged new technology. On October 21, 2011, Facebook after having been mired in whistleblower leaks, scandals, and a near-constant press cycle of relentless adverse reporting, decided to pivot away from its controversial social media business and build what they called *The Metaverse*. The metaverse itself is an idea first postulated in the science fiction novel *Snow Crash* by In the novel, the metaverse refers to a virtual world separate from the physical one, which is accessible through virtual reality terminals. Stephenson describes a bleak cyberpunk dystopia where the metaverse offers an elusive and dangerous escape from a world overrun by corruption, corporate mafias, and mercenary defense forces, and in which individuals have all retreated from public life into sovereign gated communities called burbclaves. Curiously, Facebook decided that this dystopian future was the name they wanted to attach to the pivot of the corporate brand.

Although not necessarily a crypto-based technology, the metaverse marketing seems to imagine an extension of existing virtual reality hardware, such as the Oculus Rift and Sony PlayStation VR, to include virtual environments. These "metaverse worlds" are alleged to function as either gaming environments or social environments for people to do higher-fidelity teleconferencing and participate in collaborative work-related activities. Facebook released a slick promotional video showing the company's CEO rendered in mockups of how he envisions the not yet fully formed technology.

The metaverse almost invariably shows up in crypto discourse because the metaverse pivot was announced contemporaneously to the crypto rebranding into web3. Since both concepts entered the public consciousness at roughly the same time, they have become intermingled and used interchangeably to describe some ill-defined imagined future[22].

The post hoc myth-making[24] that has emerged around the metaverse and crypto synthesis is that somehow digital assets such as NFTs will become tradable assets in Facebook's virtual worlds and that their alleged utility in virtual reality will become a way to generate income in the metaverse, which supposedly and necessarily, needs to be denominated in crypto. The myth of the metaverse has captivated the media, who have written no end of vapid think pieces feeding the vaguely colonialist rhetoric of a new virtual frontier for a new generation to colonize and capitalize. Many tech startups have since spun up companies based purely around virtual land grabs, in which plots of land in digital spaces are auctioned based on some narrative about their perceived utility in some distant future. The irony of this premise is that virtual worlds do not suffer from any concept of scarcity, except the ones their developers artificially introduce. Even if we accept the far-fetched premise of the existence of new virtual worlds, why should those worlds inherit the same hypercapitalist[12] excesses as our present world?

Stablecoins

"A lot of the evil in the world is actually not intentional. A lot of people in the financial system did a lot of damage without intending to."

– George Soros

In the digital age, whoever owns the world's data owns the future. To that end, in 2018, American social media company Facebook announced it was launching a cryptocurrency project known as Libra, which would form the basis of the singularly most extensive surveillance system outside of government. The Libra project was audacious in scope and vast in its reach for consumer data[2]. In a series of whitepapers and code releases, Facebook proposed to set up an international payment system backed[6] by a reserve of state-issued currencies such as the US dollar, euro, yen, British sterling, and Singapore dollar. The entity holding the basket of currencies would be incorporated in Geneva, Switzerland, and would serve as an independent entity to Facebook, which theoretically would manage the basket with a consortium of other Silicon Valley tech companies (Lyft, Spotify, Uber, Shopify) and several Sand Hill Road venture funds.

18.1 The Idea of Stablecoins

The impetus behind this extension of Facebook's business was a natural extension of their messaging and social media business. Facebook has a self-reported 2.7 billion users globally who already transact across a decentralized variety of payment rails. Facebook believed it would be natural to provide an alternative platform for its existing user base. This model would allow Facebook to collect interest on deposits held in the cash pool and monetize transaction flow information for their already lucrative advertising business. Complete access to the spending and financial information of 2.7 billion retail users would provide an enormous stream of actionable data for Facebook to micro-target advertisements.

For Facebook, this was a unique opportunity. If the company had access to your daily spending habits and could observe the time, frequency, and amount of all your transactions, they could infer future spending behavior as it can. An individual who buys Starbucks every morning before work could be easily extrapolated to be a coffee lover and shown advertisements for coffee-related products. However, as we have seen with metadata collection information in the past, repeated patterns or aberrations in these patterns are often sufficient contexts to make more significant deductions concerning an individual user's behavior.

Facebook is its core advertising company, and its advertising business is enormously lucrative. The microtargeting of ads to consumers generated $70.7 billion in 2019. However, as a public company there are only so many sectors that would satiate the company's expected growth. The company's expansion into the financial services sector was the natural choice given the relative stagnation of the social media market.

From a technical perspective, the company runs a black-box algorithm that consumes as much possible information about an individual consumer's internet behavior and attempts to make predictions about spending habits based on this data. The ability to feed consumers spending patterns and purchases back into the algorithm would complete the circle. The algorithm is simply a closed-loop that optimizes the presentation of Facebook content to maximize spending habits for their advertising partners. If given free rein to build this system, it would turn Facebook into the most effective digital advertising engine in existence and Facebook would become the Standard Oil of personal data.

However, the implications of Facebook's business have consistently landed the company in the midst of a growing number of scandals. Facebook's business is under constant scrutiny for abuses of user privacy and the ever-increasing amount of misinformation allowed to propagate through its platform. Researchers at Facebook came under scrutiny from the scientific community after publishing a paper *Experimental evidence of massive-scale emotional contagion through social networks*[5] in Proceedings of the Natural Academy of Sciences. In the paper, the Facebook employees outlined specifically how "emotional states can be transferred to others via emotional contagion" introduced as part of a Facebook live experiment on its users. Apart from being alarmingly creepy, this study raised quite a few ethical concerns regarding whether the users involved in the study were given informed consent to be part of the research[1]. This experiment was the first indication that Facebook's business model had moved on from simple observation and prediction to direct manipulation of user behavior. Non-consensual behavior modification is now a central part of Facebook's business model.

The second major scandal involving Facebook concerned the Cambridge Analytica data breach. In this scandal, a third-party analytics company Cambridge Analytics was able to harvest a massive amount of private data from Facebook without user consent. The data breach affected some 87 million users whose profile information was harvested for Cambridge Analytica psychometric modeling program. The clients of Cambridge Analytica were various political campaigns that may have used this information for political targeting during the 2016 elections for the United States presidency and the Brexit referendum in the United Kingdom. This scandal marked a new era of scrutiny of Facebook and the company's capacity and willingness to be ethical custodians of private personal information. The company remains in contempt of the European, British, and Canadian governments, who subpoenaed its executives to explain the data breaches of their citizens.

This degree of public scrutiny came in full force after the company announced its intentions with Libra. The project was widely criticized for its overreach, lack of compliance with existing regulations, and threats to the sovereignty of existing nations to control their currencies. European representatives nearly universally denounced the project, and several United States senators issued veiled threats to the Libra consortium members to withdraw from the project. The consortium members caved to these demands, and the more respectable companies such as PayPal, Visa, and Mastercard all withdrew from the project.

On the technical side of the Libra project, Facebook curiously attempted to build an actual cryptocurrency modeled after several stablecoin projects. The approach and methodology were similar to many public cryptocurrency projects and were likely due to the company's hiring of existing cryptographers and enthusiasts from the same community. The project's whitepaper reads like any other crypto asset whitepaper and presents with the same technical underpinnings and crypto-economic obscurantism in the tradition of many ICO proposals.

However, the leadership was aware of the limitations of what a financial services company division of Facebook could get away with from a design perspective. Since the Libra project was run as a company with a central entity subject to regulatory and legal scrutiny for safeguarding funds, the project could not conceivably be launched as a decentralized peer-to-peer network. In holding customers' funds, Facebook will still be subject to AML/KYC and sanctions enforcement regarding the company's processing of dollars and euros. This contradiction between the decentralized messaging of the product and its centralized architecture leads to the fundamental disconnect in their codebase and marketing.

The mechanism proposed for maintaining consensus of the Libra ledger state was significantly revising the models found in public cryptocurrency projects. Bitcoin allows any user running the protocol to connect and participate in the consensus state and submit transactions. However, Libra being run as a business created a context in which only large corporations would be invited to maintain the consensus state and run the servers to maintain the network. These corporations would all maintain legal contracts with the Libra entity and theoretically run individual nodes of software that Facebook provided them. The governance model of the Libra consortium was a performative farce, and the engineering behind the protocol reflected the same level of theatricality.

Instead of a consensus model like proof-of-work, which would have been unsuited and inefficient for the Libra case, Facebook invested in a not-invented-here form of a classical consensus algorithm known as Paxos; and named their derived implementation HotStuff. The goal of this setup served no purpose other than giving the appearance of decentralization. A closed network in which a fixed set of corporate validators maintained a faux-decentralized state was, for all intents and purposes, equivalent to a centralized setup of replicated servers. This performative decentralization permeates all levels of the Libra codebase and the project. In all aspects, the codebase is trying very hard to convince you it is like other public blockchain projects when it bears little similarity in practice.

The phenomenon is a clever attempt by Facebook executives to exploit regulatory arbitrage around cryptocurrency to build a project to exploit this temporary loophole and friendliness around emerging technology. The project is a stablecoin in marketing only and has cleverly used the semantic ambiguity around blockchain and cryptocurrencies in an attempt to launch a massive financial surveillance system.

The marketing around the project consisted of a particularly egregious and unethical campaign to promote Libra as a service for the unbanked and marginalized communities. From the perspective of Silicon Valley, problems of aid and development are no longer seen as problems of weak and corrupt institutions; they are recast as problems of inadequate connectivity or insufficient technology. As the Financial Times analyzed, the process of banking the unbanked is ultimately one of nation-building and financial development, not of connectivity. Many of the unbanked lack accounts because they lack the funds to put in the accounts to sustain custodianship of those funds. Facebook has shown little interest in the unbanked in any of its past activities. This attempt to position their new service as a charitable service is purely exploitative marketing.[3]

Facebook Libra was a project of paradoxes, contradictions, and gross mismanagement, which ultimately led to its failure. However, if the project had launched, it would have enabled Facebook to engage in predatory pricing, self-dealing, and the capacity to annex adjacent markets, all while not subject to Bank Holding and Secrecy acts that protect consumers deposits by virtue of being a technology company dealing in its own allegedly "sovereign" currency. Nevertheless, Facebook remains a deeply unethical company that attracts the most deranged and opportunistic employees with no regard for the integrity of democracy or public well-being. Facebook is a company that is the very embodiment of corporate irresponsibility and depravity at every level.

18.2 CENTRAL BANK DIGITAL CURRENCIES

The Facebook project and its implication as a threat to countries' national sovereignty has given rise to a recent digital transformation trend for central banks to explore similar ideas. These projects are known as *central bank digital currencies*. The proposition is simple and based on the fact that central banks typically have enormous balance sheets of their lending activities and hold the accounts for many entities that interact with the Federal Reserve or the European Central Bank. Several central banks, including the People's Bank of China and the Boston Federal Reserve, are exploring projects to this end.[4]

Advocates have generally embraced Libra and CBDCs as an "on-ramp to cryptocurrency" and praised the project for its illusory legitimacy to unrelated projects like bitcoin. However, Facebook and central banks are not building cryptocurrencies, and at best, digitizing existing accounting and payments systems. These proposed solutions bear no resemblance to bitcoin or any cryptocurrencies although and use this confusion is used as part of the blockchain meme to confuse the public.

Digital currencies are not synonymous with cryptocurrency, especially when a central issuer offers it. Digital currencies and payment rails are an essential part of public infrastructure that—especially in the United States—needs to transition from slow legacy batch systems that operate 3-4 times a week to real-time payment systems that other developed economies regularly use. These efforts are separate and entirely unrelated to cryptocurrency. Distributed ledger technology has nothing to offer central bank digital currencies as a central bank by definition, centralizes the architecture.[4]

Crypto Journalism

"Afterwards, he procures a patent, opens books for subscriptions, promising prodigious and incredible advantages to all that will venture their money on this project...and in order to support the stock price they use many other tricks and rogueries as publishing books and advertisements which are stuffed with monstrous absurdities and lies."

– Thomas Baston, 1705

Tech journalism is a small part of a larger media landscape undergoing a shift in its distribution modes. In the internet era, journalism is in a precarious state. Moreover, this state requires a reimagining of the role of journalism in the public sphere while finding a way to remain profitable. The line between journalism and commerce has become increasingly blurred with the rise of native advertising. This practice has become commonplace and is offered to commercial entities to place direct advertisements inside of publications that match the form and appearance of their surrounding content. Nowhere is this conflict of interest more evident than in the coverage of cryptocurrencies and the yellow journalism surrounding it.

We are entering a world where anyone with a keyboard and internet connection can spread misinformation faster than experts can effectively refute it. There is always a fundamental asymmetry to disinformation, as humorously noted by the popular cliche: "It takes ten times as much energy to refute bullshit as it does to produce it."

However, this trend blurs the line between journalism and commerce as promotional content has been the norm in most trade journalism. For example, there is trade journalism in interior decorating, real estate, and private wealth management. In the financial services sector, respectable and established trade publications such as The Wall Street Journal and the Financial Times cover the sizable overall state of the market and stories in the general public interest. These institutions typically follow extremely high journalistic standards and may separate reporting and editorial content. There is a high ethical standard to disclose conflicts of interest between the personal holdings of a specific journalist. Generally, reporters cannot hold the individual financial products in their articles.

However, cryptocurrency and its associated trade journalism have few, if any, restrictions on outright touting or promotion. Nor does crypto journalism have an established culture of ethics, standards, or obligations to disclose conflicts of interest. This context has resulted in a contemporary form of trade journalism that thrives in this wild west environment of volatility predictions, constant scandals, and blatant self-promotion.

19.1 CHECKBOOK JOURNALISM

Across trade journalism, so-called *pay-to-play* articles are an increasingly common practice where commercial parties will outright pay a journalist for a story written in their interests in a purely commercial transaction. The transaction is simple: the journalist exchanges their reach, influence, credibility, and expertise in the domain, and in exchange, the other party receives positive press about their product or offering. There is absolutely nothing intrinsically wrong with this practice as publications are commercial enterprises and have no legal obligation to be objective or even do reporting. However, blurring the line between outlets that practice objective journalism and pay-to-play outlets is a matter of public concern and should be disclosed when citing trade journalism.

The confusion about trade journalism as a reliable source is unfortunately common in the absence of authoritative mainstream reporting on cryptocurrency. Government bodies and financial institutions such as the International Monetary Fund, United States Securities and Exchange Commission, and FinCEN regularly cite cryptocurrency trade journalism as the basis for public policy.

During the height of the initial coin offering (ICO) bubble, there was a massive explosion in pay-to-play publications where, for a price, the outlet would spread the merits of the latest token offering to prospective investors and mirror the same pitch and investment opportunity claims as if they were statements of fact. This process of credibility purchasing, exploitation of transitive trust, and stoking a "fear of missing out" was a core part of the engine that drove the ICO bubble and was a lucrative enterprise for those participating in it. Several unethical publications silently pulled their articles touting tokens that were later the subject of lawsuits or criminal investigations.

The articles pushed by these outlets vary from the mundane to the bizarre, but several trends are apparent headline trends across most outlets. The first narrative is an almost pending corporate adoption of bitcoin or blockchain technology. This narrative ties into the legitimacy story of technology and feeds on the public repute of large corporations such as central banks, investors, and governments. These headlines are generally derivatives of the standard form "X Bank looking to Tokenize Y" or "Central Bank Z is looking into bitcoin." The content of the articles will cherry-pick quotes from seemingly mundane internal reports on emerging trends in financial services to support whatever position the outlet is looking to promote. The contents of these reports rarely ever support any one technology or even denote any action on their behalf other than continuing research and hesitation. Given that most readers will rarely read anything more than the title, the actual coherence of the content is often irrelevant. These articles exist purely as fodder to be shared on social media for sensationalist clickbait titles[4].

The second increasingly common narrative is the use of cryptocurrency as a vehicle for economic progress in developing nations. Nations such as Venezuela and Zimbabwe have suffered horribly under economic mismanagement and corrupt politicians. The currencies of these countries have experienced hyperinflation and instability. The narrative pushed by cryptocurrency outlets is that the citizens of these nations are fleeing their domestic currencies in favor of digital currencies as a flight to safety. While it is true that there are some users of cryptocurrencies in these nations, as there are in most internet-connected countries, there is absolutely no macro trend[1] of citizens toward bitcoin as a means of exchange. In Venezuela, Bloomberg reports a growing trend in the use of the dollar in the region over the bolivar[5]. There is a small percentage of bitcoin usage in this region, but relative to the total economic activity in bolivar, it represents a minute fraction of transactions.

19.2 DISCLOSURES

Outlets such as Bitcoinist, CoinTelegraph, and CoinRepublic regularly practice a form of biased trade journalism in which the specific holdings of their partners or parent companies are routinely touted as exciting or revolutionary investments. The largest trade journalism outlet, Coindesk, is operated by the cryptocurrency hedge fund Digital Currency Group.

During the height of the ICO bubble, investigative journalists looked into the prices for journalists to promote a given ICO project at various cryptocurrency outlets. Shockingly the investigation found the prices of an article from a low of $240 to a high of $4500[2]. Most outlets had no ethical standard for which to turn away pay-to-post offers. Conversely, these publications will openly condemn any position that threatens their portfolios or raises concerns about their commercial partners' specific cryptocurrency projects.

John Kay, a professor at the London School of Economics, once of financial journalism[3]:

> Psychic wealth can be created without illegality: mistake or self-delusion is enough. [...] From this perspective, the critic who exposes a fake Rembrandt does the world no favor: The owner of the picture suffers a loss, as perhaps do potential viewers, and the owners of genuine Rembrandts gain little. The finance sector did not look kindly on those who pointed out that the New Economy bubble of the late 1990s, or the credit expansion that preceded the 2008 global financial crisis.

The unfortunate truth of the world is that there is a fundamental asymmetry in returns to humoring delusion for personal gain compared to the downside of reporting reality as it is. When the emperor does not wear any clothes, it can be exceptionally lucrative to devote oneself to the fashion coverage of the imperial Haute couture wardrobe. In the same light, the trade journalism of cryptocurrency is overwhelmingly economically motivated and does not have the higher standards of established outlets. In the absence of higher standards, we should neither treat it as a reliable source nor a factual representation of events.

Initial Coin Offerings

"If you see fraud and do not say fraud, you are a fraud."
— Nassim Nicholas Taleb

During 2017-2019 there was a massive secondary bubble on top of the cryptocurrency bubble in which fledgling blockchain companies used the ethereum blockchain as part of crowd sale activities to sell custom tokens representing alleged ownership in new enterprises. The history of the Initial Coin Offering (ICO) bubble is the most explicit witness to the madness of crowds, and that truth is indeed stranger than fiction.

The simple fact remains that no company that raised funds under an ICO model has taken any profitable product to market. What is it about this fundraising scheme that makes it so pathological and attracts such low-quality ventures and entrepreneurs?

The namesake of ICO (a mutation of the term initial public offering *IPO*) comes from the traditional terminology of an IPO, an event in which a company converts private shares of its stock into a product that the general public may purchase in exchange.

The first ICO was in 2013 for a small project called Mastercoin. The project raised $2.3 million by selling a custom digital token for a specified exchange amount of bitcoin and ethereum per new token issued. This model eventually kicked off a deluge of similar investments reaching its peak in 2018. These projects were highly controversial from a legal, governance, and technical perspective and were overwhelmingly dominated by outright scams and securities law violations. The Financial Conduct Authority, a regulatory body in the United Kingdom, reports that 78% of listed ICOs were outright scams[10]. US regulators estimate the cumulative amount of money investors raised under ICOs at \$22.5 billion. The companies that raised successfully under this ICO funding model fall into three categories: blatant scams, self-aware scams, and outright naivety.[8]

For ICO exit scams, the strategy is straightforward. You construct a fantastical prospectus that makes wild claims about a product or business imply or outright state that investment will increase in value over time and incur massive returns for early investors. Then you raise the money and then hop on a plane to a country without an extradition treaty and launder the money into the local currency[28]. This is known as a *exit scam* or *rug pull.*

This is the simplest and most common form of ICO business model. The best example of this is the April 2018 Vietnamese scam for two companies named Ifan and Pincoin. The two firms are alleged to have misled approximately 32,000 investors and stolen upwards of \$660 million[2].

For projects that are not outright exit scams, the name of the game is quite simple, sell off a minority of the total supply in a presale and retain a majority of that stake. This presale could be sold to accredited investors such as venture funds and high-net-worth individuals, given a specific discount on the initial public offering price. After this presale, a public sale is offered to the general international public. This offering is usually marketed around an ICO whitepaper, a prospectus, and a technical document outlining the alleged proposed vision for the product. Typically paid advisors and influencers are given a percentage of the presale tokens in exchange for their help in touting the token. The token is then sold to the public and then traded. The capital raised may be recycled back to purchase more of the company's own token, thereby synthetically inflating the price.

The entrepreneurs and early investors can then simply release whatever information they desire to manipulate the price and dump their bags on the retail market when most opportune for them to profit. The lynchpin in this scheme is investor information asymmetry and the ability to manipulate this thinly traded market for personal gain without legal consequences associated with a regular equity sale[3].

Institutional investors, such as venture capitalists, can be legally isolated from the actions of the entrepreneurs they invest in. If the venture they invest in engages in a dubious activity without their knowledge, the fund will not be directly liable for the executives' actions if they are detached from the decision-making. Given their supposed sophistication and performed due diligence, they are legally considered capable of taking risky positions in early companies. Indeed, many venture capitalists coerced startups into raising in this model by offering preferential terms, as this model promised faster-outsized returns by offloading tokens on secondary markets and exploiting retail investor information asymmetry. This market configuration inherently creates a moral hazard for entrepreneurs who are encouraged to raise under a structure that exposes them, but not institutional backers, to legal risk.

Backroom deals during the ICO bubble have been jet fuel for producing exceptional returns. These funds can leverage their capital to obtain significant positions in these ICO presales to gain advantages over the public. From a macro perspective, this bubble has been a massive wealth transfer from the participants in general sales of tokens to those in the presale of tokens. From a purely economic perspective, this is entirely rational behavior for the funds involved. These venture funds exist to take high-risk, high-return positions in companies that will generate returns for their limited partners. However, the investor information asymmetry and the fact that the retail investors are often on the other side of these trades raises some fundamental ethical questions.

In 2020 the mobile messaging company Telegram attempted to launch a token called *Grams* in the most prominent proposed coin offering to date. The company tried to raise $1.7 billion for a presale before an emergency injunction by the SEC [1] declared that the token was unregistered security and was illegally being sold to US persons[25]. The legal documents around this case give us the most transparent insight into these deals' underlying economic structure and backroom machinations. The Financial Times reported that many of the most significant Sand Hill Road funds (Sequoia Capital, Benchmark Capital, and Kleiner Perkins) were subscribed to this presale[6].

The secondary economic question pertains to the fact that the overwhelming

---

[1] Securities and Exchange Commission v. TELEGRAM GROUP INC.

majority of these companies have produced nothing of value. The lack of any marketable blockchain artifacts raises some existential questions about the utility of this sector.

The question remains where did all this money go? Not all of it was spent on Lamborghinis, parties, and cocaine (although a fair amount was). While it is true that these companies have created jobs, however, this kind of job creation is equivalent to paying employees to dig a ditch and then fill it back up again. The parable of the broken window is an economic thought experiment regarding whether a child breaking a window is a net win for the economy simply due to the window having to be replaced. The activity of replacing the window has unseen costs that, when netted over all the participants, are in aggregate negative over the opportunity costs of other productive activities. ICOs, simply put, are a society-level misallocation of capital that incurs a massive opportunity cost in the number of productive things and companies that could be built with said capital.

Within ICO companies, this form of non-productive development is often performative and in the same economic category as the broken window metaphor. The company needs only to maintain the illusion of credibility long enough to maintain the liquidity of the initial token, allowing early investors to dump their bags. If the products produced in the prospectus never go to market, the employees are paid, but there is no economic output from this activity that contributes to the economy. Token companies act as a boutique bakery that raises billions of dollars by selling shares in a bread business but never bakes a single loaf of bread.

For coins that are neither exit scams nor thinly-veiled pump and dump schemes, there is another class of projects with slow-burn failures. This class of ventures stems from the inability to deliver on unrealistic business defined by the whitepaper. These whitepapers typically involved appeals to vague buzzword and aspirations to build software built around "decentralization" memes[30,27,19] and vague terms[1,26] such as:

- Immutable
- Decentralized
- Trustless

- Secure
- Tamper-proof
- Disintermediated
- Open/Transparent
- Neutral
- Direct transfers of value

This kind of venture may be entirely staffed with entrepreneurs and employees acting in good faith; however, the pressure from investors to increase the value of the token or to launch a high-growth business can often result in undesirable outcomes for all parties involved.

After the fundraising, the problems these companies face are simply to secure the funds and exchange a subset of cryptocurrencies for real money. Many companies raised funds before even setting up a corporate entity or opening a bank account for their business and faced the daunting prospect of where to register and bank. Several jurisdictions became ICO-friendly to encourage innovation and job growth, to collect taxes, and to expand the possibilities of having home-grown domestic startup success stories. The most popular choices for jurisdictions were the Swiss canton of Zug and the island of Malta[9]. The Swiss banking culture of client confidentiality encouraged many ICO companies to incorporate in the Zug region and then use the Swiss or Lichtenstein banking system to convert their bitcoin and ethereum into Francs and enter the traditional financial system. These funds could then be distributed to British offshore trusts, often set up in Gibraltar, to hide the funds from taxation and lawsuits.

> ICOs are a high-risk investment in startups that are sold directly to the public and circumvent the regulation on sales of equity by offering unregistered securities and often hide funds in offshore accounts in Switzerland.

However, the actual building of the business was often quite challenging for these startups. Typically startups go through a series of rounds of funding in which investors buy equity in the company in exchange for increasing sums of capital. The sums usually scale with the viability of the business, maturity of the business model, and opportunity for growth. These are customarily denoted pre-seed, seed, Series A, Series B, etc. The average Series A for an American startup is around $13 million. However, these ICO funds raised capital 10-100 times that of a typical Series A round. All of this money was raised for a company that did not have anything: no existing business, no product, no growth, no service, and no customers. Startups are challenging even for the most seasoned entrepreneurs; when first-time founders are handed hundreds of millions of dollars and simply told to deliver, the reality of this situation can often produce an impossible setup with perverse incentives[11].

The behavior seen by many of these ICO startups was characterized by executive infighting, lawsuits over corporate governance, drastic turnovers in staff, and class action suits by investors. Unconventionally these companies had such large cash reserves that they would often themselves spin-out investment vehicles to invest in other companies building on the company's proposed token or protocol. This token "turtles all the way down" approach created a cottage industry of blockchain consultants, blockchain lawyers, and blockchain developers who were more than happy to burn through the money raised. According to Bloomberg, "56% of crypto startups that raise money through token sales die within four months of their initial coin offerings"[14].

The founding teams of these ICO companies were often a zoo of disjoint personalities and backgrounds. Some ICO founding teams were entirely fictional biographies with stock photo images pulled from the internet. The Financial Times reported an ICO with fictional cartoon characters for all founders[13]. There was an unusual pattern of ICO-backed tech ventures founded entirely by lawyers and social media influencers with no technical leadership. From a technical perspective, many of these slow-burn companies attempted to build the software proposed in their initial whitepaper only to find that the underlying technology stack they initially proposed was simply too slow, immature, or impossible to support their product pitched. Many companies overpromised the capacity of so-called smart contracts to build arbitrarily complex financial products and were quickly hit by the hard limitations shortly after investigating the technology. In the absence of experienced technical leadership, many of these companies attempted to remedy the immaturity of the software themselves and hired repeated iterations of teams unsuccessfully to build what they had initially promised.

As is common in many software projects, these attempts began to grow in scope and complexity. To justify the high growth prospects of their initial raise, many companies started to launch their own bespoke currencies, which attempted to create entirely new offerings from the ground up. With absurdly large cash reserves, lack of coherent project plans, and inexperienced management, many software engineers took it on themselves to simply pilfer these companies to fund their own projects. These software teams were often defined by drastic turnover and a constant stream of leadership replacements to steer the company in a new technical direction to address the lack of marketable products.

This may sound like an absurdist farce to outsiders, but was the lived experience of many engineers and founders who participated in the 2017-2020 bubble. The absurdity of these ventures was essentially not given coverage by the tech press except in the events of large corporate scandals. Tech journalism has a propensity to cover success stories and ignore failures. During this period, most ICO companies burned their cash reserves on frivolous pursuits and lavish executive expenses and then died.

The ICO sector was notorious within the technology industry for lawsuits. From the employee's perspective, the work environment was beset with omnipresent paranoia, conspiracies, greed, and aimless technical goals that seemed performative and detached from the concealed goal of the company: inflating the corporate coin. This environment mirrored the entire philosophy of the cryptocurrency ecosystem, which is simply "number go up at any cost."

20.1 CRAZY COINS

The coin projects that came out of the bubble were a zoo of absurdity. The line between projects whose originations stem from the Dunning-Kruger effect [2] as compared to outright fraud is enormously blurry and undecidable. Particularly hilarious examples ended up defining the historical record of this absurd bubble.

---

[2] The Dunning-Kruger effect is a type of cognitive bias in which people believe that they are more intelligent and more capable than they are. Low ability people do not possess the skills needed to recognize their own incompetence.

BananaCoin was a fruity coin whose whitepaper described their currency offering as being the "Uber for bananas." Two Russian entrepreneurs started the project and invited the public to "join the organic" revolution by buying a digital token whose value was theoretically pegged to the export value of 1kg of bananas from Laos. The token quickly collapsed since perishable bananas do not form an economically sound basis for a reserve currency.

KodakCoin was a strange pivot from the Kodak camera company, whose business had been slowly degrading with shifts in consumer trends away from their traditional camera and photo processing business. Kodak's executives decided to capitalize on the two biggest buzzwords of the day, blockchain and social media, to launch a new medium of exchange for their photo-sharing site. The stock shot up 300% on the announcement but quickly collapsed to below the original announcement within months. The idea was a poorly convinced executive fantasy. It was never executed.

PotCoin was proposed as a "banking solution for the $100 billion global legal marijuana industry". In the United States, the disconnect between state legalization and federal legalization has left many financial institutions unable to bank marijuana dispensaries without running afoul of federal laws. The compliance costs for banks to transact with the sector are as high as the customers of these dispensaries. Chicago Bulls basketball player Dennis Rodman decided to promote this investment during high-profile trips to North Korea in a genuinely bizarre turn of events. Despite the sanctions and concentration camps, the North Korean state is sometimes portrayed in marijuana culture as a stoner's paradise where cannabis is legal and commonplace.

WhopperCoin was an official Burger King project which launched in Russia. The premise was deceptively simple; you would eat whoppers and earn a digital token which you could redeem for more whoppers or use to speculate with. The company made it clear that "eating Whoppers now is a strategy for financial prosperity tomorrow." This revolutionized the fast-food industry and allowed Burger King's customers to gamble with imaginary money instead of just their health.

During the height of the ICO bubble, even companies outside of the sector decided that the action was too good to not get engaged with. The New York-based ice tea producer Long Island Iced Tea Corp made the bold switch from selling refreshing tea beverages to cashing in on their newfound expertise in blockchain technology. They accomplished this by simply renaming themselves to **Long Blockchain Corp**. The company's stock was traded on the NASDAQ as LBCC and jumped 300% when the corporate renaming went public. At its peak, the company was traded at $6.91/share; however, six months later, the stock's value collapsed to penny stock levels, and it was subsequently delisted from the exchange.

In 2018 the nation of Venezuela also decided to get into the cryptocurrency business with the **Petro** coin. After 17 years and running his country into the ground, President Nicolás Maduro decided that the right answer to the country's economic problems was to issue a new digital currency backed by the nation's petroleum commodities. This project was a petrol reimagining of the Banana-Coin model. The most notable point in its proposed design was the ability to circumvent US sanctions. The government ran an ICO that raised $735 million in bitcoin, ethereum, and Russian rubles. The New York Times reported that the entire project was the brainchild of an idealistic young software developer Gabriel Jiménez who opposed the dictator but thought the currency was a viable way to bring about reform in his home. Their interests soon diverged, and Jiménez was forced to flee Venezuela and seek asylum in the United States[18].

One of the most extravagant and tragic stories involving the ICO bubble involved the company **ASKfm**. As part of generating publicity for its fundraising, it did a stunt in which the company paid four crypto enthusiasts to climb Mount Everest. The mountain climbers would then bury a hard drive containing the keys to $50,000 notional value in the company's ICO token, stored in crypto wallets. The gimmick allegedly encouraged other adventurous climbers to climb Everest to recover the "buried treasure." The company employed four sherpas—guides meant to guide climbers up the mountain—however, as part of the expedition, only three of the sherpas recovered after burying the hard drive on the mountain. The fourth sherpa, named Lam Babu, perished on the trek up to the summit after being struck with slow-blindness. His death, seemingly all for a marketing gimmick, was covered in the Financial Times[12] and generated serious controversy over what seemed like a senseless death, all for a crypto publicity stunt.

Coins associated with political leaders became a phenomenon with the launch of **TrumpCoin** and **PutinCoin**. Both were either parodies or absurdist political gestures to create national currencies for the "true patriots" of both of these authoritarian figures. On the more righteous side, **JesusCoin** made the obvious economic observation that the Church is an authority that needs to be disintermediated to do straight-through processing to the Lord. Through the holy power of blockchain, JesusCoin was able to give "record transaction speeds between you and God's son." While all of these coins seem like satire, the crypto interpretation of Poe's law led to all of them raising six to seven-figure offerings on the back of jokes and memes.

The satirical **PonzICO** released a whitepaper[4] which gives us the most accurate description of what drove the true philosophy and mentality that drove this bubble:

> In today's age, it seems better to promote the plausibility of future profit rather than waste energy on actually delivering.

20.2 Celebrity Endorsements

On the back of the speculative bubble of coin offerings, many entrepreneurs recruited a variety of people to promote these investments. These included many celebrities such as rappers and Hollywood actors who used their influence and social media presence to tout unregistered securities.

According to SEC documents, the highest-profile case involved the rapper T.I. who promoted FLiK tokens and encouraged his followers to buy into the offering for a purported new digital streaming service. The SEC alleges the rapper then secretly transferred the FLiK tokens to himself and sold them on the retail market, reaping an additional $3 million in profits.

In 2018 the government settled the case of Hollywood action star Steven Seagal. Unlike in his action movies, Seagal was not the hero and lost the final fight. In 2018 he posted a press release on his 6.7 million social media followers claiming that "Zen Master Steven Seagal Has Become the Brand Ambassador of Bitcoiin2Gen," which was an offering for an alleged "second-generation cryptocurrency." The SEC alleges the partners in the venture gave Steven an undisclosed $157,000 as a side payment for the promotion.

In the most underhyped fight of 2018, the SEC fought Floyd Mayweather over his promotion of a token called Centra sold as an unregistered security. Together with musician DJ Khaled, the SEC alleged the pair were paid an undisclosed $50,000 and $100,000 to tout the token to their 21 million Instagram followers. In a curious move, Floyd then disclosed his motivation for the promotion to all of his followers in a series of bizarre tweets which appear to implicate himself:

> I'm gonna make a $hit t$n of money on August 2nd on the [...] ICO

The SEC settled the case in 2018, and Floyd was ordered by the SEC to pay for the damages in the offering.

These cases are merely the highest-profile events that involved celebrities of note: there are thousands of other cases that authorities did not pursue. The thread running through all of these stories is that in our era, social media can be used to influence the general public to purchase financial products, however absurd and ill-conceived, purely on the fame of celebrities.

20.3 Court Cases

The cases that the government has litigated are generally high-value cases. These cases are matters of the public record; however, five specific cases stand out as setting a precedent for future sales. On October 11th, 2019, the SEC filed[22] an emergency action and obtained a restraining order against two offshore entities of the Telegram messaging company called Telegram Open Network and TON Blockchain. The SEC claimed they were conducting an unregistered, digital token offering by selling 2.9 billion digital tokens called Grams that raised $1.7 billion. These entities allegedly violated the Securities Act by failing to register their offers and sales with the SEC. On June 26th, a settlement agreement was reached, which required the return of $1.2 billion to investors while the parent entity was required to pay an $18.5 million civil penalty. [3] According to the

---

[3]Securities and Exchange Commission v. KIK INTERACTIVE INC.

TON community description, the entire purpose of the Ton projects involves the creation of and usage of digital assets and is considered the "first adopted payment cryptocurrency in the Telegram Messenger Ecosystem."

On June 4th, 2019, the SEC filed suit against Kik interactive for allegedly conducting an illegal $100 million securities offering of digital tokens. SEC claimed that Kik sold tokens to US investors without registering their offer and sale as required by US securities law. It was further allegedly proposed that Kik would integrate the tokens into their messaging app while creating a new Kik transaction service and reward other companies that would adopt it. None of these systems were built when the offer was made. In 2017 Kik's business was struggling with operations and running out of cash. In an effort to solve its predicament, Kik decided to attempt a Hail Mary pass and engage in illegal token sales as a means to turn around the company's fate. In October 2020, the court ruled that Kik had offered unregistered security; however, the case is still being settled at the time of writing.

On December 11th, 2019, the SEC charged entrepreneur Eran Eyal and his company United Data Inc, doing business under the name Shopin, for defrauding investors in an initial coin offering that raised more than $42 million from investors. According to the SEC, Shopin planned to use the funds from the sales of Shopin Tokens to create a universal profile for shoppers that would track customer purchase histories across online retails and give product recommendations[21]. However, the product was never created. The SEC further alleged that Eyal and Shopin misrepresented supposed partnerships with major retail chains, and Eyal himself misappropriated over $500,000 funds for personal use in rent, shopping, entertainment, and dating services. Eyed pleaded guilty to operating three securities fraud schemes. [4]

On May 21st, 2019, the SEC obtained a court order to stop an ongoing $40 million Ponzi scheme. The SEC charge alleged that Argyle Coin, LLC and its principal Jose Angel Aman ran a Ponzi scheme with investor funds[24]. The scheme allegedly involved the extension of a prior fraud Aman organized using two other companies he owns, Natural Diamonds Investment Co. and Eagle Financial Diamond Group. The SEC complaint stated that Aman made unreg-

---

[4]Securities and Exchange Commission v. Eyal

istered securities offerings in Natural Diamonds and Eagle, promising investors that the companies would invest in whole diamonds to cut down and sell for huge profits. The investment was claimed to be risk-free because it was back by colored diamonds, and the funds were to be used to develop the cryptocurrency business. According to the complaint, the $10 million of the funds were instead misappropriated and given to other investors for their proposed returns and Aman's personal expenses, including rent, purchasing horses, and riding lessons.[5]

On March 16th, 2020, the SEC set in place an asset freeze and other emergency relief to stop ongoing securities fraud committed by a former senator of Washington state, David Schmidt, as well as Robert Dunlap and Nicole Bowdler to sell Meta 1 Coin, a digital asset that the SEC considered to be an unregistered security offering. The SEC claimed that preposterous claims made, such as that the Meta 1 coin was backed by $1 billion in art or $2 billion of gold audited by the accounting firm KPMG but were backed by nothing. SEC also alleged that they told investors that the Meta 1 Coin was risk-free, would never lose value, and could return up to 224,923%. They had raised $9 million, and instead of distributing the coins, the investor funds were routed towards paying personal expenses. The SEC complaint further alleges that some of the investor funds were used to buy exotic vehicles such as a $215,000 Ferrari. Robert Dunlap, a Meta 1 executive trustee, in a statement to journalists, stated: "I am looking forward to dismantling the SEC as they are committing crimes against Humanity in the attempted enforcement of financial slavery," and that "Meta 1's Service and Victory For Humanity Will Be Everlasting." On an internet talk show called CryptoVisions, Bowdler told the CryptoVision's audience that "the Coin has been specifically architected out of the angelic realm." Later on, in the show, Bowdler mentioned that "the Archangel Metatron and Abraham Lincoln" revealed to her what would occur in the world's economic structure over the next 20 years.[6][23]

Each of these ICOs raised money from investors under the explicit or implicit expectation that the buyers would profit from the sale of a token on a

---

[5]Securities and Exchange Commission v. NATURAL DIAMONDS INVESTMENT CO.
[6]Securities and Exchange Commission v. META 1 COIN TRUST

secondary market due to the efforts of the token sellers. This model appeals to entrepreneurs as it increases the addressable investor pool to include international and unaccredited individuals who may not otherwise be able to participate. The token offering also does not grant any legal control or representation in the company, allowing ICO companies to run unchecked and with no corporate governance. It also appeals to investors because this virtual equity in a company is immediately liquid regardless of the company's fundamentals or economic activity. The tokens are often freely tradable, with no lock-up period, liquidation preferences, or regulation on insider sales. The moral hazard of ICO offerings is the simple fact that they do not incentivize any business development, capital formation, or economic activity in the way a standard equity offering does.

> The structure of raising shadow equity via crypto tokens does not align incentives between founders, investors, and employees and encourages a criminogenic environment in which fraud can thrive.

Companies that engage in this sale often create a Theranos-style long firm whose premise is based on increasingly large token sales on top of a company that is either empty or fraudulent. For these companies, statement is simple: *the token is the product*[17].

These recurring situations beg the fundamental question of why regulators allow these blatant scams to continue: a fundamental question of democratic institutions that speaks to the economic realism of law enforcement. The American system does not aspire to regulation by enforcement and acts extraordinarily slowly. Under the Trump administration, the federal government took a hands-off approach and hoped that some form of self-regulation would simply occur without intervention. The SEC appears to be divided between a hardline libertarian non-interventionist camp and a more proactive enforcement school of thought. In the stalemate between the two camps, the SEC appears to be incapable of fulfilling its duties.

In the absence of regularity action, all that emerged is a rapidly growing ecosystem of bucket shops that do little but hawk fraudulent securities, proliferate investment scams, and continue to harm the public while regulators sleep[29,7].

From the purely economic side of this phenomenon, regulators have limited time and resources to pursue prosecution and enforcement. Regulars are given many additional political tools to enforce rulings, however, the primary mechanism of action is to bring suits against the worst violations after the fact. Under-resourced regulators will simply often go after the top 20% of worst cases that will result in clear legal precedence and prevent future violations, but on the whole, the system lacks the resources to pursue every case. An unsettling fact of our judicial systems has always been that many individuals can and do get away with illegal activity, even in full visibility, if they are clever or just sufficiently lucky.

It is even more unsettling that defendants may also use the funds raised in an illegal offering to mount their legal defense with the spent funds unlikely to be returned in the form of damages[15]. Paradoxically, this creates a perverse incentive for fraudsters to grow the size of the fraud without regard to legality under the maxim that "the bigger you are, the softer you fall." The sad reality is that white-collar crime often pays very well in modern corporate America.

As a metaphor, in cybersecurity, a specific type of hacking attempt called a denial of service is an attack initiated by flooding a network with superfluous requests to overload systems. The effect of ICOs can be seen as a metaphorical denial of service attack on regulators. It is spamming the market with a flood of fraudulent companies beyond regulators' capacity to intervene, proving a viable "hacking" attack on the legal system itself. The surprising result of this attack is that this was an effective way to circumvent regulation and the law for many individuals.

20.4 Tokens As Illegal Securities

The economic crises of the 1920s and 1930s led to a new variety of laws to curb the excesses of wild speculation that had created the crises. The particulars of investment contracts were clarified and became a term of art to describe intangible financial products sold based on expectations of returns. This period marked a split between tangible products and investment contracts for the former retained "buyer beware" expectations while the new laws moved some of this burden to the seller of the investment contracts to prevent fraudulent sales. Most states passed legislation known as *blue sky laws* which responded to the observation that "if securities legislation was not passed, financial pirates would sell citizens everything in the state but the blue sky," much like crypto charlatans are doing today. These laws introduced the now-standard registration of securities and the introduction of regulated brokers for the selling and exchange of investment contracts.

In 1946 this resulted in a Supreme Court ruling SEC vs. Howey[20], which defined a subset of investment contracts known as *securities* if they met a specific set of criteria which came to be known as the Howey Test. This landmark case was over whether purchasers of investment units in an orange grove were purchasing securities from their stake in the managerial efforts in growing an orange grove. A product is considered a security under US law when it shares the following three characteristics:

> [A]n investment contract for purposes of the Securities Act means a contract, transaction or scheme whereby a person invests his money in a common enterprise and is led to expect profits solely from the efforts of the promoter or a third party, it being immaterial whether the shares in the enterprise are evidenced by formal certificated or by nominal interests in the physical assets employed in the enterprise.

Since then, the test has been applied to exotic investments from liquor[5] to chinchillas[16] and, most recently, to digital assets. Much of the precedent built on this definition has been an interpretation of precisely what constitutes a contract itself and what constitutes an expectation of profits in the form of marketing done on the investment. Importantly, directly marketing a product as an investment for profit is neither necessary nor sufficient cause for it to be a security.

During the 2016-2018 ICO bubble, many offerers tried to circumvent the Howey test to sell tokens under the guise of the product being a "utility token" or "fuel token,"; in which the purchase of the token allegedly serves as a means of exchange on, or provides access to a function of the network. However, the presence of external secondary markets in which these tokens were traded based on their investment potential offered reasonable cause to infer the investment potential of the token, even if it was not directly marketed as such. The whitepapers and executives overseeing these offerings would deliberately avoid terms such as "profit" and "investment" as a means to try to avoid scrutiny as security. Token investments were sold with a wink and nod to potential buyers that it was not an investment, yet the pretense was understood by everyone involved.

The other method around the securities laws is the use of dual-purpose tokens, which can be redeemed for services within a network and traded speculatively. In many of these dual-use token cases, the smoking gun is the presence of prominent venture capital investors where the expressed purpose of their investment vehicle is to return on the investment of their fund. If a messaging app offered a token that granted the alleged "utility" of being able to purchase in-app stickers, it is implausible that a fund of this size's intent is to buy hundreds of millions of dollars of stickers for its own use. Instead, they intend to use their capital and information asymmetry to gain an advantage in trading the tokens for a return after the presale. The alleged utility is simply a very thin legal cover to hide their real intent.

Any decentralized network brings additional operational risk to the business itself in internalizing operations for anti-money laundering and compliant money transmission that would typically be delegated to external payment processing partners. There is no technical necessity for network decentralization or a blockchain to achieve the ends of this proposal. The disintermediation potentials posited could equivalently be achieved by centralized database solutions far more efficiently and cost-effectively.

The implicit intent of all cryptocurrency ventures is simply to raise money from unsophisticated investors with no oversight in a new form of regulatory avoidance trying to circumvent investor protections of the Securities Act. It is an attempt to roll back regulation to the wild and free-wheeling excesses of the 1920s that ultimately led to the Market Crash of 1929.

Ransomware

"Ransomware is unique among cybercrime because in order for the attack to be successful, it requires the victim to become a willing accomplice after the fact"

– James Scott

Most bitcoin use outside of speculation is not in payments but in financial black market activities and malware. Malware is a form of software that infects computer systems and directs them to behave in ways that are contrary to user intention. Viruses are a common form of malware that consist of executable software which infects systems and instructs them to destroy or deviate from normal running behavior. The virus will often spread to other computers before executing its malicious payload. Another type of malware is surveillanceware, which allows a remote operator to observe the private user behavior on a computer or smartphone and intercept private communications and data on the device.

Malware is not a new phenomenon; it has existed since the 1990s and has seen massive proliferation since the rise of widespread internet connectivity. However, its most novel and destructive form is *ransomware*, a form of malware that infects a target's computer, potentially encrypting or threatening to delete their files in exchange for a ransom to the hackers. The invention of bitcoin and other cryptocurrencies has allowed the feasibility of this new form of malicious software to collect the funds of its victims around the world. While the software is not a new invention, if early ransomware demanded a payment, it would have had to demand small physical cash payments in person or by mail, potentially exposing the hacker to tracking and law enforcement. The alternative would be to require funds to be issued via bank transfer. However, the institution could reverse this transaction and reveal the identity of the hacker's target account to receive the funds.

Cryptocurrency provided the perfect answer that allows hackers to anonymously prey on their victims and extort cash payments from them while minimizing their exposure to being caught by law enforcement. Hackers can automate these mass attacks, and the ransomware will virally propagate itself and automatically funnel funds back to the issuer with very little intervention on the hackers' part. If there is one killer app for cryptocurrency, it is that it provides an efficient payment mechanism for extortion. Ransomware could not function effectively at scale without cryptocurrency.

21.1 CRYPTO'S KILLER APP

The first example of cryptocurrency-based ransomware was in September 2013 with the discovery of a ransomware payload known as CryptoLocker. The software would infect target computers, encrypt various local files, and demand a bitcoin payment to unlock the captured files within three days. The attack was eventually isolated to a Russian network of computers and shut down. The hackers in question were likely involved with this network; however, there were no arrests.

The attack occurred in 2017 with the rise of a new payload known as WannaCry. The payload was delivered and transmitted over the internal in a traditional virus payload and infected nearly 230,000 Windows systems worldwide. The attack demanded its victims pay $300 per system paid in bitcoin to the hackers' wallet account. The attack hit many governments and industrial systems, including Deutsche Bahn, FedEx, the Russian Ministry, and several public health care systems. Most notably, the United Kingdom National Health Care system saw some 70,000 devices infected, affecting 16 hospitals. The attack cost the British taxpayers £92 million to recover and caused significant disruption to patient care and people's lives[3].

CryptoLocker was ransomware that used a trojan to target Windows PCs in

2013 and spread via infected email attachments to lock and encrypt local storage devices. Bitcoin payments were required by a specific deadline—otherwise, the price would rise significantly. The damage is estimated to be in the range of $30 million. A ransomware attack hit over 22 Texas municipalities in August 2019. The mitigation costs and recovery are estimated to be $12 million. Although hospitals and businesses are typically targets, local governments have become the main focus of these cyber criminals more recently.

In late 2019 there was an attack on the University of California San Francisco research department performing COVID-19 vaccine development, which locked servers used by epidemiology and biostatistics departments. The university staff attempted to negotiate with the attacker for over six days and came to a ransom of $1.14 million. COVID-19 has accelerated the ransomware business targeting universities, labs, and hospitals with vaccine research data. Such ransomware groups originate from Russia and Eastern Europe and possibly from state-level actors in these regions[5,2,1].

Not all attacks result in payouts to hackers. In 2021 Ireland's Health Service was extorted for $20 million, but the government refused to pay.

21.2 THE ONCOMING STORM

Traditional kidnapping and ransom-based criminal enterprises have the unpleasant requirement of physical presence. Physical cash forces the locality and physicality of the criminal to the crime, whereas ransomware frees them from this locality restriction. If a criminal mugs a victim in the street and demands withdrawal of cash at an ATM, they will at most get the maximum ATM withdrawal amount (often $300) transaction that the victim can immediately reverse with a simple call to the bank.

With cryptocurrency enabling ransomers, it allows these criminals to proliferate behind the scenes with very little chance of getting caught. The regular financial system has innate measures to prevent this indiscriminate targeting of the innocent.

In 2021 the number of ransomware attacks exploded in number. The average ransom fee requested has increased from $5,000 in 2018 to around $200,000 in

2020. The total ransomware costs are projected to exceed $20 billion in 2021. As of 2021, the most lucrative hacks have been the following attacks:

1. January 2021 – Travelex ($2.3 million)
2. April 2021 – DC Police Department ($4 million)
3. May 2021 – Brenntag ($4.4 million)
4. July 2021 – CWT Global ($4.5 million)
5. May 2021 – Colonial Pipeline ($4.4 million)
6. March 2021 – Acer ($5 million)
7. May 2021 – JBS USA Holdings ($11 million)
8. March 2021 – CNA Financial ($40 million)

At the time of writing the ransomware industry has become a $5.2B/year industry and is only growing in both its damages and scale[4].

Financial Populism

"Man is a credulous animal, and must believe something; in the absence of good grounds for belief, he will be satisfied with bad ones."

— Bertrand Russell, *Unpopular Essays*

22.1 OCCUPY WALL STREET

On September 17th, 2011, a group of nearly a thousand irate protesters marched into the Financial District of Lower Manhattan, marking the start of an influential protest movement known as Occupy Wall Street. In their words, they had had enough of Wall Street and were finally going to make their voices heard by physically occupying territory adjacent to the world's financial hub to send a message. Occupy Wall Street was a loose coalition of Americans who self-described as the disenfranchised 99% and believed that the American economic system was no longer serving their interests and instead had been captured by corporate interests. Occupy Wall Street was a movement that resonated and was born out of America's resentment towards the large financial institutions that had received public bailouts following the 2008 subprime mortgage crisis.

For months these protestors would camp and occupy a private park in Manhattan known as Zuccotti Park, all the while the financial district was operating business as usual around them. These Manhattan protests went on for months with protestors regularly marching around Wall Street and chanting slogans such as "banks got bailed out, we got sold out" with signs with pithy sayings such as

"Privatized profits, socialized losses."

Other protest groups, taking up the common banner, would pop up in many other cities across the United States in a movement that would become known as the broader Occupy movement. These grassroots groups had their own agenda, messaging, and aims within the movement, but generally fell under the umbrella of financial populism. The movement organically crystallized around a hazy but definable reaction to the broader phenomenon of social and economic inequality, greed, corruption, and the undue influence of corporations[1] on government.

These protests would go on until November 15th, 2011, when the New York Police Department marched into the Zuccotti encampment and evicted the occupying protestors; soon after, the movement would recede from public life and largely retreated into online activism rather than street protests. Nevertheless, the movement represented a genuine political moment in American public discourse. It was the first significant mainstream movement to directly position its message as addressing the fundamental problem of income inequality–an issue that had been growing and festering in American life since the policies of the Reagan era. The memes of the "1% vs. 99%" have since become a fixture of American politics and speak to a genuine grievance at the heart of American political life[10].

Seen from an ideological point of view, Occupy Wall Street was a populist socio-political movement that overwhelmingly drew its messaging from the tradition of radical leftist movements that preceded it. However, the genuine grievances percolating about the American zeitgeist were not bracketed purely to leftist groups; the events of the global financial crisis were indiscriminate and universal in the damage they caused the public, regardless of political affiliation. Movements on the right, such as the Tea Party, also adopted financial populist language as a reaction against the perceived injustice of the Obama administration's bailout package and recovery plans. It was a rare moment in America where both the left and the right were, for equally legitimate reasons, furious at the fact that the public had been swindled by reckless Wall Street speculation— much of which was entirely based on crimes that would be later uncovered by post-crisis financial journalism.

A valid criticism of the Occupy movement was that, in hindsight, the campaign had no clear goals or vision of what success or positive change would entail. Occupy was primarily a youth movement made up of individuals who overwhelmingly did not understand the complexity of the global financial system, regulation, or the principal causes of the financial crisis but were personally impacted by all these factors. The campaign was a reactionary movement against a not-well-understood injustice that had been exacted against them but which almost none of them could articulate the actual problem or proposed solution. The exposition of the movement's ideas led to many misconceptions and debatably amounted to little tangible change in regulation or policy.

22.2 WALLSTREETBETS AND BITCOIN

The phenomenon of cryptocurrency was developing simultaneously to the Occupy movement and represents in some sense an orthogonal vision that originates at much the same reactionary starting point although it proceeds down an entirely different path to the present moment[4]. Cryptocurrency was itself a reaction to the global financial crisis, and the Times of London headline about the bank bailout was embedded as a memo in the first block on the bitcoin blockchain. The political imagination of Satoshi—and many crypto apostles who followed his vision—was that the financial system could not be reformed. Nothing less than the wholesale destruction of corrupt financial institutions[5] would achieve their goals. Wall Street and the Federal Reserve needed to be entirely destroyed, and, like a phoenix, a new digital financial system would arise from the ashes: a new economic order free of the corruption and unregulated excesses that led to the public bailouts. History, it seems, is not without a sense of irony as although the crypto movement started as a reaction to the speculative excesses of Wall Street, fast-forwarding thirteen years and crypto became the very apotheosis of the greed and hypercapitalist speculative excesses it was originally reacting against. It was as if the protestors in Occupy Wall Street were slowly, one by one, seduced into becoming a Wolf of Wall Street variety hedge fund trader by the siren song of the chance to be the criminal rather than the victim this time around[2].

The overarching theme of both crypto and Occupy movement is financial populism[8], an ideology that corresponds to a general set of appeals to the notion that the "the common man" who has been taken for fools by the rich and powerful, and should now reassert their will over the financial elites. This ideology manifested in ideations to enact additional financial regulations through the democratic process, all the way up to vigilante justice against the perceived financial elites. Rational people may disagree about the ends taken by financial populism, however, just as with many other doctrines, these ideas are based on a kernel of truth about genuine grievances and accurate analysis of the flaws in the American economic system manifest in the lived experience of many followers.

The American public's rage toward Wall Street and the elected officials are, in many ways, highly justified. In response to the financial crisis, the American government created the Troubled Asset Relief Program (TARP) in the form of a \$700 billion government bailout to purchase toxic assets from financial institutions to stabilize the economy. While, in hindsight, the package may have been necessary, it only reaffirmed the notion that the financial sector plays by a different set of rules than the public; rules that encourage risk-taking because public taxpayer money is always available whenever the situation becomes too dire. Economists use the term *moral hazard* to describe conditions where a party will take risks because the cost incurred will not be felt by the party taking the risk. The clearest example of these excesses was when in 2009, a year after the bank rescue program, Goldman Sachs paid out \$16.7 billion in bonuses to bank employees, seemingly as compensation for their extreme risk-taking leading up to the crisis. These bonuses paid out, seemingly on the back of the taxpayer, enraged the public. Despite all the public anger, the Obama administration did not prosecute any of the high-level executives involved in the events leading up to 2008. Instead the courts prosecuted a single executive, Kareem Serageldin, who was sentenced to 30 months in prison for conspiracy to falsify books and records at Credit Suisse. In what many perceive to be an affront to justice, the rest of the sector was graciously given a bailout and a slap on the wrist despite the public outcry for the Obama administration to collect banker scalps.

However, the full brunt of the financial crisis fell on millennials, those born between 1981 to 1996, who entered the workforce during the height of the financial crisis. Millennials entered the job market during the worst downturn since the Great Depression, saddled with deep unsustainable student debt, and headed straight into dead-end jobs. Many millennials are now a lost generation of individuals with seemingly no means to claw themselves out of the debt trap and achieve the level of financial stability that their parents and grandparents were able to aspire to. The anger and resentment towards Wall Street run deep in the public consciousness and reverberates in the political rhetoric of populist leaders like Trump, who promised simplistic policies to "Make America Great Again" and roll the economy back to an imagined golden era of the past, one without the corruption and excesses of Wall Street. However, when Trump was elected in 2016 on the back of his populist message, his administration engorged the worst excesses of the financial elites. President Trump filled his cabinet with a noxious swamp of unbounded psychopaths and amoral sycophants, which marked an era of unprecedented corruption and unparalleled incompetence in government.

In January 2021, the undercurrents of financial populism found a new form when day traders on the popular Reddit forum WallStreetBets decided to engage in a short squeeze of the GameStop (NYSE: GME) stock. Several prominent hedge funds had taken a short position in the stock, expecting it to go down given the poor fundamentals and hostile business environment to brick and mortar stores during the coronavirus pandemic. The Reddit retail traders decided to coordinate on the internet forum to buy the stock en masse and drive the price up, forcing the hedge funds to cover their short positions, thus causing them to incur enormous losses. In January, the stock price jumped from $17.25 to over $500 a share. The media picked up and proliferated the market mania and the populist narrative of the "little man" getting revenge against hedge funds, creating even more speculative interest in the stock. Many other investors saw aberrant market conditions and a speculative bubble growing and decided to try and time the bubble, thus increasing the scale and scope of the mania. Reddit co-founder Alexis Ohanian gave an interview on CNBC in which he declared the Gamestop bubble to be "a chance for Joe and Jane America—the retail buyers of stock—to flex back and push back on these hedge funds."

Despite the narrative of a populist uprising, the so-called Gamestop Revolution had little effect on the broader market[6]. Instead, the vast majority of retail investors who chose to participate in the Gamestop bubble ended up losing money[7], as is characteristic of other historical bubbles. In the aftermath of the bubble popping, the Wall Street Journal reports that many of the brokers and market makers made outsized profits off the increased volume in trades; the Journal wrote that "Citadel Securities executed 7.4 billion shares of trades for retail investors. That was more than the average daily volume of the entire U.S. stock market in 2019". It also reported that Wall Street investment bank Morgan Stanley "doubled its net profit in the first quarter of 2021 to $4.1 billion." At the end of the day, the real winners of the GameStop bubble were the same entrenched institutions[9] as before, and the public learned the hard lesson that day trading is not an effective means of protest against the financial establishment.

Financial populism is a manifestation of the despair of the general population in the wake of the neoliberal policies that have dominated public policy since the 1970s. The economist Thomas Piketty[11] compellingly argues that the decline in economic growth will lead to outsize concentrations of wealth, which manifests as economic and political power. This process becomes self-reinforcing in an era of slowdowns in technological progress and demographic shifts. Capital accumulation becomes entrenched and generational, and this process threatens to capture democracy. Financial populism is a reaction to this fundamental economic shift that can be framed in terms of six key components of the ideology:

1. Economic anxiety and collective rage at a perceived captured financial system.

2. A belief that elites are rigging the financial system for their own advantage.

3. A nostalgia for a perceived "golden era" in which the inequities and asymmetry of the financial system were not present.

4. Distrust of the sense-making done by the media, who are seen as corrupted by the elites, and a belief that technology[3] is a means to level the playing field against the elites.

5. An interweaving of memes to convey the populist message in a lowest-common-denominator form that appeals to a broad base.

GameStop, Occupy Wall Street, and cryptocurrency are manifestations of financial populism in different forms. However, cryptocurrency is the purest distillation of these ideas into a purely narrative-driven speculative asset built around the commodification of populist rage. The crypto bubble is built around a speculative financial product that is fun to gamble on and combined with a moral cause that resonates with financial populists under the banner of a righteous cause. This mix of moralism and speculation is a particularly intoxicating brew that is a very potent catalyst for extreme behavior. Nevertheless, the ineffectiveness of financial populism and its complete inability to effect reform or change has since morphed into a darker ideology, rooted not in revolution or transformation, but one that revels in despair—the ideology of financial nihilism.

Financial Nihilism

"In progressive societies the concentration may reach a point where the strength of number in the many poor rivals the strength of ability in the few rich; then the unstable equilibrium generates a critical situation, which history has diversely met by legislation redistributing wealth or by revolution distributing poverty."

> – Will Durant, *The Story of Civilization*

Crypto is a symptom of the problems of our era, of a post-truth world awash in crackpottery, and a breakdown of trust in our institutions. For the first time in a generation, Americans feel the economic crunch like never before. Now well into their thirties, the millennial generation has been hammered by both the 2008 financial crisis and the coronavirus pandemic. Study after study confirms that Americans are more atomized, lonely, depressed, and desperate. At a certain level, the psychological state of market participants also begins to alter the markets and the fabric of the financial landscape itself.

The United States is increasingly going down the path toward creating a profoundly unequal society and, if left unchecked, a devolution into a neo-feudal civilization where corporate interests completely capture public institutions. For the first time, Americans see their prosperity decrease relative to their parents and grandparents. People increasingly feel that the size of the pie is decreasing, that the economy is a zero-sum game, and that the system is rigged, and—from many perspectives—they are not wrong.

23.1 ALIENATION

The divide between the winners of capitalism and the losers in the new tech-led economy is increasingly becoming an uncrossable chasm. In 2020, the top 20% of the population earned 52.2% of all American income, while the top 1% owned 34.5% of all household wealth. On top of income disparity, the disparity in asset ownership is even more pronounced; the wealthiest 10% of American households now own 89% of all American stocks; a level of inequality not seen since the Gilded Age of the late 1800s. Americans are saddled with a collective $1.75 trillion in student loans, a pit from which many of them will simply never be able to climb out. American workers have grappled with decades of wage stagnation since the 1970s and are increasingly relying on multiple jobs or the gig economy to make ends meet. For many young people, the future stretches ahead as little more than a sequence of dead-end jobs, each more alienating than the last, with no end in sight.

This feeling of economic anxiety and financial desperation, coupled with the vastly insufficient social safety net of the United States, has led people to adapt their investing and spending behavior to match their circumstances. Americans' median bank account balance is $5,300, and for some people taking their meager savings to a metaphorical casino and placing small bets with even a re-mote chance of parabolic upsides does not seem irrational. "When you ain't got nothing, you got nothing to lose."

The economic context of low-interest rates, vast income inequality, an in-creasingly looming climate catastrophe on the horizon, and the inability to get ahead has started to warp the philosophy and worldview people see capitalism through. In philosophy, *nihilism* is the rejection of all moral principles, in the belief that life is meaningless, there is no purpose other than to destroy, and nothing in the world has any actual existence. Nihilism is an anti-philosophy, an intellectual dead-end from which no other observations can be derived. The financial form of nihilism takes these ideas and applies them to the concept of value and markets.

The core thesis of financial nihilism is an extreme extrapolation of an old idea, the *subjective theory of value.* An asset has intrinsic value if its value can be measured objectively. A radical reading of the subjective theory of value asserts that any objective measure of value cannot exist, and the subjective preferences of the buyer entirely determine that market value and the seller, revealed through the autonomous operation of the free market. Dogecoin, diamonds, and dollars all have the same intrinsic value of zero because everything has zero intrinsic value. Markets simply trade in memes, some more popular than others, but none having any objective status or corresponding to any truth. Any investment scheme is thus assumed to be a grift a priori. After all, it is an attempt to get others to believe in some collective delusion which is assumed to be a Ponzi structure because everything is a Ponzi. The entire economy is thus nothing more than a Keynesian beauty contest for collective delusions. The role of the individual in late capitalism is to be nothing more than a maggot eating the corpse of civilization while the world boils itself to death in an orgy of greed and corruption.

Needless to say, this is a bleak worldview. However, out of this nihilism arises a powerful impulse to gamble out of pure existential boredom. The millennial investing strategy is often characterized by two concepts that grow out of financial nihilism:

FOMO, or *fear of missing out*, is the cognitive bias[2] that everybody else is building wealth on gambling and that if one does not jump in, one will lose one's only chance at getting rich.

YOLO, or *you only live once*, is the perspective that extreme risks are worth bearing because, in a world of zero interest rates, there is no point in either selling one's labor or accumulating wealth through compounding interest. Instead, one's only chance to get rich is purely by gambling everything on low-probability, ultra-high-return wagers in moonshot investments.

The crypto thought leader Micahel Saylor gave the most apparent embodiment of both of these investment principles at a Bitcoin conference:

> Once you know how it all ends, the only use of time is ... how do I buy more bitcoin? But take all your money and buy bitcoin. Then take all your time, figure out how to borrow more money to buy more bitcoin. Then take all your time and figure out what you can sell to buy bitcoin. And if you absolutely love the thing, that you

don't want to sell it, go mortgage your house and buy bitcoin with it. And if you've got a business that you love because your family works for the business and it's in your family for 37 years, and you can't bear to sell it, mortgage it, finance it, and convert the proceeds into the hardest money on earth, which is bitcoin.

Subsequently, one crypto investor allegedly mortgaged his house to do just this, and tweeted:

Longing #Bitcoin here with a mortgage on my home.
Target 288k.
Stop loss: Homeless.
Either humanity is winning or I am sinking with this ship. There is no Plan C. Let's go.

Now there is a kernel of truth that some individuals do make money investing in Ponzi schemes. In Bernie Madoff's 20-year stint running a Ponzi scheme, some of Madoff's early investors cashed out of the fund early, before the house of cards collapsed and walked away with billions of dollars. These people legitimately made a return from a Ponzi investment, and the uncomfortable truth is that investment fraud can vault some fortunate people into whole other socioeconomic strata if they get lucky and time a Ponzi scheme correctly. However, there is a moral component to this type of investment since the returns the small group of individuals receives are done on the back of the scheme's operators defrauding the vast majority of other participants, which is why these schemes are illegal.

23.2 Everything is a Ponzi

For financial nihilists, the moral component of investing in Ponzi schemes is a non-issue because "everything is a Ponzi scheme". The crypto media outlet Coindesk famously published an article defending a particular crypto investment from accusations of being a Ponzi scheme by outright declaring, **Yes, it's a Ponzi scheme. But who cares? So are the dollars in your pocket.** Instead of 401k, a diversified portfolio of mutual funds, and a mortgage, for a nihilist, it is an entirely natural alternative to constructing a portfolio of CumRocket, Shibu

Inu, SafeMoon, and a hundred other blatant scams in the hope that one of the scams works out.

The Bloomberg columnist Matt Levine wrote a particularly apt analysis of the meme-investment phenomenon in his newsletter entitled, *Dogecoin Is Up Because It's Funny*:

> Just imagine traveling 10 years back in time and trying to explain this to someone; just imagine what an idiot you'd feel like. "There's going to be this online currency that people think is a form of digital gold, and then there's going to be a different online currency that is a parody of the first one based on a meme about a talking Shiba Inu, and that one will have a market capitalization bigger than 80% of the companies in the S&P 500, and its value will fluctuate based on things like who is hosting 'Saturday Night Live' and whether people tweet a hashtag about it on the pot-joke holiday, and Bloomberg will write articles and banks will write research notes about those sorts of catalysts, and it will remain a perfectly ridiculous content-free parody even as people properly take it completely seriously because there are billions of dollars at stake."

The absurdity is the very point[3] of these investments. The belief that a digital token based on an internet meme of a talking dog could displace the dollar as the world's reserve currency is a point that many investors argue in online forums, entirely in earnest[4]. In an upside-down world where people have been locked in their homes for two years hiding from a global pandemic, while the world boils itself, and markets increasingly reward those who do no work, why not have a laugh about a talking dog? The entire thing seems ridiculous; it is absurd, but from a particular perspective, not any more so than the plight of many disenfranchised young people[1], who live a life of complete loneliness and alienation, in a hypercapitalist neoliberal hell from which there is no escape.

Crypto may seem like the ultimate form of revenge to force the elites to recognize the absurdity of late capitalism by day trading completely absurd financial products to the point where the establishment takes notice. The European Central Bank has to issue a statement on bitcoin, Bloomberg is forced to cover investments whose only fundamentals are a talking dog, and JP Morgan is forced to give analyst opinions on products that are seemingly "memed into existence" by internet trolls. However, absurd joke investments under capitalism do not lead to revolution, wealth redistribution, or justice; they lead to even more extreme capitalism. Despite its destructive temperament, financial nihilism cannot destroy anything, only worsen the situation for those who can least bear extreme financial risks. The same elites these disenfranchised day traders think they are sending a message to are the ones running the platforms they trade on and rigging the markets to their advantage, with far more wealth flowing to them because of the lack of regulation. Creating synthetic asset bubbles and trading in zero-sum investments is not sending a message to anyone; it simply enriches the already wealthy by enabling even more predation on the poor.

Crypto fraud is a novel form of scam that taps deeply into the systemic despair of our era. Karl Marx would probably be spinning in his grave, knowing that future generations learned how to transmute capitalist alienation itself into a fictitious commodity to be sold back to the public only as a means to entrench the power of capitalists, like some perpetual motion machine of eternal predation. Financial nihilism is the social lubricant that oils the entire machine and keeps the grift wheels spinning.

Late anthropologist David Graeber often remarked, "The ultimate, hidden truth of the world is that it is something that we make and could just as easily make differently." Nihilism, despair, and the complete rejection of objective truth is not a productive approach to philosophy, finance, or any other aspect of life. The world has a structure to it, and through the capacities of reason and science, we can understand both the world and the human condition, and through reason, we can improve our condition to build a better future. While democracy is not perfect, it is perfectible. Even if none of this were true, it is still better to labor under a delusion of misplaced hope and optimism than to wallow in aimless despair. Financial nihilism is a worldview that, although understandable, can be outright rejected.

Regulation

"Agencies tasked with protecting the public interest come to identify with the regulated industry and protect its interests against that of the public. The result: Government fails to protect the public."
– Gerald P. O'Driscoll

We live in a new golden age of fraud. Never since the 1920s has financial fraud and grifting been so ingrained in public as today. Yet, the cryptocurrency bubble is entirely built on a single foundation: securities fraud. The investment narrative of cryptoassets derives from an uncomfortable truth; selling unregulated financial assets to unsophisticated investors is a great way to raise large amounts of money quickly and with little overhead and oversight. In the 1920s, people raised money from the public on the back of promises of "easy money" from non-existent oil wells, distant gold mines in foreign countries, and snake oil cure-alls. And yet nothing has changed. Today, we have promises of investments[5] to build financial perpetual motion machines created on the back of promises of decentralized networks[2], a new digital economy, and blockchain snake oil cures for whatever problem one sees in the world.

The Securities Framework put in place by our grandparents following the Market Crash of 1929 is based on universal truths about the nature of capitalism. Unless otherwise restrained, entrepreneurs will invariably misrepresent the nature of their business to investors. Investors can only make informed investment decisions if there are full, fair, and truthful disclosures about the nature of the products they are being sold.

There is both an information and time asymmetry between those who have domain expertise about a line of a business and those who have capital willing to be put into new investments. In the absence of any regulatory framework, there is a perverse incentive for entrepreneurs to misrepresent the success and efficacy of their products to obtain more capital. As is evident throughout all historical financial bubbles covered in this book, markets do not work effectively when vast information asymmetries or perverse corporate structures incentivize fraud. Crypto fundraising is an absolute nightmare scenario from a fraud mitigation perspective[4].

The initial coin offering bubble of 2018 gave us the most unambiguous evidence of how crypto creates a criminogenic environment for fraud. By allowing potentially anonymous entrepreneurs to raise crypto-denominated capital, from all manner of international investors, with no due diligence, reporting obligations, registration requirements, or fiduciary obligations to their investors, we saw exactly what one might expect: a giant bubble of outright scams. Some studies put the number of outright ICO scams at 80%. These companies had no pretense of any economic activity, and the founders simply wanted to abscond with investor money. The rest of the 20% merely fall under the category of illegal securities offerings, companies that sold digital shares as a proxy for equity in a common venture to American investors.

Crypto assets meet the United States legal test, called the Howey Test, which defines which types of financial assets are classified as securities and fall under the Securities Act of 1933 and the remit of the Securities and Exchange Commission. The Howey test defines security as:

1.   An investment of money by a person;

2.   in a common enterprise;

3.   where the person is led to expect profits;

4.   to be derived from the entrepreneurial or managerial efforts of the promoters of the project

Crypto tokens do not just pop out of the ether fully formed. They are investments spun up by software engineers that run on a blockchain network and are sold to the public for the pursuit of price appreciation. Every crypto project launched since bitcoin has engaged in entrepreneurial or managerial efforts that primarily determined the token's value and thus are clearly securities contracts[3]. The public is not buying crypto tokens as collectibles or commodities to fulfill some human need; they are buying crypto tokens to make a financial return in real dollars[6].

Nevertheless, the United States agency responsible for regulating securities has had an exceptionally incoherent approach to enforcing existing securities law. The current chairman of the SEC, Gary Gensler, has made ample lip service to the existing framework, stating:

> My predecessor, Jay Clayton, said and I will reiterate: Without pre-judging any one token, most crypto tokens are investment contracts under this regime that the Supreme Court put out called the Howey Test,

Yet from a matter of public interest concern, the SEC has allowed companies such as Coinbase, Kraken, and Binance to run crypto exchange businesses, list as public United States companies, and sell securities to United State persons, which, at least in his words, are allegedly breaking the law. This incoherence in stated policy and enforced policy is creating a corporate culture in which many United States startups where the rule of law is no longer applicable to their business, simply by virtue of merely declaring themselves "blockchain startups" as a means to circumvent the Securities Act.

24.1 SHADOW EQUITY & SECURITIES FRAUD

In Silicon Valley venture capital circles, a new form of investing has gained popularity, a form that explicitly exploits lax enforcement of the securities framework as a core part of their business model. Usually, when early companies raise capital, such as founding a tech startup, venture capitalists will purchase equity in the company. This equity is either in direct stock or the right to buy the stock in the future at a significant discount. At some point, if the company is successful, the venture capital investors can either sell their stock to the public in an initial public offering, in which the company lists on a stock exchange; or if the company is acquired, the stock will exchange either for cash or converted into shares in the acquiring company. This mechanism allows venture capital investors to profit, often significantly, from their investments in the company in conjunction with the success of the founders they invest in. The venture investing model is an integral part of the United States tech economy and an engine for enormous prosperity and growth.

However, in the post-2018 era, the outsized venture returns seen in the previous era have largely fallen by the wayside. The unicorns—companies valued at over $1 billion—that were once darlings of Silicon Valley, Peleton, WeWork, Uber, and Lyft have not performed like the giants of the dot-com era when IPOing; the unicorn stampede has become a bloodbath in the public markets. Venture capitalists chasing the double-digit yields of the past have turned into increasingly more bizarre, risky, and unsustainable business models as part of their portfolio building. For venture capitalists dipping their toes into crypto investing, this has increasingly meant not investing in equity in their portfolio companies but instead investing in crypto tokens as a proxy for equity, a controversial mechanism known as *shadow equity*.

In the United States, regular equity is regulated under the securities framework, which involves a vast array of common-sense investor protections. The first is that issuers of the equity have a fiduciary obligation to their shareholders and can be held liable if they misrepresent the risks in the company or its financial reporting. In addition, all shareholders of the same class of shares must receive fair and equal treatment in both the information they receive from the company and their proportional representation in the governance of the company. After 90 years of precedent, securities law forms this basis of corporate governance and is a very successful check against misaligned incentives that may lead to fraud.

However, with shadow equity companies are now effectively issuing shares represented by cryptoassets or smart contracts, which are securities yet receive none of the investor protections of regular equity. Instead of a traditional equity raise, venture capital firms approach founders of crypto companies and do backroom deals that exchange capital for a percentage of the tokens that the company will issue in a sale known as a *pre-mine*. For instance, if a company issues 30 million shadow equity "share" tokens, it might allocate 20% or more of these tokens to its investors before selling them directly to the public.

With a regular equity investment in a private company, the stock is not immediately liquid or available for sale until an IPO or an acquisition event. The horizon for such events is typically around a decade before early investors, and founders can cash out. However, with shadow equity, there are no restrictions on inside or secondary sales, allowing founders and investors to sell at any point they desire as the sales are effectively unregulated. This structure creates a perverse incentive in that the value of the shadow equity is entirely uncorrelated to the success of the supposed underlying business. Crypto companies with seemingly no business, cashflows, customers, or products regularly have valuations of their shadow equity in billions of dollars, seemingly detached from any business success or even economic activity. This model only works because there is a large unregulated secondary market for these tokens that the public can speculate on, wholly detached from any business fundamentals.

Regular equity aligns the incentives of founders, investors, and employees by tieing their stock compensation to the company's overall success. If the company is successful, profitable, and builds a product that people need, then its stock will be valuable in proportion to its success. However, the incentive structure of shadow equity does the opposite. Shadow creates a form of moral hazard in which the insiders to the project, venture investors and founders, are incentivized to make the shadow equity appreciate. At the same time, the public speculators are used as exit liquidity, all while there is little incentive to build any tangible product. With a shadow equity-funded company, the stock is the company's product.

Since the rise of the "web3" marketing campaign, many high-profile venture capital firms, although not all, have engaged in mass securities fraud to juice the returns on their portfolio. Investors' returns on shadow equity are directly offering these investments to the public far faster than any other traditional form of venture investment. A typical web3 company can have a pre-mine sale, raise $50 million, offer the token to the public in a giant marketing push, and watch the price temporarily soar 10-20x in value in a massive pump while insiders take their profits, and before it all collapses down to pennies on the share; and all this before any pretense of a product is even built. Shadow equity is a somewhat pathological form of fundraising that raises serious moral hazard concerns and fundamental questions about reconciling crypto fundraising with the premises of equity completely divorced from capital formation or productive enterprise.

24.2 INDUSTRY LOBBYING EFFORTS

The American political context is fraught with uncertainty and sclerosis. There is a dangerous line of thinking that the United States has entered a new postmodern political era, an era in which the appearance of governing is more potent than actually governing. The SEC's patchwork of the federal government's enforcement of securities law and nonchalant approach to scofflaw fundraising appears to speak to this indictment.

Subversive opportunists have taken the regulatory uncertainty to enrich themselves and commit fraud in broad daylight, not unlike the American gangsters of the 1920s Prohibition Era. For the rest of the law-abiding public, we're simply left extrapolating from tidbits of information about the enforcement of laws that have been on the books for almost a century. The current attitude of federal regulators towards crypto seems to be a combination of wait-and-see and benign neglect, with a view that the crypto bubble is essentially a transient speculative mania and "the fire can be left to burn itself out" without government intervention. However, the public harm and danger of this strategy are immense.

All the while, the cryptocurrency industry has been lobbying lawmakers left and right, attempting to pass beneficial laws which will allow them to circumvent securities laws and create loopholes for them to continue the gravy train perpetuated by open and ubiquitous fraud. The revolving door between government agencies and crypto companies has been prolific in the last few years. Currently, the government risks falling into an irreparable state of regulatory capture where agencies are run by the entities they allegedly regulate.

Much of the crypto lobbyist effort for the last few years has focused on three objectives:

1. Pushing the narrative of not wanting to stifle American innovation by asserting that all new technology is unqualifiedly good and beyond reproach.

2. Offers to politicians to create new crypto jobs for constituents

in jurisdictions with loose regulation.

3.   Funding candidates open to crypto-friendly regulation and putting industry insiders into positions of power in the administration.

24.3 A FRAMEWORK FOR DISCUSSION

Instead, there should be a serious policy debate in Congress about the nature of how cryptoassets can or should fit into public life. Effective lawmaking and general consensus-building must frame this debate around the issues discussed throughout this book, but primarily around five major questions:

1.   How do financial assets with no income and intrinsic value fit into markets?

2.   Are the externalities associated with cryptoassets a net negative or net positive for the world?

3.   How do we reconcile the runaway energy costs associated with Proof of Work mining schemes with our climate goals?

4.   How do we protect the public against crypto investment fraud?

5.   How do we prevent hyper-volatile speculative coins, and cryptoassets subject to extreme run risk, from creating systemic risk in the broader economy?

24.4 REGULATORY APPROACH

Answering these questions will force lawmakers to engage in a level of public debate[1] and education around the abstract nature of market crimes and capitalism, which will be incredibly fraught in this political climate. However, it would be a challenging debate since there are strong libertarian undercurrents in American society that are unfriendly to even the premise of government intervention in markets, both from the technolibertarian side of Silicon Valley and in the ascendant MAGA right-wing nationalist movement. The congressperson who champions this cause will have to bridge the political divide and focus on the underlying problems of financial stability, the efficacy of the dollar as the world reserve currency, and the continued operation of fair, transparent, and efficient capital markets. However positively, these are universal ideals that transcend political boundaries and are essential to every American no matter their affiliation.

To that end, there are three clear actions that the federal government and Congress need to address to curtail the vast amount of crypto fraud running rampant in today's markets. The path forward is threefold:

(1) Regulate cryptoassets as securities and enforce the registration laws.

Cryptoassets are clearly securities contracts. They meet both the legal and practical qualifications for being regulated, just like any other investment contract. To investors, they present with much the same presentation of opportunity: to generate a return based on the efforts of others, but with far more extreme risk. The existing securities framework would vastly mitigate these risks and protect the public from harms that have been well-understood by economists and lawyers for 100 years now.

Crypto exchanges are currently acting as vertically integrated broker-dealers, market makers, and clearing houses which introduces vast conflicts of interest prohibited in every other market that trades in securities. In addition, the capacity to trade against the exchange's own clients and use non-public information in proprietary trades produces a criminogenic environment ripe for fraud. The amount of pump and dumps and market manipulation present in crypto markets is unprecedented and is primarily created and done by exchange operators themselves. Massive amounts of non-public asymmetric information, economic cartels, and manipulation are not conducive to either capital formation or financial stability.

Exchanges that want to do business with Americans should use entities set up on American soil and registered with the SEC. Instead crypto exchanges are attempting to perform *regulatory arbitrage*, using the rules of one jurisdiction to avoid regulation in another. These entities should not be hiding in tax havens using regulatory arbitrage to conceal themselves in jurisdictions with loose financial regulation as they are currently doing. Handling the money on behalf of and safeguarding investments of American citizens must always be done through subordinating corporations to both the judgments of the courts and compliance with the law.

(2) Ban surrogate money schemes derived from sovereign currencies.

As found in many stablecoin projects, surrogate money schemes attempt to create dollar-like products that mimic public money. However, the products are not backed by the full faith and credit of the United States Government, and in many cases not even backed by any hard assets. Stablecoins are subject to extreme risk of runs, much like we saw in bank runs in the Great Depression, an event not seen in the United States in 90 years. There is no reason to return to an era where runs are possible, as the markets already have similar significant risks from money market mutual funds (MMMF), which behave much the same way that stablecoins do and have well-known risks. During the financial crisis and the 2020 coronavirus pandemic, MMMFs required government bailouts. The funds "broke the buck" and required the United States Treasury to guarantee all $3.8 trillion in outstanding MMMF liabilities. These structures are incredibly prone to risk and create a moral hazard if taxpayer bailouts become increasingly common. The creation of stablecoins in almost precisely the same system, but instead backed by even riskier assets like Chinese commercial paper and other cryptoassets, which take the run risk of MMMF and expand it exponentially. Attempting to integrate these stablecoins into the larger economy exponentially broadens the risk of MMMFs to consumers and the economy at large. On top of this, the proliferation of private money simply weakens the dollar's strength both domestically and abroad. Stablecoins are the financial product for which the upside is entirely illusory, and the downsides are catastrophic. The proliferation or integration of stablecoins is not in the interests of the United States from both a financial stability and foreign policy perspectives.

(3) Firewall cryptoassets away from the banking sector and the broader market.

The Glass-Steagal Act, put in place after the Great Depression, set "firewalls" between different divisions of the banks. The separation of the entities' commercial and investment banking divisions and the restrictions on which types of securities they could handle provided an efficient framework for safeguarding the economy in the post-Depression recovery era. In much the same way, the United States banking system needs to be firewalled off from the extreme volatility of cryptoassets. Banks should not handle or custody cryptoassets for their clients, create financial products derived from cryptoassets, and should not have any exposure to cryptoassets at all. This ensures that if/when the crypto market implodes, banks are not taken down by the collapse, thus avoiding the conditions that may lead to another financial crisis.

24.5 COMPLETE BAN

Alternatively, the United States could consider a path similar to what China recently enacted[7] or to the historical American Executive Order 6102, which forbade ownership of gold. Despite the rhetorical claims to "not throw the baby out with the bathwater," there is, after 13 years of crypto, very little evidence that there is any baby at all. Introducing completely non-economic digital speculative "playthings" introduces nothing to an economy other than slightly more exotic gambling games. In fact, there is a strong argument that such activities may come at an enormous opportunity cost, in the capital and talent that get diverted to ever-more extravagant ways to financialize digital nothingness. We can create an entire industry speculating on the volatility of nothingness and turn every fictional thing into a tradable token, but should we?

The only overall outcome of this program is the equivalent of digging digital ditches and filling them up again. Perhaps our society has better things to do than digging deeper and deeper ditches and filling them up again. And quite possibly, the Americans should simply ban crypto and play intellectual catch up with what seems like the rather sensible policy the Chinese have concluded on for the same universal common-sense financial and public harm mitigation reasons.

Conclusion

Crypto is a gripping story full of sound and fury, hope and fear, hype and noise, greed and idealism, yet despite all that, it is a tale signifying nothing in the end. Crypto is not just an experiment in anarcho-capitalism that did not work; it is an experiment that can never work and will never work. Crypto was promised as the technology of the future, yet it is a technology that can never escape its negative externalities or its entanglement with the terrible ideas of the past. Crypto is not the future of finance: it is the past of finance synthesized with the age-old cry of the populist strongman, *To Make Money Great Again*.

Crypto presents a radical revisioning of our financial system[6]. While the ideas of blockchain technology may be new, most of its stated ambitions are not; they are informed by ideas in economics and finance that go back centuries. The world has a storied past of experimentation with private money[4] issuance and soft-touch investment frameworks, and the consequences and lessons of these historical events shape our current laws today. While times may change, human nature and the capacity for fraud[5] and conflicts of interest abound in every business that handles investments; cryptoassets may be new, but the same concerns arise today just as they did during economic crises in the 1800s and the 1920s. We would do well to learn from the manias, panics, and crashes of the past, lest we repeat these very same tragedies with digital assets.

While our existing financial system is undeniably profoundly flawed, not optimally inclusive, and sometimes highly rigged in favor of the already wealthy; crypto offers no solution to its problems other than to create an even worse system subject to unquantifiable software risk, profound conflicts of interest, and an incentives structures that would exasperate wealth inequality to levels not seen since the Dark Ages[10]. Put simply, Wall Street is bad, but crypto is far worse.

Not all innovation is unqualifiedly good[11]; not everything that we can build should be built. The history of finance and software is full of dead ends, false starts, and wrong turns. Today, we face a critical choice concerning the nature of cryptoassets and our financial markets, which will impact our future and our place in the global financial system. Regardless of political affiliation, everyone has the same fundamental needs from our financial system. We all need transparent, inclusive, fair, and efficient markets which serve the public interests and enable real innovation to thrive. At all levels of sophistication and from all walks of life, every type of investor needs to be given truthful, fair, and full information about their investments and protected against fraud and unnecessary risk by our public institutions. Crypto's very design is entirely antithetical to building or improving any of our existing markets and only serves to add more opaqueness[9], systemic risk, and fraud[3,14].

All scientists and engineers are duty-bound to our profession and our communities to ensure that the public good is the central concern during all professional computing work. As a technologist, cryptoassets present our industry with an immense challenge[12,7] and fundamental questions about the nature of responsible innovation. As a profession, every technical artifact we create is imbued with both the capacity for productive use as well as misuse. Inventions have both utility and externalities, and it falls on our shoulders to balance the two to make assessments about their responsible integration into the public sphere to prevent harm[2].

Software engineering is a new discipline, and other fields such as medicine, chemistry, and physics have had to grapple with these hard questions for centuries. However, sometimes a discipline produces an artifact for which the negative externalities so vastly outweigh the potential uses that a fundamental re-analysis must be performed and the debate brought into the public sphere. Some innovations can never escape their negative externalities and must be dealt with on a regulatory level to mitigate their misuse. Crypto assets are a highly controversial technology for their objectively false promises of radical disruption coupled with their immense potential for public harm.

If integrated into the larger financial system, these products present an enormous risk to regulators and everyday investors. It remains an open question what the intrinsic value[8] of such assets is and if a product that can flash crash to zero in mere seconds has any suitable place on either banks' balance sheets or individual investors' retirement accounts. The 2008 subprime mortgage crisis still lingers in the public consciousness, and the lessons of this crisis must inform our experiments at increased financialization.

Despite thirteen years of development, there is widespread debate over the proposed upside of cryptoassets from technical and financial considerations. While the aspirations of technologies may be genuine, the reality of the technology and its applications are vastly overstated and not in line with what is possible. Blockchain-based technologies have severe limitations and design flaws that preclude almost all applications that deal with public customer data and regulated financial transactions. Real-world applications of blockchain technology within financial services are sparse and ambiguous as to whether they are an improvement on existing non-blockchain solutions. Most senior software engineers now strongly reject the entire premise of a blockchain-based financial system because the idea rests on both economic and technical absurdities.

The catastrophes and externalities related to crypto are neither isolated nor are they growing pains of a nascent technology; instead, these are the violent throws of a technology that is not built for its purpose and is forever unsuitable as a foundation for large-scale economic activity. Technologies that serve the public must always have mechanisms for fraud mitigation and allow a human-in-the-loop[1] to reverse transactions. Blockchain technology, the foundation of all cryptoassets, cannot, and will not, have transaction reversal or data privacy mechanisms because they are antithetical to its base design. The software behind crypto is architecturally unsound, and the economics are incoherent.

The theoretical upsides of every crypto project are entirely illusory. It is a solution in search of a problem[13]. Its very foundations are predicated on logical contradictions and architectural flaws that more technology cannot fix and will never be resolved. The impact of crypto's externalities is massive and becomes more pronounced every day it is allowed to continue to exist. Crypto is a project that will always create more net suffering by its very design because its design is antithetical to both the rule of law and the foundations of liberal democracy. Technologists working on cryptoassets and web3 are not building a brighter and more egalitarian future; they are only creating a path back to serfdom, where the landed elite are now tech platforms that control the means of communication, the money supply, and the levers of the state itself.

A tech-led plutocracy is not a future we want to build, and despite the inevitablist rhetoric of its supporters, crypto does not have to be part of our future. Crypto has no physical existence; it is a meme, an idea—and an incoherent one at that—which is no more eternal or permanent than the notion of the divine right of kings to rule once was. Crypto is an idea that is as senseless and ephemeral as every other collective delusion throughout history that has since passed into the intellectual dustbin of history, and this time is not different.

Acknowledgements

Many thanks to all those who helped with editing, citations and research. Adam Wespeiser, Brian Goetz, Ravi Mohan, Neil Turkewitz, James King, Alan Graham, Geoffrey Huntley, Rufus Pollock, Paul Hattori, Grady Booch, and Dave Troy. And to the many other crypto critics who laid the intellectual foundation myself and others to follow.

Bibliography

SOURCES

Chapter 2: Introduction

[1] Stephen Diehl. *The Case Against Crypto*. URL: https://www.stephendiehl.com/blog/against-crypto.html (visited on 02/17/2022).

[2] Anton Klarin. "The decade-long cryptocurrencies and the blockchain roller-coaster: Mapping the intellectual structure and charting future directions". In: *Research in International Business and Finance* 51 (March 2020). ISSN: 02755319. DOI: 10.1016/j.ribaf.2019.101067.

[3] Robert J Shiller. "Narrative economics". In: *American Economic Review* 107.4 (2017), pp. 967–1004.

Chapter 3: History of Crypto

[1] David Chaum. "Blind signature system". In: *Advances in cryptology*. Springer, 1984, pp. 153–153.

[2] Matthew Leising. *Crypto Assets of $50 Billion Moved From China in the Past Year*. Publication Title: Bloomberg. Aug. 2020. URL: http://www.bloomberg.com/news/articles/2020-08-20/crypto-assets-of-50-billion-moved-from-china-in-the-past-year.

[3] Satoshi Nakamoto. *Bitcoin: A peer-to-peer electronic cash system*. Manubot, 2008.

[4]   Nathaniel Popper. *The untold story of bitcoin*. Allen Lane, 2015.

Chapter 4: Historical Market Manias

[1]   Edward J Balleisen. "Fraud: An American History from Barnum to Mad-off". In: *Fraud*. Princeton University Press, 2017.

[2]   Alan S Blinder. *After the music stopped: The financial crisis, the response, and the work ahead*. 79. Penguin Books, 2013.

[3]   Michael Demmler and Amilcar Orlian Fernández Domínguez. "Bitcoin and the South Sea Company: A comparative analysis". In: *Revista Finan-zas y Política Económica* 13.1 (2021). Publisher: Universidad Católica de Colombia, pp. 197–224.

[4]   Gerald P Dwyer. "Wildcat Banking, Banking Panics, and Free Banking in the United States". In: (1996), p. 20.

[5]   David Faber. *And then the roof caved in: How Wall Street's greed and stu-pidity brought capitalism to its knees*. John Wiley & Sons, 2009.

[6]   Inês Faria. "When tales of money fail: the importance of price, trust, and sociality for cryptocurrency users". In: *Journal of Cultural Economy* 0.0 (2021). Publisher: Taylor & Francis, pp. 1–12. ISSN: 17530369. DOI: 10.1080/17530350.2021.1974070. URL: https://doi.org/10.1080/17530350.2021.1974070.

[7]   John Kenneth Galbraith. *A short history of financial euphoria*. Penguin, 1994.

[8]   Brandon L Garrett. "Too big to jail". In: *Too Big to Jail*. Harvard Univer-sity Press, 2014.

[9]   Thomas Gibson. *The Cycles of Speculation*. Moody Corporation, 1907.

[10]   Janet Gleeson. *Millionaire: The Philanderer, Gambler, and Duelist Who Invented Modern Finance*. Simon and Schuster, 2001.

[11]   Gary B. Gorton and Jeffery Zhang. "Taming Wildcat Stablecoins". In: *SSRN Electronic Journal* (2021). DOI: 10.2139/ssrn.3888752.

[12] Michael Hiltzik. *Iron empires: Robber barons, railroads, and the making of modern America.* Houghton Mifflin, 2020.

[13] Robert C Hockett. "Money's Past is Fintech's Future: Wildcat Crypto, the Digital Dollar, and Citizen Central Banking". In: (2019).

[14] Craig Jarvis. *Crypto Wars The Fight for Privacy in the Digital Age: A Political History of Digital Encryption.* CBC PRESS, 2021.

[15] Charles P Kindleberger, Panics Manias, and A Crashes. *History of Financial Crises.* 1996.

[16] Alex Kolchinski. *Crypto is an Unproductive Bubble.* Alex Kolchinski. Mar. 18, 2022. URL: https://alexkolchinski.com/2022/03/18/crypto-is-an-unproductive-bubble/ (visited on 03/19/2022).

[17] Edwin Lefevre. *Reminiscences of a stock operator.* Vol. 175. John Wiley & Sons, 2004.

[18] Thomas Levenson. *Money for Nothing: The South Sea Bubble and the Invention of Modern Capitalism.* Head of Zeus Ltd, 2020.

[19] Hyman P Minsky. "The financial instability hypothesis". In: *In Handbook of Radical Political.* Citeseer, 1993.

[20] Anne L Murphy. *The origins of English financial markets: Investment and speculation before the South Sea Bubble.* Cambridge University Press Cambridge, 2009.

[21] Frank Partnoy. *The match king: Ivar Kreuger, the financial genius behind a century of Wall Street scandals.* PublicAffairs, 2010.

[22] Carlota Perez. *Technological revolutions and financial capital.* Edward Elgar Publishing, 2003.

[23] Jed S Rakoff. "The financial crisis: why have no high-level executives been prosecuted?" In: *The New York Review of Books* 9.2 (2014), p. 7.

[24] Carmen M Reinhart and Kenneth S Rogoff. *This time is different: A panoramic view of eight centuries of financial crises.* National Bureau of Economic Research, 2008.

[25]   Arthur J Rolnick and Warren Weber. "Free banking, wildcat banking, and shinplasters". In: *Quarterly Review* 6 (Fall 1982). Publisher: Federal Reserve Bank of Minneapolis.

[26]   J. Barkley Rosser, Marina V. Rosser, and Mauro Gallegati. "A Minsky-Kindleberger Perspective on the Financial Crisis". In: *Journal of Economic Issues* 46.2 (June 2012), pp. 449–458. ISSN: 0021-3624, 1946-326X. DOI: 10.2753/JEI0021-3624460220. (Visited on 05/17/2022).

[27]   Daniel Sanches. "The Free-Banking Era: A Lesson for Today?" In: (), p. 6.

[28]   Graham Steele. "The Miner of Last Resort: Digital Currency, Shadow Money and the Role of the Central Bank". In: *Technology and Government, Emerald Studies in Media and Communications, Forthcoming* (2021).

[29]   Robin Wigglesworth. "Albanian lessons for regulators nervously eyeing the crypto world". In: *Financial Times* (July 5, 2021). URL: https://www.ft.com/content/810367e5-e0b1-4221-b303-f3012a177437 (visited on 03/02/2022).

[30]   Mitchell Zuckoff. *Ponzi's scheme: The true story of a financial legend.* Random House, 2005.

Chapter 5: Economic Problems

[1]   David Andolfatto. *Economist's View: 'Why Gold and Bitcoin Make Lousy Money'.* URL: https://economistsview.typepad.com/economistsview/2013/04/why-gold-and-bitcoin-make-lousy-money.html (visited on 04/23/2022).

[2]   Bank of International Settlements. "Cryptocurrencies: looking beyond the hype". In: Bank for International Settlements Basel, 2018. URL: https://www.bis.org/publ/arpdf/ar2018e5.htm.

[3]   BankUnderground. *The seven deadly paradoxes of cryptocurrency.* Bank Underground. Nov. 13, 2018. URL: https://bankunderground.co.uk/2018/11/13/the-seven-deadly-paradoxes-of-cryptocurrency/ (visited on 04/30/2022).

[4] Ben Bemanke and Harold James. "The Gold Standard, Deflation, and Financial Crisis in the Great Depression: An International Comparison". In: *Financial Markets and Financial Crises*. University of Chicago Press, Jan. 1991, pp. 33–68. (Visited on 03/14/2022).

[5] Eric Budish. *The economic limits of bitcoin and the blockchain*. National Bureau of Economic Research, 2018.

[6] Paul Davidson. *Is bitcoin 'money'? The Post Keynesian view*. URL: https://rwer.wordpress.com/2013/11/27/14335/ (visited on 04/23/2022).

[7] Chris Dillow. *The Bitcoin paradox*. (Visited on 04/27/2022).

[8] Stefan Eich. "The currency of politics". In: *The political theory of money from Aristotle to Keynes* (2018).

[9] Paul Einzig. *Primitive money: In its ethnological, historical and economic aspects*. Elsevier, 2014.

[10] Garrick Hileman. "Alternative Currencies: A Historical Survey and Taxonomy". ISSN: 1556-5068 Publication Title: SSRN Electronic Journal. 2017.

[11] Franz J Hinzen, Kose John, and Fahad Saleh. "Proof-of-work's limited adoption problem". In: *NYU Stern School of Business* (2019).

[12] Mrinalini Krishna. *When FDR Abandoned the Gold Standard*. Investopedia. Apr. 20, 2017. URL: https://www.investopedia.com/news/when-fdr-abandoned-gold-standard/ (visited on 03/07/2022).

[13] Louis Larue. ""A conceptual framework for classifying currencies"." In: *International Journal of Community Currency Research* 24.1 (2020), pp. 45–60. ISSN: 00487112.

[14] Louis Larue. "The case against alternative currencies". In: *Politics, Philosophy & Economics* 0.0 (), p. 1470594X211065784.

[15] Igor Makarov and Antoinette Schoar. "Trading and arbitrage in cryptocurrency markets". In: *Journal of Financial Economics* 135.2 (2020). Publisher: Elsevier, pp. 293–319.

[16]   Dan McCrum. "Bitcoin's place in the long history of pyramid schemes". In: *Financial Times* (Nov. 10, 2015). URL: https : / / www . ft . com / content / 1877c388 - 8797 - 11e5 - 90de - f44762bf9896 (visited on 05/04/2022).

[17]   Michael McLeay, Amar Radia, and Ryland Thomas. "Money creation in the modern economy". In: *Bank of England Quarterly Bulletin* (2014), Q1.

[18]   Michael McLeay, Amar Radia, and Ryland Thomas. "Money in the modern economy: an introduction". In: *Bank of England Quarterly Bulletin* (2014), Q1.

[19]   Cullen O Roche. "Understanding the Modern Monetary System". In: (2011). URL: http://ssrn.com/paper=1905625.

[20]   Nouriel Roubini. "The Great Crypto Heist". In: *Project Syndicate* 16 (2019).

[21]   Christopher Shea. "Survey: No Support for Gold Standard Among Top Economists". In: *Wall Street Journal* (Jan. 23, 2012). ISSN: 0099-9660. URL: https : / / www . wsj . com / articles / BL - IMB - 3067 (visited on 04/27/2022).

[22]   Shane Shifflett and Paul Vigna. "Some traders are talking up cryptocurrencies, then dumping them, costing others millions". In: *The Wall Street Journal* (2018).

[23]   Thomas S Umlauft. "Is Bitcoin Money? An Economic-Historical Analysis of Money, Its Functions and Its Prerequisites". In: Discussion paper prepared for the "Prices, Business Fluctuations and Cycles ...", 2018.

[24]   Yanis Varoufakis. *Yanis Varoufakis on Crypto & the Left, and Techno-Feudalism.* Jan. 26, 2022. URL: https : / / the - crypto - syllabus . com / yanis - varoufakis-on-techno-feudalism/ (visited on 04/05/2022).

Chapter 6: Technical Problems

[1]   Stephen Diehl. *The Handwavy Technobabble Nothingburger.* Nov. 24, 2021. URL: https://www.stephendiehl.com/blog/nothing-burger.html (visited on 02/25/2022).

[2]   Sabine Dörry, Gary Robinson, and Ben Derudder. "There is no Alternative: SWIFT as Infrastructure Intermediary in Global Financial Markets". In: *Financial Geography Working Paper Series* (December 2018). ISBN: 22.

[3]   Frida Erlandsson and Gabriela Guibourg. "Times are changing and so are payment patterns". In: *Economic Commentaries* 6 (2018).

[4]   Brian P. Hanley. "The False Premises and Promises of Bitcoin". In: (July 4, 2018). arXiv: 1312.2048. URL: http://arxiv.org/abs/1312.2048 (visited on 03/21/2022).

[5]   Jona Harris and Aviv Zohar. "Flood & Loot: A Systemic Attack On The Lightning Network". In: *arXiv preprint arXiv:2006.08513* (2020).

[6]   Franz J Hinzen, Kose John, and Fahad Saleh. "Proof-of-work's limited adoption problem". In: *NYU Stern School of Business* (2019).

[7]   Lily Katz. "Bitcoin Acceptance Among Retailers Is Low and Getting Lower". In: *Bloomberg.com* (July 2017). Publisher: Bloomberg. URL: https://www.bloomberg.com/news/articles/2017-07-12/bitcoin-acceptance-among-retailers-is-low-and-getting-lower.

[8]   Olga Kharif. "Bitcoin's rally masks an uncomfortable fact: almost nobody uses it". In: *Bloomberg.com* (May 2019). Publisher: Bloomberg. URL: https://www.bloomberg.com/news/articles/2019-05-31/bitcoin-s-rally-masks-uncomfortable-fact-almost-nobody-uses-it.

[9]   Roman Matzutt et al. "A quantitative analysis of the impact of arbitrary blockchain content on bitcoin". In: *International Conference on Financial Cryptography and Data Security*. Springer, 2018, pp. 420–438.

[10]   David Rosenthal. *Economies of Scale in Peer-to-Peer Networks*. DSHR's Blog. Oct. 7, 2014. URL: https://blog.dshr.org/2014/10/economies-of-scale-in-peer-to-peer.html (visited on 02/25/2022).

[11]   David Rosenthal. *EE380 Talk (Can We Mitigate Cryptocurrencies' Externalities?)* DSHR's Blog. Feb. 9, 2022. URL: https://blog.dshr.org/2022/02/ee380-talk.html (visited on 02/25/2022).

[12] David Rosenthal. *Ethereum Has Issues*. URL: https://blog.dshr.org/2022/04/ethereum-has-issues.html (visited on 04/15/2022).

[13] David Rosenthal. *Stanford Lecture on Cryptocurrency*. URL: https://blog.dshr.org/2022/02/ee380-talk.html (visited on 03/02/2022).

[14] Nicholas Weaver. "Risks of cryptocurrencies". In: *Communications of the ACM* 61.6 (2018). Publisher: ACM New York, NY, USA, pp. 20–24.

[15] Molly White. *Abuse and Harassment on the Blockchain*. Molly White. Jan. 22, 2022. URL: https://blog.mollywhite.net/abuse-and-harassment-on-the-blockchain/ (visited on 02/25/2022).

[16] Molly White. *Anonymous Cryptocurrency Wallets Are Not So Simple*. Molly White. Feb. 12, 2022. URL: https://blog.mollywhite.net/anonymous-crypto-wallets/ (visited on 02/25/2022).

Chapter 7: Valuation Problems

[1] Olivier J Blanchard and Mark W Watson. "Bubbles, rational expectations and financial markets". In: *NBER working paper* (w0945 1982).

[2] Gary Silverman. "Crypto Has 'No Inherent Worth' But Is Good to Trade, Says Man Group Chief". In: *Financial Times* (July 26, 2021). URL: https://www.ft.com/content/9275baf4-0422-43a1-b8c9-9317882ca874 (visited on 02/18/2022).

[3] Nassim Nicholas Taleb. "Bitcoin, Currencies, and Fragility". In: (July 4, 2021). arXiv: 2106.14204. URL: http://arxiv.org/abs/2106.14204 (visited on 02/25/2022).

Chapter 8: Environmental Problems

[1] Matteo Benetton, Giovanni Compiani, and Adair Morse. "When Cryptomining Comes to Town: High Electricity-Use Spillovers to the Local Economy". In: *SSRN Electronic Journal* (2021). DOI: 10.2139/ssrn.3779720.

[2]   B. Dindar and Ö. Gül. "The detection of illicit cryptocurrency mining farms with innovative approaches for the prevention of electricity theft". In: *Energy & Environment* (April 2021). Publisher: SAGE Publications Sage UK: London, England, p. 0958305X211045066. ISSN: 0958-305X. DOI: 10.1177/0958305x211045066.

[3]   Ulrich Gallersdörfer et al. "Energy Consumption of Cryptocurrencies Beyond Bitcoin". In: *Joule* 4.2018 (Sept. 2020). Publisher: Cell Press, pp. 2018–2021. ISSN: 2542-4351. DOI: 10.1016/j.joule.2020.07.013.

[4]   David Gerard. *Attack of the 50 foot blockchain: Bitcoin, blockchain, Ethereum & smart contracts.* David Gerard, 2017.

[5]   Andrew L. Goodkind, Benjamin A. Jones, and Robert P. Berrens. "Cryptodamages: Monetary value estimates of the air pollution and human health impacts of cryptocurrency mining". In: *Energy Research and Social Science* 59 (March 2019 2020). Publisher: Elsevier, p. 101281. ISSN: 22146296. DOI: 10.1016/j.erss.2019.101281. URL: https://doi.org/10.1016/j.erss.2019.101281.

[6]   Peter Howson. "Climate Crises and Crypto-Colonialism: Conjuring Value on the Blockchain Frontiers of the Global South". In: *Frontiers in Blockchain* 3 (May 2020). DOI: 10.3389/fbloc.2020.00022.

[7]   Rabin K. Jana et al. "Determinants of electronic waste generation in Bitcoin network: Evidence from the machine learning approach". In: *Technological Forecasting and Social Change* 173 (2021). ISSN: 00401625. DOI: 10.1016/j.techfore.2021.121101.

[8]   "Key World Energy Statistics 2019". In: Backup Publisher: IEA Paris, France. International Energy Agency, 2019.

[9]   Sinan Küfeoğlu and Mahmut Özkuran. "Bitcoin mining: A global review of energy and power demand". In: *Energy Research and Social Science* 58 (2019). Publisher: Elsevier, p. 101273. ISSN: 22146296. DOI: 10.1016/j.erss.2019.101273.

[10] Camilo Mora et al. "Bitcoin emissions alone could push global warming above 2 C". In: *Nature Climate Change* 8.11 (2018). Publisher: Nature Publishing Group, pp. 931–933.

[11] Mark Peplow. *Bitcoin poses major electronic-waste problem*. Publication Title: Chemical & Engineering News. Mar. 2019.

[12] Christian Stoll, Lena Klaaßen, and Ulrich Gallersdörfer. "The Carbon Footprint of Bitcoin". In: *Joule* 3.7 (2019), pp. 1647–1661. ISSN: 25424351. DOI: 10.1016/j.joule.2019.05.012.

[13] Paul Vigna. "Most bitcoin trading faked by unregulated exchanges, study finds". In: *Wall Street Journal* (2019).

[14] Alex de Vries. "Bitcoin's energy consumption is underestimated: A market dynamics approach". In: *Energy Research & Social Science* 70 (2020). Publisher: Elsevier, p. 101721.

[15] Alex de Vries. "Renewable energy will not solve bitcoin's sustainability problem". In: *Joule* 3.4 (2019). Publisher: Elsevier, pp. 893–898.

[16] Alex de Vries and Christian Stoll. "Bitcoin's growing e-waste problem". In: *Resources, Conservation and Recycling* 175 (September 2021). Publisher: Elsevier B.V., p. 105901. ISSN: 18790658. DOI: 10.1016/j.resconrec.2021.105901. URL: https://doi.org/10.1016/j.resconrec.2021.105901.

[17] Nicholas Weaver. *Blockchains and Cryptocurrencies: Burn It With Fire*. Apr. 20, 2018. URL: https://www.youtube.com/watch?v=xCHab0dNnj4 (visited on 02/25/2022).

Chapter 9: Cryptocurrency Culture

[1] Fiona Allon. "Money after Blockchain: Gold, Decentralised Politics and the New Libertarianism". In: *Australian Feminist Studies* 33.96 (2018). Publisher: Taylor & Francis, pp. 223–243. ISSN: 14653303.

[2] Patrick D. Anderson. "Privacy for the weak, transparency for the powerful: the cypherpunk ethics of Julian Assange". In: *Ethics and Information Technology* 23.3 (2021). Publisher: Springer, pp. 295–308. ISSN: 15728439. DOI: 10.1007/s10676-020-09571-x.

[3] Hannah Arendt. *What is Freedom? Between Past and Future: Eight exercises in political thought*. 1993.

[4] Julian Assange et al. *Cypherpunks: Freedom and the Future of the Internet.* OR books, 2016.

[5] Andrew M. Bailey, Bradley Rettler, and Craig Warmke. "Philosophy, politics, and economics of cryptocurrency I: Money without state". In: *Philosophy Compass* 16.11 (2021), pp. 1–15. ISSN: 17479991. DOI: 10.1111/phc3.12785.

[6] Andrew M. Bailey, Bradley Rettler, and Craig Warmke. "Philosophy, politics, and economics of cryptocurrency II: The moral landscape of monetary design". In: *Philosophy Compass* 16.11 (2021), pp. 1–15. ISSN: 17479991. DOI: 10.1111/phc3.12784.

[7] Tom Barbereau et al. "Decentralised Finance's Unregulated Governance: Minority Rule in the Digital Wild West". In: *Available at SSRN* (2022). DOI: https://papers.ssrn.com/sol3/papers.cfm?abstract_id=4001891.

[8] John Perry Barlow. "A Declaration of the Independence of Cyberspace". In: *Duke Law & Technology Review* 18.1 (2019), pp. 5–7.

[9] Jamie Bartlett. "Forget far-right populism – crypto-anarchists are the new masters". In: *The Observer* (June 4, 2017). ISSN: 0029-7712. URL: https://www.theguardian.com/technology/2017/jun/04/forget-far-right-populism-crypto-anarchists-are-the-new-masters-internet-politics (visited on 04/28/2022).

[10] Matthew Bellinger. "The Rhetoric of Bitcoin: Money, Politics, and the Construction of Blockchain Communities". ISBN: 978-0-438-86971-4 Publication Title: ResearchWorks Archive. PhD thesis. 2018. 223 pp. DOI: https://digital.lib.washington.edu/researchworks/handle/1773/43342. URL: https://digital.lib.washington.edu/researchworks/handle/1773/43342.

[11] Enrico Beltramini. "Against technocratic authoritarianism. A short intellectual history of the cypherpunk movement". In: *Internet Histories* 5.2 (2021). Publisher: Taylor & Francis, pp. 101–118. ISSN: 24701483. DOI: 10.1080/24701475.2020.1731249.

[12] Enrico Beltramini. "The Cryptoanarchist Character of Bitcoin's Digital Governance". In: *Anarchist Studies* 29.2 (2021). Publisher: Lawrence and Wishart, pp. 75–99. DOI: 10.3898/AS.29.2.03.

[13] Ben S. Bernanke. *Essays on the Great Depression*. Princeton University Press, 2004.

[14] Ian Bogost. "Cryptocurrency might be a path to authoritarianism". In: *The Atlantic* 30 (2017).

[15] Laizeau T Boon-Falleur M. "Trustless libertarians ? Attitudes about trust, politics, science and the environment in the blockchain community". 2021. URL: https://psyarxiv.com/ka7st.

[16] Ann Brody and Stéphane Couture. "Ideologies and Imaginaries in Blockchain Communities: The Case of Ethereum". In: *Canadian Journal of Communication* 46.3 (2021). ISSN: 0705-3657. DOI: 10.22230/cjc.2021v46n3a3701.

[17] Maja Hojer Bruun, Astrid Oberborbeck Andersen, and Adrienne Mannov. "Infrastructures of trust and distrust: The politics and ethics of emerging cryptographic technologies". In: *Anthropology Today* 36.2 (2020). Publisher: Wiley Online Library, pp. 13–17. ISSN: 14678322. DOI: 10.1111/1467-8322.12562.

[18] Giorel Curran and Morgan Gibson. "WikiLeaks, Anarchism and Technologies of Dissent". In: *Antipode* 45.2 (2013). Publisher: Wiley Online Library, pp. 294–314. ISSN: 00664812. DOI: 10.1111/j.1467-8330.2012.01009.x.

[19] Stefan Eich. "Old Utopias, New Tax Havens: The Politics of Bitcoin in Historical Perspective". In: *Regulating Blockchain: Techno-Social and Legal Challenges* (2019). ISBN: 978-0-19-187820-6, pp. 85–98. URL: https://www.oxfordscholarship.com/view/10.1093/oso/9780198842187.001.0001/oso-9780198842187-chapter-5.

[20] Inês Faria. "Trust, reputation and ambiguous freedoms: financial institutions and subversive libertarians navigating blockchain, markets, and regulation". In: *Journal of Cultural Economy* 12.2 (2019). Publisher: Taylor & Francis, pp. 119–132. ISSN: 17530369. DOI: 10.1080/17530350.2018.1547986. URL: https://doi.org/10.1080/17530350.2018.1547986.

[21] Sandra Faustino. "How metaphors matter: an ethnography of blockchain-based re-descriptions of the world". In: *Journal of Cultural Economy* 12.6 (2019). Publisher: Taylor & Francis, pp. 478–490. ISSN: 17530369. DOI: 10.1080/17530350.2019.1629330.

[22] Justin Fletcher. "Currency in Transition: An Ethnographic Inquiry of Bitcoin Adherents". In: (2013). DOI: https://stars.library.ucf.edu/etd/2748/.

[23] Helmut Frisch. *Theories of inflation*. Cambridge University Press, 1983.

[24] David Golumbia. "Bitcoin as politics: Distributed right-wing extremism". In: *MoneyLab Reader: An Intervention in Digital Economy, Amsterdam: Institute of Network Cultures* (2015).

[25] David Golumbia. "Cyberlibertarianism: The extremist foundations of 'digital freedom.'" In: *Clemson University Department of English* (2013).

[26] David Golumbia. "Cyberlibertarians' Digital Deletion of the Left: Technological Innovation Does Not Inherently Promote the Left's Goals". In: *Retrieved* 2.10 (2013), p. 2014.

[27] David Golumbia. *The Politics of Bitcoin: Software as Right-wing Extremism*. University of Minnesota Press, 2016.

[28] Andy Greenberg. *This Machine Kills Secrets: Julian Assange, the Cypherpunks, and Their Fight to Empower Whistleblowers*. Penguin Randon House, 2012. DOI: https://www.penguinrandomhouse.com/books/309904/this-machine-kills-secrets-by-andy-greenberg/. URL: https://www.penguinrandomhouse.com/books/309904/this-machine-kills-secrets-by-andy-greenberg/.

[29] Keith Hart. "Money from a cultural point of view". In: *HAU: Journal of Ethnographic Theory* 5.2 (2015). Publisher: University of Chicago Press, pp. 411–416.

[30] John Harvey and Ines Branco-Illodo. "Why Cryptocurrencies Want Privacy: A Review of Political Motivations and Branding Expressed in "Privacy Coin" Whitepapers". In: *Journal of Political Marketing* 19.1 (2020). Publisher: Taylor & Francis, pp. 107–136. ISSN: 15377865. DOI: 10.1080/15377857.2019.1652223.

[31]   Z. Isadora Hellegren. "A history of crypto-discourse: encryption as a site of struggles to define internet freedom". In: *Internet Histories* 1.4 (2017). Publisher: Taylor & Francis, pp. 285–311. ISSN: 24701483. DOI: 10.1080/24701475.2017.1387466.

[32]   Syed Omer Husain, Alex Franklin, and Dirk Roep. "The political imaginaries of blockchain projects: discerning the expressions of an emerging ecosystem". In: *Sustainability Science* 15.2 (2020). ISBN: 1162502000786, pp. 379–394. ISSN: 18624057. DOI: 10.1007/s11625-020-00786-x.

[33]   Syed Omer Hussain. "Prefigurative Post-Politics as Strategy: The Case of Government-Led Blockchain Projects". In: *The Journal of The British Blockchain Association* 3.1 (2020). Publisher: The British Blockchain Association, pp. 1–11. ISSN: 25163949. DOI: 10.31585/jbba-3-1-(2)2020.

[34]   Sarah Jeong. "The Bitcoin protocol as law, and the politics of a stateless currency". In: *Available at SSRN 2294124* (2013).

[35]   Artyom Kosmarski and Nikolay Gordiychuk. *Anthropology and blockchain.* ISSN: 14678322 Issue: 6 Pages: 1–3 Publication Title: Anthropology Today Volume: 37. 2021. DOI: 10.1111/1467-8322.12683.

[36]   Paul Krugman. "Bitcoin is basically a Ponzi scheme". In: *The Seattle Times* 30 (2018). URL: https://www.seattletimes.com/opinion/bitcoin-is-basically-a-ponzi-scheme/.

[37]   Paul Krugman. "Technobabble, Libertarian Derp and Bitcoin". In: *The New York Times* 21 (2021). URL: https://www.nytimes.com/2021/05/20/opinion/cryptocurrency-bitcoin.html.

[38]   Paul Krugman. "The Brutal Truth About Bitcoin". In: *The New York Times* 21 (2021).

[39]   Christopher J Lawrence and Stephanie Lee Mudge. "Movement to market, currency to property: the rise and fall of Bitcoin as an anti-state movement, 2009–2014". In: *Socio-Economic Review* 17.1 (2019). Publisher: Oxford University Press, pp. 109–134.

[40]   Tim May. *Cyphernomicon.* 1994.

[41] Timothy May. "The crypto anarchist manifesto". In: *High Noon on the Electronic Frontier: Conceptual Issues in Cyberspace* (1992). Publisher: MIT Press Cambridge, MA.

[42] Michael McLeay, Amar Radia, and Ryland Thomas. "Money creation in the modern economy". In: *Bank of England Quarterly Bulletin* (2014), Q1.

[43] Arvind Narayanan. "What happened to the crypto dream?, part 1". In: *IEEE security & privacy* 11.2 (2013). Publisher: IEEE, pp. 75–76.

[44] "Perspective | Bitcoin is teaching libertarians everything they don't know about economics". In: *Washington Post* (). ISSN: 0190-8286. URL: https://www.washingtonpost.com/news/wonk/wp/2018/01/08/bitcoin-is-the-new-middle-ages/ (visited on 03/03/2022).

[45] Tom Redshaw. "Bitcoin beyond ambivalence: Popular rationalization and Feenberg's technical politics". In: *Thesis Eleven* 138.1 (2017). Publisher: SAGE Publications Sage UK: London, England, pp. 46–64. ISSN: 14617455. DOI: 10.1177/0725513616689390.

[46] Wessel Reijers and Mark Coeckelbergh. "The Blockchain as a Narrative Technology: Investigating the Social Ontology and Normative Configurations of Cryptocurrencies". In: *Philosophy and Technology* 31.1 (2018). Publisher: Philosophy & Technology, pp. 103–130. ISSN: 22105441. DOI: 10.1007/s13347-016-0239-x.

[47] Wessel Reijers, Fiachra O'Brolcháin, and Paul Haynes. "Governance in Blockchain Technologies & Social Contract Theories". In: *Ledger* 1 (2016), pp. 134–151. ISSN: 2379-5980. DOI: 10.5195/ledger.2016.62.

[48] Cullen O Roche. "Understanding the Modern Monetary System". In: (2011). URL: http://ssrn.com/paper=1905625.

[49] David Sanz Bas. "Hayek and the cryptocurrency revolution". In: *Iberian Journal of the History of Economic Thought* 7.1 (2020), pp. 15–28. ISSN: 2386-5768. DOI: 10.5209/ijhe.69403.

[50] Christopher Shea. "Survey: No Support for Gold Standard Among Top Economists". In: *Wall Street Journal* (Jan. 23, 2012). ISSN: 0099-9660. URL: https://www.wsj.com/articles/BL-IMB-3067 (visited on 04/27/2022).

[51] Matthew A. Zook and Joe Blankenship. "New spaces of disruption? The failures of Bitcoin and the rhetorical power of algorithmic governance". In: *Geoforum* 96 (August 2018). Publisher: Elsevier, pp. 248–255. ISSN: 00167185. DOI: 10.1016/j.geoforum.2018.08.023. URL: https://doi.org/10.1016/j.geoforum.2018.08.023.

Chapter 10: Ethical Problems

[1] Claer Barrett. "Why young investors bet the farm on cryptocurrencies". In: *Financial Times* (May 28, 2021). URL: https://www.ft.com/content/162839aa-0437-478b-a4d4-4a8d7ab71458 (visited on 02/18/2022).

[2] Massimo Bartoletti et al. "Dissecting Ponzi schemes on Ethereum: identification, analysis, and impact". In: *Future Generation Computer Systems* 102 (2020). Publisher: Elsevier, pp. 259–277.

[3] Nellie Bowles. "Everyone Is Getting Hilariously Rich and You're Not". In: *New York Times* (2018).

[4] Shaen Corbet et al. "The destabilising effects of cryptocurrency cybercriminality". In: *Economics Letters* 191 (2020). Publisher: Elsevier, p. 108741.

[5] Nigel Dodd. "The social life of Bitcoin". In: *Theory, culture & society* 35.3 (2018). Publisher: Sage Publications Sage UK: London, England, pp. 35–56.

[6] Rachel Ehrenfeld. *Evil Money: Encounters along the money trail.* SP Books, 1994.

[7] Yaya Fanusie and Tom Robinson. "Bitcoin laundering: an analysis of illicit flows into digital currency services". In: *Center on Sanctions and Illicit Finance memorandum, January* (2018).

[8] Matthew Field. *The weird world of Bitcoin 'whales': The 2,500 people that control 40pc of the market.* The Telegraph. Jan. 22, 2022. URL: https://www.telegraph.co.uk/technology/2021/01/22/weird-world-bitcoin-whales-2500-people-control-40pc-market/ (visited on 05/09/2022).

[9]   Financial Conduct Authority. *Guidance on Cryptoassets*. Financial Conduct Authority, 2019. URL: https://www.fca.org.uk/publication/consultation/cp19-03.pdf#page=11.

[10]   Emily Fletcher, Charles Larkin, and Shaen Corbet. "Countering money laundering and terrorist financing: A case for bitcoin regulation". In: *Research in International Business and Finance* 56 (January 2021). Publisher: Elsevier B.V., p. 101387. ISSN: 02755319. DOI: 10.1016/j.ribaf.2021.101387. URL: https://doi.org/10.1016/j.ribaf.2021.101387.

[11]   Sean Foley, Jonathan R Karlsen, and Tālis J Putniņš. "Sex, drugs, and bitcoin: How much illegal activity is financed through cryptocurrencies?" In: *The Review of Financial Studies* 32.5 (2019). Publisher: Oxford University Press, pp. 1798–1853.

[12]   John Fry and Eng-Tuck Cheah. "Negative bubbles and shocks in cryptocurrency markets". In: *International Review of Financial Analysis* 47 (2016). Publisher: Elsevier, pp. 343–352.

[13]   David Gerard. *Attack of the 50 foot blockchain: Bitcoin, blockchain, Ethereum & smart contracts*. David Gerard, 2017.

[14]   Peter Howson and Alex de Vries. "Preying on the poor? Opportunities and challenges for tackling the social and environmental threats of cryptocurrencies for vulnerable and low-income communities". In: *Energy Research and Social Science* 84 (xxxx 2022), p. 102394. ISSN: 22146296. DOI: 10.1016/j.erss.2021.102394.

[15]   Syed Omer Husain, Alex Franklin, and Dirk Roep. "The political imaginaries of blockchain projects: discerning the expressions of an emerging ecosystem". In: *Sustainability Science* 15.2 (2020). ISBN: 1162502000786, pp. 379–394. ISSN: 18624057. DOI: 10.1007/s11625-020-00786-x.

[16]   Viktoria Ivaniuk. "Cryptocurrency Exchange Regulation – An International Review". In: *Magda Dziembowska, Robert Dziembowski, Apelacja w postępowaniu* (2020), p. 67.

Bibliography

[17] Izabella Kaminska. "Mavrodi's MMM Global pyramid scheme collapses, unsurprisingly". In: *Financial Times* (Apr. 11, 2016). URL: https://www.ft.com/content/8499c0a3-8367-30c4-9e07-3e5689cd584e (visited on 05/04/2022).

[18] Florian Knauer and Andreas Mann. "What is in It for Me? Identifying Drivers of Blockchain Acceptance among German Consumers". In: *The Journal of the British Blockchain Association* (2019). Publisher: The British Blockchain Association, p. 10484.

[19] Dániel Kondor et al. "Do the rich get richer? An empirical analysis of the Bitcoin transaction network". In: *PloS one* 9.2 (2014). Publisher: Public Library of Science, e86197.

[20] J.P. Koning. *Bitcoin Financial Literacy and Crypto-Twitter*. Publication Title: American Institute for Economic Research. Sept. 2020. URL: https://www.aier.org/article/bitcoin-financial-literacy-and-crypto-twitter/.

[21] Paul Langley. "Assets and assetization in financialized capitalism". In: *Review of International Political Economy* 28.2 (2020). Publisher: Routledge, pp. 382–393. ISSN: 14664526. DOI: 10.1080/09692290.2020.1830828. URL: https://doi.org/10.1080/09692290.2020.1830828.

[22] Seung Cheol Lee. "Magical capitalism, gambler subjects: South Korea's bitcoin investment frenzy". In: *Cultural Studies* 0.0 (2020). Publisher: Taylor & Francis, pp. 1–24. ISSN: 14664348. DOI: 10.1080/09502386.2020.1788620. URL: https://doi.org/10.1080/09502386.2020.1788620.

[23] A Moiseienko and O Kraft. *From Money Mules to Chain-Hopping: Targeting the Finances of Cybercrime*. 2018.

[24] Mike Orcutt. *This is how North Korea uses cutting-edge crypto money laundering to steal millions*. Publication Title: MIT Technology Review. Apr. 2020. URL: http://www.technologyreview.com/2020/03/05/916688/north-korean-hackers-cryptocurrency-money-laundering/.

[25] Luke Ottenhof. "Crypto-colonialists use the most vulnerable people in the world as guinea pigs". In: *VICE Media* (2021).

[26] Georgios A Panos and Tatja Karkkainen. "Financial Literacy and Attitudes to Cryptocurrencies". In: *Available at SSRN 3482083* (2019).

[27] Nathaniel Popper. "Terrorists Turn to Bitcoin for Funding, and They're Learning Fast". In: *The New York Times* (2019), pp. 92–4.

[28] Elizabeth M. Renieris. *Why a Little-Known Blockchain-Based Identity Project in Ethiopia Should Concern Us All.* Centre for International Governance Innovation. URL: https://www.cigionline.org/articles/why-a-little-known-blockchain-based-identity-project-in-ethiopia-should-concern-us-all/ (visited on 02/22/2022).

[29] Justin Scheck and Shane Shifflett. "How dirty money disappears into the black hole of cryptocurrency". In: *Wall Street Journal* 28 (2018).

[30] Ruchira Sharma. *'Crypto Ruined My Life': The Mental Health Crisis Hitting Bitcoin Investors.* Vice. Feb. 16, 2022. URL: https://www.vice.com/en/article/akvn8z/crypto-bad-for-mental-health (visited on 02/23/2022).

[31] Steve Stecklow et al. "Chaos and hackers stalk investors on cryptocurrency exchanges". In: *Reuters, September* 29 (2017).

[32] "Virtual Assets and Virtual Asset Service Providers". In: (2019). Publisher: Financial Action Task Force. URL: https://www.fatf-gafi.org/media/fatf/documents/recommendations/RBA-VA-VASPs.pdf.

[33] Nicholas Weaver. "Risks of cryptocurrencies". In: *Communications of the ACM* 61.6 (2018). Publisher: ACM New York, NY, USA, pp. 20–24.

[34] Langdon Winner. "Do Artifacts Have Politics?" In: *Daedalus* 109.1 (1980). Publisher: The MIT Press, pp. 121–136. ISSN: 0011-5266. URL: https://www.jstor.org/stable/20024652 (visited on 04/25/2022).

[35] Pengcheng Xia et al. "Don't Fish in Troubled Waters! Characterizing Coronavirus themed Cryptocurrency Scams". In: *arXiv preprint arXiv:2007.13639* (2020).

Bibliography

Chapter 11: The Cult of Crypto

[1] William J Bernstein. *The Delusions of Crowds: Why People Go Mad in Groups*. Grove Press, 2021.

[2] Balázs Bodó. "Mediated trust: A theoretical framework to address the trustworthiness of technological trust mediators". In: *New Media and Society* 23.9 (2021). Publisher: SAGE Publications Sage UK: London, England, pp. 2668–2690. ISSN: 14617315. DOI: 10.1177/1461444820939922.

[3] Sandra Faustino, Inês Faria, and Rafael Marques. "The myths and legends of king Satoshi and the knights of blockchain". In: *Journal of Cultural Economy* 0.0 (2021). Publisher: Taylor & Francis, pp. 1–14. ISSN: 17530369. DOI: 10.1080/17530350.2021.1921830. URL: https://doi.org/10.1080/17530350.2021.1921830.

[4] Lorenzo Franceschi-Bicchierai, Jordan Pearson, and Jason Koebler. *Leaked 'Shill Price List' Shows Wild World of Crypto Promos*. Vice. Apr. 18, 2022. URL: https://www.vice.com/en/article/pkp9wg/leaked-shill-price-list-shows-wild-world-of-crypto-promos (visited on 04/25/2022).

[5] Mark Glongloff. *Bitcoin, GameStop Are More Cults Than Investments*. URL: https://www.bloomberg.com/opinion/articles/2021-03-02/bitcoin-btc-gamestop-gme-are-more-cults-than-investments (visited on 03/02/2022).

[6] David Golumbia. "Cyberlibertarians' Digital Deletion of the Left: Technological Innovation Does Not Inherently Promote the Left's Goals". In: *Retrieved* 2.10 (2013), p. 2014.

[7] David Golumbia. "Zealots of the blockchain: The true believers of the Bitcoin cult". In: *The Baffler* 38 (2018). Publisher: JSTOR, pp. 102–111.

[8] Rath Johanna. "Substituting trust by technology: A comparative study". ISSN: 00029211 Publication Title: ICAE Working Paper Series, No. 107 Provided. 2020. URL: https://www.econstor.eu/handle/10419/216850.

[9] Amanda Montell. *Cultish*. HarperAudio, 2021.

[10]   Laurie Penny. *Four Days Trapped at Sea With Crypto's Nouveau Riche*. Publication Title: BREAKERMAG. Dec. 2018. URL: https://breakermag. com/trapped-at-sea-with-cryptos-nouveau-riche/.

[11]   Jamie Powell. "Crypto-shills". In: *Financial Times* (2019). URL: https: //ftalphaville.ft.com/2018/11/29/1543469404000/Crypto- shills/.

[12]   Yanis Varoufakis. *Yanis Varoufakis on Crypto & the Left, and Techno-Feudalism*. Jan. 26, 2022. URL: https://the-crypto-syllabus.com/yanis- varoufakis-on-techno-feudalism/ (visited on 04/05/2022).

[13]   Siddharth Venkataramakrishnan and Robin Wigglesworth. "Inside the cult of crypto". In: *Financial Times* (Sept. 10, 2021). URL: https://www. ft.com/content/9e787670-6aa7-4479-934f-f4a9fedf4829 (visited on 03/04/2022).

[14]   Gili Vidan and Vili Lehdonvirta. "Mine the gap: Bitcoin and the maintenance of trustlessness". In: *New Media and Society* 21.1 (2019), pp. 42–59. ISSN: 14617315. DOI: 10.1177/1461444818786220.

[15]   Joe Weisenthal. *Bitcoin Is a Faith-Based Asset*. URL: https://www.bloomberg. com/news/articles/2021-01-21/bitcoin-is-a-faith-based- asset-joe-weisenthal (visited on 03/02/2022).

[16]   Martin Wolf. "The libertarian fantasies of cryptocurrencies". In: *Financial Times* (Feb. 2019). URL: https://www.ft.com/content/eeeacd7c- 2e0e-11e9-ba00-0251022932c8.

Chapter 12: Casino Capitalism

[1]   Edward Chancellor. "Devil take the hindmost: A history of financial speculation". In: (1999). Publisher: Macmillan London.

[2]   Shaanan Cohney et al. "Coin-operated capitalism". In: *Columbia Law Review* 119.3 (2019). Publisher: JSTOR, pp. 591–676.

[3]   Marieke De Goede. *Virtue, fortune, and faith: A geneaology of finance*. Vol. 24. U of Minnesota Press, 2001.

[4] Mark Fisher. *Capitalist realism: Is there no alternative?* John Hunt Publishing, 2009.

[5] Marcy Gordon. *SEC Investigating Gibson Greetings On Derivative Investments.* AP NEWS. Section: Archive. URL: https://apnews.com/article/ 2d76c5b226fe682058b02df15dbc74cd (visited on 05/11/2022).

[6] William H Janeway. *Doing capitalism in the innovation economy: Markets, speculation and the state.* Cambridge University Press, 2012.

[7] Carlota Perez. *Technological revolutions and financial capital.* Edward Elgar Publishing, 2003.

Chapter 13: Crypto Exchanges

[1] Hilary J. Allen. "DeFi: Shadow Banking 2.0?" In: *SSRN Electronic Journal* (2022). ISSN: 1556-5068. DOI: 10.2139/ssrn.4038788. URL: https: //www.ssrn.com/abstract=4038788 (visited on 04/21/2022).

[2] Benjamin Braun and Daniela Gabor. "Central banking, shadow banking, and infrastructural power". In: (2019). DOI: 10.31235/osf.io/nf9ms.

[3] Christopher P. Buttigieg et al. "Anti-money laundering regulation of crypto assets in Europe's smallest member state". In: *Law and Financial Markets Review* 13.4 (2019). Publisher: Taylor & Francis, pp. 211–227. ISSN: 17521459. DOI: 10.1080/17521440.2019.1663996.

[4] Lin William Cong et al. "Crypto Wash Trading". In: *Available at SSRN 3530220* (2020).

[5] Douglas J. Cumming, Sofia Johan, and Anshum Pant. "Regulation of the Crypto-Economy: Managing Risks, Challenges, and Regulatory Uncertainty". In: *Journal of Risk and Financial Management* 12.3 (2019). Publisher: Multidisciplinary Digital Publishing Institute, p. 126. ISSN: 1911-8074. DOI: 10.3390/jrfm12030126.

[6] Anirudh Dhawan and Talis J. Putnins. "A New Wolf in Town? Pump-and-Dump Manipulation in Cryptocurrency Markets". In: *SSRN Electronic Journal* (2020). ISSN: 1556-5068. DOI: 10.2139/ssrn.3670714. URL: https://www.ssrn.com/abstract=3670714 (visited on 02/22/2022).

[7] Stephen Diehl. *The Internet's Casino Boats.* URL: https://www.stephendiehl.com/blog/casino-boats.html (visited on 02/25/2022).

[8] Cory Doctorow. *When Crypto-Exchanges Go Broke, You'll Lose It All.* URL: https://onezero.medium.com/when-crypto-exchanges-go-broke-youll-lose-it-all-53cfd3c4476 (visited on 04/25/2022).

[9] Brian D. Feinstein and Kevin Werbach. "The Impact of Cryptocurrency Regulation on Trading Markets". In: *SSRN Electronic Journal* 7.1 (2020). Publisher: Oxford University Press, pp. 48–99. DOI: 10.2139/ssrn.3649475.

[10] JT Hamrick et al. "An examination of the cryptocurrency pump and dump ecosystem". In: (2018). URL: http://ssrn.com/paper=3303365.

[11] JT Hamrick et al. "The economics of cryptocurrency pump and dump schemes". In: (2018). Publisher: CEPR Discussion Paper No. DP13404.

[12] Matthew Hougan et al. "Economic and Non-Economic Trading in Bitcoin". In: (2019). Publisher: Bitwise Asset Management.

[13] Viktoria Ivaniuk. "Cryptocurrency Exchange Regulation – An International Review". In: *Magda Dziembowska, Robert Dziembowski, Apelacja w postępowaniu* (2020), p. 67.

[14] Kristin N. Johnson. "Decentralized Finance: Regulating Cryptocurrency Exchanges". In: *SSRN Electronic Journal* (2021). ISSN: 0043-5589. DOI: 10.2139/ssrn.3831439.

[15] Josh Kamps and Bennett Kleinberg. "To the moon: defining and detecting cryptocurrency pump-and-dumps". In: *Crime Science* 7.1 (2018). Publisher: Springer, p. 18.

[16] Sumeet Singh Lamba. *FOMO: Marketing to Millennials.* Notion Press, 2021.

[17] Tao Li, Donghwa Shin, and Baolian Wang. "Cryptocurrency pump-and-dump schemes". In: *Available at SSRN 3267041* (2019).

[18]   Ephrat Livni and Andrew Ross Sorkin. "The Dramatic Crash of a Buzzy Cryptocurrency Raises Eyebrows". In: *The New York Times* (June 28, 2021). ISSN: 0362-4331. URL: https : / / www . nytimes . com / 2021 / 06 / 28 / business / dealbook / icp-cryptocurrency-crash . html (visited on 02/22/2022).

[19]   Ben McKenzie and Jacob Silverman. *Why users are pushing back against the world's largest crypto exchange.* Washington Post. Section: Outlook. Apr. 1, 2022. URL: https : / / www . washingtonpost . com / outlook / 2022 / 04 / 01 / binance-may-19-lawsuit-cryptocurrency/ (visited on 05/12/2022).

[20]   Patricia Kowsmann {and} Caitlin Ostroff. "Binance Froze When Bitcoin Crashed. Now Users Want Their Money Back." In: *Wall Street Journal* (July 11, 2021). ISSN: 0099-9660. URL: https : / / www . wsj . com / articles / binance-froze-when-bitcoin-crashed-now-users-want-their-money-back-11626001202 (visited on 04/05/2022).

[21]   Matt Ranger. *An Anatomy of Bitcoin Price Manipulation.* Single Lunch. Jan. 9, 2022. URL: https://www.singlelunch.com/2022/01/09/an-anatomy-of-bitcoin-price-manipulation/ (visited on 04/24/2022).

[22]   Nouriel Roubini. "The Great Crypto Heist". In: *Project Syndicate* 16 (2019).

[23]   Fabian Schär. "Decentralized finance: on blockchain-and smart contract-based financial markets". In: *Federal Reserve Bank of St. Louis Review* 103.2 (2021), pp. 153–174. ISSN: 00149187. DOI: 10.20955/r.103.153-74.

[24]   Shane Shifflett and Paul Vigna. "Some traders are talking up cryptocurrencies, then dumping them, costing others millions". In: *The Wall Street Journal* (2018).

[25]   Gary Silverman. "Crypto's wild ride raises new liquidity concerns". In: *Financial Times* (Dec. 11, 2021).

[26]   Steve Stecklow et al. "Chaos and hackers stalk investors on cryptocurrency exchanges". In: *Reuters, September* 29 (2017).

[27]   Paul Vigna. "Most bitcoin trading faked by unregulated exchanges, study finds". In: *Wall Street Journal* (2019).

[28] Molly White. *Cryptocurrency off-ramps, and the shift towards centralization*. Molly White. Feb. 12, 2022. URL: https://blog.mollywhite.net/off-ramps/ (visited on 02/25/2022).

[29] Jiahua Xu and Benjamin Livshits. "The anatomy of a cryptocurrency pump-and-dump scheme". In: *28th USENIX Security Symposium*. 2019, pp. 1609–1625.

Chapter 14: Digital Gold

[1] Fiona Allon. "Money after Blockchain: Gold, Decentralised Politics and the New Libertarianism". In: *Australian Feminist Studies* 33.96 (2018). Publisher: Taylor & Francis, pp. 223–243. ISSN: 14653303.

[2] Dirk G. Baur and Thomas Dimpfl. "The volatility of Bitcoin and its role as a medium of exchange and a store of value". In: *Empirical Economics* 61.5 (2021). Publisher: Springer, pp. 2663–2683. ISSN: 14358921. DOI: 10.1007/s00181-020-01990-5.

[3] Michael Cembalest. *The Maltese Falcoin: On Cryptocurrencies and Blockchains*. Feb. 3, 2022, p. 31. URL: https://privatebank.jpmorgan.com/content/dam/jpm-wm-aem/global/pb/en/insights/eye-on-the-market/the-maltese-falcoin.pdf.

[4] Ben Kaiser, Mireya Jurado, and Alex Ledger. "The looming threat of China: An analysis of chinese influence on bitcoin". In: (2018).

[5] Mike Orcutt. *Coronavirus is forcing fans of Bitcoin to realize it's not a 'safe haven' after all*. Publication Title: MIT Technology Review. Apr. 2020. URL: http://www.technologyreview.com/2020/03/19/905207/coronavirus-is-forcing-fans-of-bitcoin-to-realize-its-not-a-safe-haven-after-all/..

[6] John Plender. "Crypto vs gold: the search for an investment bolt hole". In: *Financial Times* (Apr. 1, 2022). URL: https://www.ft.com/content/d497772f-7422-4372-b72d-f74f96884466 (visited on 04/01/2022).

[7]   Refk Selmi, Jamal Bouoiyour, and Mark E. Wohar. ""Digital Gold" and geopolitics". In: *Research in International Business and Finance* 59 (2022). Publisher: Elsevier, p. 101512. ISSN: 02755319. DOI: `10.1016/j.ribaf.2021.101512`.

Chapter 15: Smart Contracts

[1]   Ryan Clements. "Built to Fail: The Inherent Fragility of Algorithmic Stablecoins". In: *SSRN Electronic Journal* 11 (2021). Publisher: HeinOnline, p. 131. DOI: `10.2139/ssrn.3952045`.

[2]   Cory Doctorow. *The Inevitability of Trusted Third Parties*. URL: `https://onezero.medium.com/the-inevitability-of-trusted-third-parties-a51cbcffc4e2` (visited on 04/19/2022).

[3]   Pieter Hartel, Ivan Homoliak, and Daniël Reijsbergen. "An Empirical Study Into the Success of Listed Smart Contracts in Ethereum". In: *IEEE Access* 7 (2019). Publisher: IEEE, pp. 177539–177555.

[4]   *Hyperledger Fabric Documentation*. 2017. URL: `https://hyperledger-fabric.readthedocs.io/`.

[5]   Ephrat Livni and Andrew Ross Sorkin. "The Dramatic Crash of a Buzzy Cryptocurrency Raises Eyebrows". In: *The New York Times* (June 28, 2021). ISSN: 0362-4331. URL: `https://www.nytimes.com/2021/06/28/business/dealbook/icp-cryptocurrency-crash.html` (visited on 02/22/2022).

[6]   Andrea Pinna et al. "A massive analysis of ethereum smart contracts empirical study and code metrics". In: *IEEE Access* 7 (2019). Publisher: IEEE, pp. 78194–78213.

[7]   US Securities, Exchange Commission, et al. "SEC issues investigative report concluding DAO tokens, a digital asset, were securities". In: *US Securities and Exchange Commission* 25 (2017), pp. 2017–131.

[8]   Angela Walch. "Software Developers as Fiduciaries in Public Blockchains". In: *Regulating Blockchain. Techno-Social and Legal Challenges, ed. by Philipp Hacker, Ioannis Lianos, Georgios Dimitropoulos & Stefan Eich, Oxford University Press, 2019.* (2019).

Chapter 16: Blockchainism

[1]   Asvatha Babu. "Behind the Veil of Decentralization: Analyzing Blockchain Frames and Sponsors in US News". Publication Title: SSRN Electronic Journal. 2020.

[2]   Jon Baldwin. "In digital we trust: Bitcoin discourse, digital currencies, and decentralized network fetishism". In: *Palgrave Communications* 4.1 (2018). Publisher: Palgrave, pp. 1–10.

[3]   Balázs Bodó. "The commodification of trust". In: *SSRN Electronic Journal* 1 (2021). ISSN: 1556-5068. DOI: 10.2139/ssrn.3843707.

[4]   Leif Gensert. *Blockchain Is Merely a Marketing Instrument.* Leif Thoughts - Schlockchain. Section: blog. Apr. 3, 2018. URL: https://leif.io/blog/2018/04/03/blockchain-is-merely-a-marketing-instrument/ (visited on 03/18/2022).

[5]   Harry Halpin. "Deconstructing the decentralization trilemma". In: *ICETE 2020 - Proceedings of the 17th International Joint Conference on e-Business and Telecommunications* 3 (2020). ISBN: 9789897584459 _eprint: 2008.08014, pp. 505–512. DOI: 10.5220/0009892405050512.

[6]   Robert Herian. "Blockchain, GDPR, and fantasies of data sovereignty". In: *Law, Innovation and Technology* 12.1 (2020). Publisher: Taylor & Francis, pp. 156–174. ISSN: 1757997X. DOI: 10.1080/17579961.2020.1727094. URL: https://doi.org/10.1080/17579961.2020.1727094.

[7]   Adrianne Jeffries. "Blockchain is Meaningless". In: *The Verge* 7 (2018), p. 2018. URL: https://www.theverge.com/2018/3/7/17091766/blockchain-bitcoin-ethereum-cryptocurrency-meaning.

[8] Matt Levine. *Web3 Takes Trust Too*. Jan. 10, 2022. URL: https://www.bloomberg.com/opinion/articles/2022-01-10/web3-takes-trust-too (visited on 02/25/2022).

[9] Sarah Manski and Michel Bauwens. "Reimagining New Socio-Technical Economics Through the Application of Distributed Ledger Technologies". In: *Frontiers in Blockchain* 2 (January 2020), pp. 1–17. DOI: 10.3389/fbloc.2019.00029.

[10] Florian Martin-Bariteau. "Blockchain and the European Union General Data Protection Regulation: The CNIL's Perspective". In: *SSRN Electronic Journal* 1 (2018). ISSN: 1556-5068. DOI: 10.2139/ssrn.3275783.

[11] Michel Rauchs et al. "2nd Global Enterprise Blockchain Benchmarking Study". In: (2019). URL: http://ssrn.com/paper=3461765.

[12] Bruce Schneier. *There's No Good Reason to Trust Blockchain Technology*. Publication Title: Wired Magazine. 2019. URL: https://www.wired.com/story/theres-no-good-reason-to-trust-blockchain-technology/.

[13] Soatok. *Against Web3 and Faux-Decentralization*. Dhole Moments. Oct. 19, 2021. URL: https://soatok.blog/2021/10/19/against-web3-and-faux-decentralization/ (visited on 02/25/2022).

[14] Kai Stinchcombe. *Blockchain is Not Only Crappy Technology But a Bad Vision for the Future*. Medium. Apr. 5, 2018. URL: https://medium.com/@kaistinchcombe/decentralized-and-trustless-crypto-paradise-is-actually-a-medieval-hellhole-c1ca122efdec (visited on 02/25/2022).

[15] Kai Stinchcombe. *Ten Years In, Nobody Has Come Up With a Use for Blockchain*. Hackernoon. Dec. 22, 2017. URL: https://hackernoon.com/ten-years-in-nobody-has-come-up-with-a-use-case-for-blockchain-ee98c180100 (visited on 02/25/2022).

[16] Angela Walch. "Deconstructing 'Decentralization': Exploring the Core Claim of Crypto Systems". In: *C. Brummer (ed.), Crypto Assets: Legal and Monetary Perspectives* (2019), pp. 1–36. DOI: https://papers.ssrn.com/sol3/papers.cfm?abstract_id=3326244.

[17]   Molly White. *Blockchain-based Systems Are Not What They Say They Are*. Molly White. Jan. 9, 2022. URL: https://blog.mollywhite.net/ blockchains-are-not-what-they-say/ (visited on 02/25/2022).

Chapter 17: Frauds & Scams

[1]   Edward J Balleisen. "Fraud: An American History from Barnum to Madoff". In: *Fraud*. Princeton University Press, 2017.

[2]   William K Black. *The best way to rob a bank is to own one*. University of Texas Press, 2013.

[3]   Shaen Corbet. *Understanding cryptocurrency fraud: The challenges and headwinds to regulate digital currencies*. Vol. 2. Walter de Gruyter GmbH & Co KG, 2021. ISBN: 3-11-071857-X.

[4]   Donald R Cressey. "Other people's money; a study of the social psychology of embezzlement." In: (1953). Publisher: Free Press.

[5]   Dan Davies. *Lying for Money: How Legendary Frauds Reveal the Workings of Our World*. Profile Books, 2018.

[6]   Anirudh Dhawan and Talis J. Putnins. "A New Wolf in Town? Pump-and-Dump Manipulation in Cryptocurrency Markets". In: *SSRN Electronic Journal* (2020). ISSN: 1556-5068. DOI: 10.2139/ssrn.3670714. URL: https://www.ssrn.com/abstract=3670714 (visited on 02/22/2022).

[7]   JT Hamrick et al. "An examination of the cryptocurrency pump and dump ecosystem". In: (2018). URL: http://ssrn.com/paper=3303365.

[8]   JT Hamrick et al. "The economics of cryptocurrency pump and dump schemes". In: (2018). Publisher: CEPR Discussion Paper No. DP13404.

[9]   GS Hans. "How and Why Did It Go So Wrong?: Theranos as a Legal Ethics Case Study". In: *Ga. St. UL Rev.* 37 (2020). Publisher: HeinOnline, p. 427.

[10]   Marianne Jennings. *The seven signs of ethical collapse: How to spot moral meltdowns in companies... Before it's too late*. Macmillan, 2006.

[11]   Josh Kamps and Bennett Kleinberg. "To the moon: defining and detecting cryptocurrency pump-and-dumps". In: *Crime Science* 7.1 (2018). Publisher: Springer, p. 18.

[12]   Tao Li, Donghwa Shin, and Baolian Wang. "Cryptocurrency pump-and-dump schemes". In: *Available at SSRN 3267041* (2019).

[13]   Harry Markopolos. *No one would listen: A true financial thriller*. John Wiley & Sons, 2011.

[14]   Kanis Saengchote. "A DeFi Bank Run: Iron Finance, IRON Stablecoin, and the Fall of TITAN". In: *IRON Stablecoin, and the Fall of TITAN (July 16, 2021)* (2021).

[15]   Justin Scheck and Shane Shifflett. "How dirty money disappears into the black hole of cryptocurrency". In: *Wall Street Journal* 28 (2018).

[16]   Jiahua Xu and Benjamin Livshits. "The anatomy of a cryptocurrency pump-and-dump scheme". In: *28th USENIX Security Symposium*. 2019, pp. 1609–1625.

[17]   Dirk A Zetzsche et al. "The ICO Gold Rush: It's a scam, it's a bubble, it's a super challenge for regulators". In: *University of Luxembourg Law Working Paper* 11 (2017), pp. 17–83.

[18]   Mitchell Zuckoff. *Ponzi's scheme: The true story of a financial legend*. Random House, 2005.

Chapter 18: Web3

[1]   Tracy Alloway and Joe Weisenthal. "Sam Bankman-Fried Described Yield Farming and Left Matt Levine Stunned". In: *Bloomberg.com* (Apr. 25, 2022). URL: https://www.bloomberg.com/news/articles/2022-04-25/sam-bankman-fried-described-yield-farming-and-left-matt-levine-stunned (visited on 05/16/2022).

[2]   Tom Barbereau et al. "DeFi, Not So Decentralized: The Measured Distribution of Voting Rights". In: *Proceedings of the 55th Hawaii International Conference on System Sciences*. 2022. DOI: https://scholarspace.manoa.hawaii.edu/handle/10125/80074.

[3] Balázs Bodó and Heleen Janssen. "Here Be Dragons – Maintaining Trust in the Technologized Public Sector". In: *SSRN Electronic Journal* (2021). ISSN: 1556-5068. DOI: 10.2139/ssrn.3868208.

[4] Martin Brennecke et al. "The De-Central Bank in Decentralized Finance: A Case Study of MakerDAO". In: *55th Hawaii International Conference on System Sciences (2022)*. 2022. DOI: 10.24251/HICSS.2022.737. URL: https://www.researchgate.net/publication/354736149_The_De-Central_Bank_in_Decentralized_Finance_A_Case_Study_of_MakerDAO.

[5] Paul Butler. *"Play-to-earn" and Bullshit Jobs*. URL: https://paulbutler.org/2021/play-to-earn-and-bullshit-jobs/ (visited on 03/02/2022).

[6] Pınar Çağlayan Aksoy and Zehra Özkan Üner. "NFTs and copyright: challenges and opportunities". In: *Journal of Intellectual Property Law & Practice* 16.10 (2021), pp. 1115–1126. ISSN: 1747-1532. DOI: 10.1093/jiplp/jpab104.

[7] Joshua Fairfield. "Tokenized: The Law of Non-Fungible Tokens and Unique Digital Property". In: *Indiana Law Journal* (2021), pp. 1–99. DOI: https://papers.ssrn.com/sol3/papers.cfm?abstract_id=3821102. URL: https://papers.ssrn.com/sol3/papers.cfm?abstract_id=3821102.

[8] Youssef Faqir-Rhazoui, Javier Arroyo, and Samer Hassan. "A comparative analysis of the platforms for decentralized autonomous organizations in the Ethereum blockchain". In: *Journal of Internet Services and Applications* 12.1 (2021). ISBN: 1317402100139 Publisher: Journal of Internet Services and Applications. ISSN: 18690238. DOI: 10.1186/s13174-021-00139-6.

[9] David Graeber. "Bullshit jobs: the rise of pointless work, and what we can do about it". In: (2019). Publisher: Penguin.

[10] Kelvin F K Low. "The Emperor's New Art: Cryptomania, Art & Property". In: *Art & Property* (2021). DOI: https://papers.ssrn.com/sol3/papers.cfm?abstract_id=3978241. URL: https://papers.ssrn.com/sol3/papers.cfm?abstract_id=3978241.

[11] Simon Mackenzie and Diāna Bērziņa. "NFTs: Digital things and their criminal lives". In: *Crime, Media, Culture* (2021). Publisher: SAGE Publications Sage UK: London, England, p. 17416590211039797. ISSN: 17416604.

[12] Paris Marx. *Why Web3, the Blockchain and Crypto Internet, Is Doomed to Fail.* URL: https://www.businessinsider.com/web3-blockchain-crypto-internet-doomed-fail-doesnt-live-up-hype-2022-3?r=US&IR=T (visited on 03/29/2022).

[13] Christopher Mims. *NFTs, Cryptocurrencies and Web3 Are Multilevel Marketing Schemes for a New Generation - WSJ.* Wall Street Journal. Feb. 19, 2022. URL: https://www.wsj.com/articles/nfts-cryptocurrencies-and-web3-are-multilevel-marketing-schemes-for-a-new-generation-11645246824 (visited on 03/14/2022).

[14] Evgeny Morozov. *Web3: A Map in Search of Territory.* The Crypto Syllabus. Jan. 13, 2022. URL: https://the-crypto-syllabus.com/web3-a-map-in-search-of-territory/ (visited on 03/03/2022).

[15] Tim O'Reilly. *Why It's Too Early to Get Excited About Web3.* O'Reilly Media. Dec. 13, 2021. URL: https://www.oreilly.com/radar/why-its-too-early-to-get-excited-about-web3/ (visited on 02/25/2022).

[16] Dan Olson. *Line Goes Up – The Problem With NFTs.* Jan. 21, 2022. URL: https://www.youtube.com/watch?v=YQ_xWvX1n9g (visited on 03/02/2022).

[17] Rufus Pollock. *Reflections on the Blockchain · Rufus Pollock Online.* mainly a critique of early DAOs and techno-solutionism. July 2, 2016. URL: https://rufuspollock.com/2016/07/02/reflections-on-the-blockchain/ (visited on 02/25/2022).

[18] "Sam Bankman-Fried Described Yield Farming and Left Matt Levine Stunned". In: *Bloomberg.com* (Apr. 25, 2022). URL: https://www.bloomberg.com/news/articles/2022-04-25/sam-bankman-fried-described-yield-farming-and-left-matt-levine-stunned (visited on 04/25/2022).

[19] Tante. *The Third Web.* Nodes in a social network. long critical essay including detailed history by Tante. Dec. 17, 2021. URL: https://tante.cc/2021/12/17/the-third-web/ (visited on 02/25/2022).

[20]   Yanis Varoufakis. *Yanis Varoufakis on Crypto & the Left, and Techno-Feudalism.* Jan. 26, 2022. URL: https://the-crypto-syllabus.com/yanis-varoufakis-on-techno-feudalism/ (visited on 04/05/2022).

[21]   Angela Walch. "Software Developers as Fiduciaries in Public Blockchains". In: *Regulating Blockchain. Techno-Social and Legal Challenges, ed. by Philipp Hacker, Ioannis Lianos, Georgios Dimitropoulos & Stefan Eich, Oxford University Press, 2019.* (2019).

[22]   Richard Waters. "Web3 is yet to take off despite the hype". In: *Financial Times* (Apr. 8, 2022). URL: https://www.ft.com/content/16eaf1b9-08fb-4454-a4eb-ac662cdd8590 (visited on 04/08/2022).

[23]   Nicholas Weaver. *The Web3 Fraud.* USENIX. Dec. 16, 2021. URL: https://www.usenix.org/publications/loginonline/web3-fraud (visited on 02/25/2022).

[24]   Alice Yuan Zhang. *Unpacking the Myth of Web3: Decentralization of What?* aliceyuanzhang. Apr. 29, 2022. URL: https://aliceyuanzhang.com/decentralization.

Chapter 19: Stablecoins

[1]   Catherine Flick. "Informed consent and the Facebook emotional manipulation study". In: *Research Ethics* 12.1 (2016). Publisher: SAGE Publications Sage UK: London, England, pp. 14–28.

[2]   David Gerard. *Libra Shrugged: How Facebook Tried to Take Over the Money.* David Gerard, 2020.

[3]   Brendan Greeley. "Facebook's Libra will not help the unbanked". In: *Financial Times* 18 (2019).

[4]   John Kiff et al. "A Survey of Research on Retail Central Bank Digital Currency". In: (2020). URL: http://ssrn.com/paper=3639760.

[5]   Adam DI Kramer, Jamie E Guillory, and Jeffrey T Hancock. "Experimental evidence of massive-scale emotional contagion through social networks". In: *Proceedings of the National Academy of Sciences* 111.24 (2014). Publisher: National Acad Sciences, pp. 8788–8790.

[6]   Bruce Mizrach. "Stablecoins: Survivorship, Transactions Costs and Ex-
        change Microstructure". In: *SSRN Electronic Journal* (2021). DOI: `10 .`
        `2139/ssrn.3835219`.

Chapter 20: Crypto Journalism

[1]   Brian Ellsworth. "Special report: in Venezuela, new cryptocurrency is
        nowhere to be found". In: *Reuters* (2018), pp. 30–08.

[2]   Corin Faife. *We Asked Crypto News Outlets If They'd Take Money to Cover
        a Project. More Than Half Said Yes.* Publication Title: BREAKERMAG.
        Dec. 2018. URL: `https://breakermag.com/we-asked-crypto-news-`
        `outlets-if-theyd-take-money-to-cover-a-project-more-`
        `than-half-said-yes/`.

[3]   John Kay. *Why we shouldn't borrow money from the future.* World Eco-
        nomic Forum. URL: `https://www.weforum.org/agenda/2015/10/`
        `why-we-shouldnt-borrow-money-from-the-future/` (visited on
        05/02/2022).

[4]   "Synthetic reverse FUD". In: *Financial Times* (May 13, 2022).

[5]   Alex Vasquez. *There Are More Dollars in Venezuela Now Than There Are
        Bolivars.* Publication Title: Bloomberg.com. Dec. 2019. URL: `https://`
        `www.bloomberg.com/news/articles/2019-12-03/there-are-`
        `more-dollars-in-venezuela-now-than-there-are-bolivars`.

Chapter 21: Initial Coin Offerings

[1]   Moritz Becker. "Blockchain and the Promise (s) of Decentralisation : A
        Sociological Investigation of the Sociotechnical Imaginaries of Blockchain".
        In: *Proceedings of the STS Conference Graz 2019.* 2019, pp. 6–30. ISBN:
        978-3-85125-668-0. DOI: `10 . 3217 / 978 - 3 - 85125 - 668 - 0 - 02`. URL:
        `https://diglib.tugraz.at/download.php?id=5e2997b7bb322&`
        `location=browse`.

[2]   Hugo Benedetti and Leonard Kostovetsky. "Digital tulips? Returns to investors in initial coin offerings". In: *Returns to Investors in Initial Coin Offerings (May 20, 2018)* (2018).

[3]   Dmitri Boreiko and Dimche Risteski. "Serial and large investors in initial coin offerings". In: *Small Business Economics* (2020). Publisher: Springer, pp. 1–19.

[4]   Josh Cincinnati. *PonzICO: Let's Just Cut to the Chase.* 2017.

[5]   *Continental Marketing Corp. v. Securities and Exchange Commission.* Issue: No. 9199 Pages: 466 Publication Title: F. 2d Volume: 387. 1967.

[6]   Chloe Cornish and Richard Waters. "Silicon Valley investors line up to back Telegram ICO". In: *Financial Times* (Jan. 2018). URL: https://www.ft.com/content/790d9506-0175-11e8-9650-9c0ad2d7c5b5.

[7]   Anastasiia Morozova Cristina Cuervo. *Regulation of Crypto Assets.* Jan. 2020. URL: https://www.imf.org/en/Publications/fintech-notes/Issues/2020/01/09/Regulation-of-Crypto-Assets-48810.

[8]   Abe De Jong, Peter Roosenboom, and Tom van der Kolk. "What Determines Success in Initial Coin Offerings?" In: (2018). URL: http://ssrn.com/paper=3250035.

[9]   Julianna Debler. "Foreign initial coin offering issuers beware: the Securities and Exchange Commission is watching". In: *Cornell Int'l LJ* 51 (2018). Publisher: HeinOnline, p. 245.

[10]   Financial Conduct Authority. *Guidance on Cryptoassets.* Financial Conduct Authority, 2019. URL: https://www.fca.org.uk/publication/consultation/cp19-03.pdf#page=11.

[11]   Sabrina T Howell, Marina Niessner, and David Yermack. "Initial coin offerings: Financing growth with cryptocurrency token sales". In: *The Review of Financial Studies* (2018).

[12]   Jemima Kelly. "A crypto stunt gone tragically wrong". In: *Financial Times* (May 25, 2018).

[13] Jemima Kelly. *The ICO whose team members are literally cartoon characters.* Publication Title: Financial Times. Sept. 2019. URL: https://www.ft.com/content/57805b32-0bbe-34cb-940c-66cdd1aec5e2.

[14] Olga Kharif. *Half of ICOs Die Within Four Months After Token Sales Finalized.* Publication Title: Bloomberg.com. July 2018. URL: https://www.bloomberg.com/news/articles/2018-07-09/half-of-icos-die-within-four-months-after-token-sales-finalized.

[15] Michael Levi. *Regulating fraud: White-collar crime and the criminal process.* Routledge, 2013.

[16] *Miller v. Central Chinchilla Group, Inc.* Issue: No. 73-1731 Pages: 414 Publication Title: F. 2d Volume: 494. 1974.

[17] Paul P Momtaz. "Entrepreneurial finance and moral hazard: evidence from token offerings". In: *Journal of Business Venturing* (2020). Publisher: Elsevier, p. 106001.

[18] Nathaniel Popper. "The Coder and the Dictator". In: *New York Times* (Mar. 2020). URL: https://www.nytimes.com/2020/03/20/technology/venezuela-petro-cryptocurrency.html.

[19] Nathan Schneider. "Decentralization: an incomplete ambition". ISSN: 17530369 Issue: 4 Publication Title: Journal of Cultural Economy Volume: 12. 2019.

[20] *SEC v. WJ Howey Co.* Issue: No. 843 Pages: 293 Publication Title: US Volume: 328. 1946.

[21] *Securities and Exchange Commission v. Eyal.* Issue: No. 19 Civ. 11325 (LLS). 2020.

[22] *Securities and Exchange Commission v. KIK INTERACTIVE INC.* Issue: No. 19 Civ. 5244 (AKH). 2020.

[23] *Securities and Exchange Commission v. META 1 COIN TRUST.* Issue: No. 1: 20-CV-273-RP. 2020.

[24] *Securities and Exchange Commission v. NATURAL DIAMONDS INVESTMENT CO.* Issue: Case No. 9: 19-CV-80633-ROSENBERG/REINHART. 2020.

[25] *Securities and Exchange Commission v. TELEGRAM GROUP INC.* Issue: No. 19 Civ. 9439 (PKC). 2020.

[26] Angela Walch. "Blockchain's treacherous vocabulary: One more challenge for regulators". In: *Journal of Internet Law* 21.2 (2017).

[27] Angela Walch. "Deconstructing 'Decentralization': Exploring the Core Claim of Crypto Systems". In: *C. Brummer (ed.), Crypto Assets: Legal and Monetary Perspectives* (2019), pp. 1–36. DOI: `https://papers.ssrn.com/sol3/papers.cfm?abstract_id=3326244`.

[28] David Yaffe-Bellany. "Millions for Crypto Start-Ups, No Real Names Necessary". In: *The New York Times* (Mar. 2, 2022). ISSN: 0362-4331. URL: `https://www.nytimes.com/2022/03/02/technology/cryptocurrency-anonymity-alarm.html` (visited on 03/02/2022).

[29] Dirk A Zetzsche et al. "The ICO Gold Rush: It's a scam, it's a bubble, it's a super challenge for regulators". In: *University of Luxembourg Law Working Paper* 11 (2017), pp. 17–83.

[30] Zhexi Zhang. "The Aesthetics of Decentralization". PhD thesis. MIT, 2019. DOI: `https://dspace.mit.edu/handle/1721.1/123614`. URL: `https://dspace.mit.edu/handle/1721.1/123614`.

Chapter 22: Ransomware

[1] MIKE McQuade. *The untold story of NotPetya, the most devastating cyber-attack in history.* 2018.

[2] Kartikay Mehrotra. *UCSF Hack Shows Evolving Risks of Ransomware in the Covid Era.* Publication Title: Bloomberg.com. Aug. 2020. URL: `https://www.bloomberg.com/news/features/2020-08-19/ucsf-hack-shows-evolving-risks-of-ransomware-in-the-covid-era`.

[3] Nathaniel Popper. "Ransomware Attacks Grow, Crippling Cities and Businesses". In: *New York Times* (Feb. 2020).

[4] Bander Ali Saleh Al-rimy, Mohd Aizaini Maarof, and Syed Zainudeen Mohd Shaid. "Ransomware threat success factors, taxonomy, and countermeasures: A survey and research directions". In: *Computers & Security* 74 (2018). Publisher: Elsevier, pp. 144–166.

[5] Pengcheng Xia et al. "Don't Fish in Troubled Waters! Characterizing Coronavirus themed Cryptocurrency Scams". In: *arXiv preprint arXiv:2007.13639* (2020).

Chapter 23: Financial Populism

[1] Kurt Andersen. *Evil geniuses: The unmaking of America: A recent history*. Random House, 2020.

[2] Diane-Laure Arjaliès. ""At the Very Beginning, There's This Dream." the Role of Utopia in the Workings of Local and Cryptocurrencies". In: *Handbook of Alternative Finance*. February. 2020.

[3] Jon Baldwin. "In digital we trust: Bitcoin discourse, digital currencies, and decentralized network fetishism". In: *Palgrave Communications* 4.1 (2018). Publisher: Palgrave, pp. 1–10.

[4] Jamie Bartlett. "Forget far-right populism – crypto-anarchists are the new masters". In: *The Observer* (June 4, 2017). ISSN: 0029-7712. URL: https://www.theguardian.com/technology/2017/jun/04/forget-far-right-populism-crypto-anarchists-are-the-new-masters-internet-politics (visited on 04/28/2022).

[5] Carola Binder. "Technopopulism and Central Banks". In: *SSRN Electronic Journal* (2021). DOI: https://papers.ssrn.com/sol3/papers.cfm?abstract_id=3823456. URL: https://papers.ssrn.com/sol3/papers.cfm?abstract_id=3823456.

[6] Spencer Jakab. *The Revolution That Wasn't: How GameStop and Reddit Made Wall Street Even Richer*. Penguin Business, Jan. 27, 2022.

[7]   Spencer Jakab. "Who Really Got Rich From the GameStop Revolution?" In: *Wall Street Journal* (Jan. 31, 2022). ISSN: 0099-9660. URL: https://www.wsj.com/articles/who-really-got-rich-from-the-gamestop-revolution-11643432418 (visited on 05/04/2022).

[8]   Miles Johnson. "Bitcoin is a faith-based financial asset for a populist era". In: *Financial Times* (Dec. 2, 2017). URL: https://www.ft.com/content/ca13d594-d6ac-11e7-8c9a-d9c0a5c8d5c9 (visited on 04/28/2022).

[9]   Jongchul Kim. "Propertization: The Process by Which Financial Corporate Power Has Risen". In: *SSRN Electronic Journal* (2018), pp. 58–82. ISSN: 1556-5068. DOI: 10.2139/ssrn.2478294.

[10]   Michael Levitin. *Occupy Wall Street Did More Than You Think*. The Atlantic. Section: Ideas. Sept. 14, 2021. URL: https://www.theatlantic.com/ideas/archive/2021/09/how-occupy-wall-street-reshaped-america/620064/ (visited on 04/28/2022).

[11]   Thomas Piketty. "Capital in the twenty-first century". In: *Capital in the twenty-first century*. Harvard University Press, 2018.

Chapter 24: Financial Nihilism

[1]   David Bandurski. *The 'lying flat' movement standing in the way of China's innovation drive*. Brookings. July 8, 2021. URL: https://www.brookings.edu/techstream/the-lying-flat-movement-standing-in-the-way-of-chinas-innovation-drive/ (visited on 04/25/2022).

[2]   Sumeet Singh Lamba. *FOMO: Marketing to Millennials*. Notion Press, 2021.

[3]   Charlie Warzel. *The Absurdity is the Point*. Galaxy Brain. May 11, 2021. URL: https://warzel.substack.com/p/the-absurdity-is-the-point (visited on 03/02/2022).

[4]   Jen Wieczner. *Why Dogecoin, the Joke Crypto, Is Forcing People to Take It Seriously*. Intelligencer. Apr. 17, 2021. (Visited on 04/17/2022).

Chapter 25: Regulation

[1] Ulrich Bindseil, Patrick Papsdorf, and Jürgen Schaaf. *The encrypted threat: Bitcoin's social cost and regulatory responses.* Jan. 7, 2022. URL: https://www.suerf.org/docx/f_88b3febc5798a734026c82c1012408f5_38771_suerf.pdf (visited on 02/25/2022).

[2] Dmitri Boreiko, Guido Ferrarini, and Paolo Giudici. "Blockchain Startups and Prospectus Regulation". In: *European Business Organization Law Review* 20.4 (2019). Publisher: Springer, pp. 665–694. ISSN: 17416205. DOI: 10.1007/s40804-019-00168-6.

[3] Chris Brummer. *Cryptoassets: legal, regulatory, and monetary perspectives.* Oxford University Press, 2019.

[4] Ryan Clements. "Emerging Canadian Crypto-Asset Jurisdictional Uncertainties and Regulatory Gaps". In: *Banking and Finance Law Review* 37 (2021).

[5] Michèle Finck. *Blockchain Regulation and Governance in Europe.* Publication Title: Blockchain Regulation and Governance in Europe. Cambridge University Press, 2018. DOI: 10.1017/9781108609708.

[6] Howell E. Jackson and Morgan Ricks. *Locating Stablecoins within the Regulatory Perimeter.* Aug. 2021. URL: https://corpgov.law.harvard.edu/2021/08/05/locating-stablecoins-within-the-regulatory-perimeter.

[7] *What's behind China's cryptocurrency ban?* World Economic Forum. URL: https://www.weforum.org/agenda/2022/01/what-s-behind-china-s-cryptocurrency-ban/ (visited on 05/25/2022).

Chapter 26: Conclusion

[1] Hilary Allen. *Driverless Finance.* Oxford University Press, 2022.

[2] Rupert Goodwins. *The dark equation of harm versus good means blockchain's had its day.* Dec. 6, 2021. URL: https://www.theregister.com/2021/12/06/the_dark_equation_of_harm/ (visited on 02/25/2022).

[3] Brian P. Hanley. "The False Premises and Promises of Bitcoin". In: (July 4, 2018). arXiv: 1312.2048. URL: http://arxiv.org/abs/1312.2048 (visited on 03/21/2022).

[4] Jemima Kelly. "Why I'm still not taking crypto seriously". In: *Financial Times* (Apr. 27, 2022). URL: https://www.ft.com/content/f220f44f-3627-4797-b6fe-9253563db49d (visited on 04/28/2022).

[5] Robert McCauley. *Why bitcoin is worse than a Madoff-style Ponzi scheme.* Dec. 22, 2021. URL: https://www.ft.com/content/83a14261-598d-4601-87fc-5dde528b33d0 (visited on 05/09/2022).

[6] Saule T Omarova. "New tech v. new deal: Fintech as a systemic phenomenon". In: *Yale J. on Reg.* 36 (2019). Publisher: HeinOnline, p. 735.

[7] David Rosenthal. *EE380 Talk (Can We Mitigate Cryptocurrencies' Externalities?)* DSHR's Blog. Feb. 9, 2022. URL: https://blog.dshr.org/2022/02/ee380-talk.html (visited on 02/25/2022).

[8] Robert J. Shiller. "What Is Bitcoin Really Worth? Don't Even Ask." In: *The New York Times* (Dec. 15, 2017). ISSN: 0362-4331. URL: https://www.nytimes.com/2017/12/15/business/bitcoin-investing.html (visited on 04/17/2022).

[9] Jacob Silverman. *Crypto Is Making Everything Worse.* Jacobin. URL: https://jacobinmag.com/2022/03/cryptocurrency-bitcoin-speculative-asset-digitization-metaverse (visited on 03/20/2022).

[10] Evan Soltas. *Bitcoin Really Is an Existential Threat to the Modern Liberal State.* URL: https://www.bloomberg.com/opinion/articles/2013-04-05/bitcoin-really-is-an-existential-threat-to-the-modern-liberal-state (visited on 04/23/2022).

[11] C.W. Walker Walker. *'Unnecessary complexity': the crypto industry's continuing efforts to avoid regulation.* LSE Business Review. Oct. 13, 2021. (Visited on 05/16/2022).

[12] Nicholas Weaver. *Blockchains and Cryptocurrencies: Burn It With Fire.* Apr. 20, 2018. URL: https://www.youtube.com/watch?v=xCHab0dNnj4 (visited on 02/25/2022).

[13]   Ed Zitron. *Solutions That Create Problems*. Ed Zitron's Where's Your Ed
       At. Feb. 23, 2022. URL: https://ez.substack.com/p/solutions-
       that-create-problems (visited on 02/23/2022).

[14]   Ed Zitron. *The Infinite Exploitation Of Cryptocurrency*. Where's Your Ed
       At. Mar. 30, 2022. URL: https://ez.substack.com/p/the-infinite-
       exploitation-of-cryptocurrency?s=r.

Index

CPSIA information can be obtained
at www.ICGtesting.com
Printed in the USA
LVHW101042031222
734518LV00019B/540